BITCOIN VS ALTCOINS

THE BATTLE FOR DOMINANCE

Phil Champagne

e53 publishing

Published by e53 Publishing, LLC

Cover design by Ricardo Galvão, Vivianne Champagne and Konsensus.Network

Interior design by Konsensus.Network

ISBN 978-0-99-606134-6 Hardcover
     978-0-99-606133-9 Paperback
     978-0-99-606135-3 E-book

e 53 publishing

To my father Jean-Paul and my mother Suzanne. I miss you guys!

TABLE OF CONTENTS

Disclaimer: I am not a financial advisor, please consult your financial advisor for any final actions you might take. For simplicity, I will often phrase sentences in a certain way, but you should do your own research.

—

For access to easy clickable links, check out the book's website at
http://bitcoinvsaltcoinsbook.com/footnotes/

FOREWORD

In 1637, a French mathematician named Pierre de Fermat jotted down a note in the margin of a famous book called Arithmetica by the Greek mathematician Diophantus. The note, originally in Latin, read: "I have discovered a truly remarkable proof of this theorem which this margin is too small to contain." The theorem that Fermat was referring to was a mathematical puzzle. The puzzle, which was later referred to as Fermat's Last Theorem, states that no three positive integers a, b, and c can satisfy the equation $a^n + b^n = c^n$ for any integer value of n greater than 2. Or more simply, there are no whole number solutions to this equation when n is greater than 2. Evidently, this note remained in Fermat's copy of Arithmetica for the next 33 years when it was finally discovered by his son Samuel Fermat five years after Pierre had died. The discovery prompted intense interest among mathematicians of the time who were left puzzled by Fermat's cryptic statement and lack of proof.[1]

Fast forward 349 years to 1986 and the mathematical theorem still wasn't solved. But this time, there was a relentless Princeton professor of mathematics that was focused upon the problem at hand. His name was Andrew Wiles, and there was something about Fermat's Last Theorem that captured his imagination and interest even when he was a graduate school student. Although the problem remained unsolved, Wiles was convinced he could pull it off. For years he toiled over the problem. He solicited help from students like Richard Taylor and other professors like John Coates. One of the biggest challenges of the problem was the sheer complexity. One of Wiles's most significant setbacks came in 1993 when he thought he had finally solved the problem, only to discover a flaw in his proof.

---

[1] Simon Singh, Fermat's Enigma: The Epic Quest to Solve the World's Greatest Mathematical Problem (Fourth Estate, 1997)

The gap in his argument related to the behavior of certain geometric objects called elliptic curves. Wiles was trying to prove the theorem by developing a new mathematical tool called the "modularity theorem," which relates elliptic curves to modular forms, a type of mathematical function. However, while working on the proof, some of his calculations weren't checking out. At this point, Wiles had been working on this specific problem for seven years of his life, even taking a sabbatical from his teaching position at Princeton, just to focus on the problem full-time.[2]

Despite Wiles's numerous setbacks, he was finally able to solve the problem later in 1993 by connecting the two seemingly unrelated areas of mathematics (elliptic curves and modular forms). For three and a half centuries, this obscure math problem perplexed the smartest mathematicians. And once it was solved, the discovery ushered in important implications for many areas of mathematics, including number theory, algebraic geometry, representation theory, and modern-day encryption protocols. More specifically, the modularity theorem has enabled the development of more secure encryption protocols such as Elliptic Curve Digital Signature Algorithm (ECDSA) and the Elliptic Curve Diffie-Hellman (ECDH). And for all the bitcoiners out there, yes, bitcoin uses ECDSA for key generation and digital signature verification. So why am I telling you this long historical story about mathematics and some obscure puzzle that took centuries to solve? Simple. It's a story about focusing on a problem and solving it. And unsurprisingly, without properly defining what the problem is, it can never be solved. In Wiles' case, the definition of the problem was quite simple, yet the solution was absurdly difficult to uncover. When it comes to bitcoin, I'd argue we presently have the opposite situation. The complex solution has already been uncovered thanks to the brilliance of Satoshi Nakamoto, but the world is struggling to understand what the problem even is. Sure, some people can sense something is wrong and they know something needs to be solved, but many can't pinpoint *what* needs to be solved.

---

[2]"The Story of Fermat's Last Theorem" by Simon Singh and John Lynch, published on the dailymotion.com website, accessed on February 28, 2023. (Link: https://www.dailymotion.com/video/x1btavd)

We've all seen the plight of most citizens clinging to liberal or conservative politicians thinking they hold the keys that can miraculously solve the world's growing dysfunction and problems with an ever-growing list of new policies and legislation. But in that relentless search, an empty feeling is left on citizens because the elected officials aren't properly defining *the* problem; instead, they are placing blame and superficially addressing downstream issues.

So what is the problem and why does the "clown world" seem to be getting stronger each and every day? Well, I'd propose the problem is quite simple: it's the money. More specifically, the world desperately needs a scarce, saleable, fungible, portable, divisible, permissionless, secure money.

Whether people understand the problem or not, there's a massive battle taking place in the world right now. The battle is between net producers and net consumers. The net producers are exporting their scarce natural resources and goods to places where there are net consumers. Interestingly, the net consumers around the world insist on paying for those scarce resources with fiat money. Fiat money that has a tremendous amount of credit that sits at its base layer, yielding very low interest rates. How much? Only hundreds of trillions of dollars' worth. The problem for net consumers is that net producers are tired of being paid in these low-yielding, fiat digital monetary units that keep getting debased to offset their inability to exchange production in-kind. And now that inflation is starting to exceed interest rates, the hundred trillion dollar pile of made-up fiat units become a melting ice cube. So, this is the quandary that plagues the world. It's also the reason we are seeing net producing countries shut off their flow of natural resources unless settlement is now conducted in their local currency, gold, or bitcoin. Because if the net consumers of the world insist on paying for scarce natural resources with an ever-expanding supply of made-up digital fiat monetary units, what they are really insisting is they should be allowed to violate the first law of thermodynamics. A law which states, "the total energy in a system remains constant, although it may be converted from one form to another."

So, this brings me to bitcoin versus altcoins. What *is* the problem that desperately needs to be solved? Do we need a better notary service for artwork (NFTs) so we understand who owns the rights? Is that the issue plaguing the world right now? Of course not, and of course anything's better than the AAA office putting a rubber stamp and signature on a piece of paper and logging it in their oversized legal pad with Billy's initials.

Do we need decentralized exchanges so anyone in the world can own global businesses that make profits and preserve an owner's purchasing power? Yes, probably. When I look around the world and see that half the globe is unbanked and can't gain access to equity ownership in premium companies like Apple, Exxon, TSM, etc., it's easy to recognize there's a huge disadvantage for preserving one's work and energy. Is this the core issue that's preventing the world from moving forward with global cooperation and efficiency? I don't think so. Instead, I think it's a potential downstream effect of actually solving *the* problem and likely an outcome once everyone's operating off a reliable, secure, and permissionless unit of account.

Do we need a decentralized form of scarce money? And of course, this is my point, yes. Without establishing a base settlement layer that's undeniably decentralized and secure, the global system of exchange runs the risk of breaking out into a cardiac arrest type event. Any type of money that's built with a "spectrum of decentralization", opposed to absolute decentralization, is the equivalent of building a skyscraper on bedrock that deflects. Michael Saylor has done a fabulous job of providing civil-engineering examples for people who struggle to understand the implications of complex software layers and complex economic conditions that are not built on sound engineering principles.

When I look across the wide breadth of altcoin projects rooted in the Proof of Stake consensus mechanism, I see a lot of the same systems that still violate the first law of thermodynamics. Now, many altcoin evangelists will claim that Proof of Stake protocols allow for flexibility and the ability to "create their own physical reality," but this is a dangerous claim. No matter how much people wish they could leave physical reality to market their token's agility and "smartness", the real world and real natural resources powering their computers, or printing this book, still exist and pose a real cost to the people producing such goods and services.

Nancy Leveson is a professor of aeronautics and astronautics at MIT, and she's an expert in the field of system safety engineering. In her book, An Introduction to System Safety Engineering, she writes, "The flexibility of software encourages us to build much more complex systems than we have the ability to engineer. Theoretically, a large number of tasks can be accomplished with software, and distinguishing between what can be done and what should be done is very difficult... When we are limited to physical materials, the difficulty or even impossibility of building anything we might think about building limits what we attempt. Software temptations are virtually irresistible. The apparent ease of creating arbitrary behavior makes us arrogant. We become sorcerer's apprentices, foolishly believing that we can control any amount of complexity. Our systems will dance for us in ever more complicated ways. We don't know when to stop... A project's specification rapidly becomes a wish list. Additions to the list encounter little or no resistance. We can always justify just one more feature, one more mode, one more gee-whiz capability. And don't worry, it'll be easy – after all, it's just software. In one stroke, we are free of nature's constraints. This freedom is software's main attraction, but unbounded freedom lies at the heart of all software difficulty... We would be better off if we learned how and when to say no..."[3]

Unlike Fermat's Last Theorem, the definition of what bitcoin intends to solve isn't as clearly defined as $a^n + b^n = c^n$ in the minds of the global population. Even more confusing is the competing self-interest of altcoin marketers that obfuscate the bitcoin problem statement in the name of promoting their pre-mined, gee-wiz coin that often doesn't improve upon existing centralized systems. Could other decentralized protocols materialize out of this movement? Of course! Look at the decentralized social media

---

[3]Nancy Leveson, "An Introduction to System Safety Engineering" (Addison-Wesley Professional, 2011), quoted in Jason Lowery, "Softwar" (CreateSpace Independent Publishing Platform, 2017), 266.

protocol called Nostr, it's a perfect example. Did it need a pre-mined token to achieve what it's done? Nope. In fact, it's already using scarce bitcoin lightning sats instead of empty meaningless likes on Twitter.

So, when I look at the debate between bitcoin and altcoins, my message is simple. There's a really big problem in the world right now – a problem so big it comes around once in a millennia. Global money is broken. Bitcoin is offering a solution to that enormous problem. Altcoins won't solve that problem because they lack bitcoin's security, decentralization, and subsequent scarcity. Other protocols can still exist and offer solutions, but to other problems. Problems of much smaller magnitude from the global lens.

By Preston Pysh
28 FEB 2023
TheInvestorsPodcast.com

1

WHAT IS THIS BOOK ABOUT?

For the first few years after the 2008 release of Satoshi Nakamoto's white paper, "Bitcoin: A Peer-to-Peer Electronic Cash System," the buzz within the cryptography community was all about bitcoin. Anyone introduced to this revolutionary concept learned about bitcoin and nothing else. Today, however, people are likely to encounter a multitude of other "crypto-currencies." Of course, most will have heard about bitcoin, but, upon investigation, they will most likely have run into articles about Ethereum or some other cryptocurrency. Or perhaps their friends will have told them about this amazing altcoin that they had invested in and how much profit they had made from it and how much better it was than bitcoin. The question arises, is bitcoin after all an outdated first draft of the crypto concept, or is it sufficiently resilient to remain the dominant cryptocurrency?

Unceremoniously launched in early 2009, bitcoin's source code created a silent revolution. Bitcoin was a new form of currency, and, as such, it prompted hot debates. It was not merely a new computer operating system or computer language but rather a technology capable of disrupting the existing financial system and a source of power to the rich and powerful players who controlled it.

> Bitcoins naturally reside in the electronic world and thus require a derivative to function in the physical world. The inverse is true for physical commodities such as gold and silver.

Bitcoin signaled the emergence of a new form of currency, one whose characteristics are better suited to an electronically oriented society than are those of gold and silver. Bitcoin is native in the electronic world, and it requires derivatives to be exchanged in the physical form. Conversely, in the case of gold and silver, it is the opposite. With banks in the past serving as a trusted third party holding the physical gold in exchange for paper or digital notes to facilitate exchanges. Similarly, if you want to transact bitcoin without internet access, you need a form of trust of a third party or the giver of the bitcoin. For example, the person sending you bitcoins could do so using a paper wallet, which operates like a check in which you trust it will not bounce back.

> Note: A paper wallet is where a copy of a bitcoin address and a private key are stored on a piece of paper that can be given to anyone. The person receiving this information must trust that the bitcoins will not be spent by the giver of the paper since they might have made a copy of the private key.

When it came to using gold and silver as money, the distinction was easy, and there weren't really better choices on the periodic table. Gold is rare enough, beautiful, a metal solid at room temperature, does not rust, and has been desired for its value for thousands of years. Silver, a bit less rare, provides similar features. Copper and any other metal was either too abundant to be used as money or did not have the best attributes, like mercury, being liquid at room temperature.

Bitcoin, on the other hand, is a combination of a protocol, open-source software, and the network of nodes running it, all securing a set of rules which include a limit on the total supply of bitcoins. A node is any computer that runs the bitcoin software and contains a copy of its blockchain. Bitcoin currency's rarity (supply cap) is set with a hard limit as part of the protocol. As is the nature of open-source software, bitcoin software, too, can be replicated to produce another variant of bitcoin. So, when you talk about bitcoin to your uncle who is invested in gold and silver, he sees thousands of cryptocurrencies listed on websites like coingecko.com or coinmarketcap.com. To him, bitcoin doesn't sound very rare. – In the top several listings alone, he sees bitcoin, Bitcoin Cash, Litecoin and so on. Realistically, how could a newbie make any sense out of this?

Bitcoin's network effects explain its dominance, but even if the phenomenon is well known, many argue bitcoin is still a technology that could be displaced by a better one later, just like My Space was displaced by Facebook. But bitcoin's protocol is different, when the main goal is to store wealth in a system that must be trusted not to be subverted. The network effect is primary, and the bells and whistles become second. By bells and whistles, I'm referring to transactions per second, smart contracts, and other fancy new features added. When the goal is to create and maintain a store of value, you want something that is conservative; one where changes are rare and vetted for quite some time.

This brings us up to the subject of altcoins. Before the end of 2017, altcoins did not really compete against bitcoin for the limelight. In market capitalization – which is the total cost if one wanted to buy the entire existing supply of an asset at the current market price – bitcoin was the uncontested top dog.

Note: Market cap calculations can fool someone if one disregards how distributed the coins are. For example, if my cousin and I launch a coin with a supply of one million coins, give ourselves half each, and I sell one coin to my sister for $1,000, this illiquid market with an exceptionally low distribution shows a ridiculously high market cap of $1 billion.

Prior to 2017, Ethereum, Litecoin, XRP and all the others had a fraction of the market share of the total cryptocurrency space, while bitcoin dominated. At that time, the question for most new investors was whether or not to invest in bitcoin. Few looked at much else. But mid-2017, an altcoin frenzy started when, in less than one month, some made gains over a factor of 10 or more. Suddenly many newcomers were incentivized to take a closer look at altcoins, bypassing bitcoin, for the pure speculative gain. In addition, there was an intense debate among bitcoin investors, miners, and developers about whether or not to increase bitcoin's block size to increase the number of transactions it could support. During that same period, there was some congestion (heavy usage) on the bitcoin network, hiking the cost of a bitcoin transaction as high as $100. Some speculated that "big blockers" were artificially generating new transactions just to push their argument in favor of a bitcoin software hard fork update that would increase the size of the block. Eventually, this dissension led to the creation of a hard fork, Bitcoin Cash, while the original bitcoin stayed unchanged. All existing prior transactions on the bitcoin blockchain were identical so people ended up having both Bitcoin Cash coins (BCH) and bitcoins (BTC). For those interested in reading more about that period of bitcoin history, I suggest *The Blocksize War* by Jonathan Bier.

This entire episode created a war of ideology from which new terms like "bitcoin maximalist" and "shitcoins" emerged. The term bitcoin maximalist describes those who promote and believe bitcoin is the only viable currency and a foundation for a new monetary system while everything else is a "shitcoin." The term "shitcoin" is well supported. It is true there have been countless scams and ridiculous copycats that almost resemble a pyramid scheme. For example, the shitcoin creator is heavily incentivized to acquire ownership of a coin before heavily promoting it, and then selling it on the open market, basically a classic pump and dump scheme. On the other hand, some other cryptocurrencies have legitimate new functionality, which, from a technological point of view, is positive. Just like in its early days when bitcoin was seen as an experiment, the same can be true for some altcoins today. However, a departure from this creation of new currency with a new blockchain arose in 2018, with the launch of the Liquid Network. The Liquid Network is a blockchain where the currency used is a coin called LBTC. LBTC is pegged one-to-one to bitcoin, as such, it is called a side chain of bitcoin. Interestingly, the Liquid Network uses a consensus algorithm similar to a controversial altcoin called XRP. We will cover these two in greater detail in a later chapter.

Those new to the cryptocurrency world in general might not be familiar with the strong on-going debate regarding the validity of some or all of the cryptocurrency blockchain projects. The stock and commodity markets seem free of these kinds of vitriolic "wars of word" and ideology, perhaps due to their nature. A friend might be invested in Airline company B while you are invested in Airline company A or even Train company C. Even if your friend thinks your investment is futile, he will simply, at worst, mention this politely. By comparison, if you look at the bitcoin-related discussion on Twitter, the term "shitcoin" is used freely. Peter Schiff – a prominent gold-bug – sees all cryptocurrencies eventually going to zero and may have used the term shitcoin for all of them, including bitcoin.

Within cryptocurrency, we are observing as the nascent asset class experiences an internal war – like if gold bugs and silver bugs were throwing dirt at each other. Understanding why this war continues becomes very important if you want to look at the cryptocurrency space in general. We will elaborate more in the following chapters as to why bitcoiners see the dilution of investment in other altcoins as a problem. Different elements fuel this intense debate. Among them is the importance of decentralization of a cryptocurrency, meaning how no small group could collude together to control any aspects of the blockchain and its network, no matter what.

Understanding and assessing decentralization is critical to the analysis of a cryptocurrency. Governments themselves are certainly very centralized, particularly the federal government. Governments have immense power in setting laws, and regulations, and as such, it has been a target of collusion with the military industrial complex, big pharma, and of course the banking cartel, just to list a few. If a dominant cryptocurrency can have a backdoor that allows for operations that could provide any kind of advantage to a group or organization over everyone else, it will be abused. For many bitcoin maximalists, a cryptocurrency is either fully decentralized or fully centralized. Others see decentralization as a gradient, where some are more decentralized than others. Some altcoin investors despise what bitcoin represents. Among the top criticisms towards bitcoin is the belief that Proof of Work siphons energy out of the grid. These critics are either confused about how energy markets work, supporters of Proof of Stake, or perhaps invested in a cryptocurrency like XRP, which is neither Proof of Work nor Proof of Stake, but rather, a "Federated Byzantine agreement consensus." With a word like "federated," it sounds more centralized, but we will not get ahead of ourselves, chapter 7 is dedicated to this topic and will help you form your own opinion.

Regardless of whether you are a supporter or detractor of the bitcoin network, you can recognize that it is truly an amazing innovation, underpinned by multiple components such as an ever-evolving series of blocks appended one after the other, forming a blockchain. And because it is not centrally controlled, a consensus mechanism via Proof of Work, combined with a timing mechanism, provides an agreement by all parties about the latest state. Ironically, in the cryptocurrency lexicon, the arrival of the term blockchain dominated more than bitcoin itself, so much so that some in the banking industry would learn about blockchain before they even heard about bitcoin. It is difficult to imagine today, but this is the kind of thing you might have heard in 2016: "I have heard about blockchain, but what is bitcoin you are talking about?" It is as if some in the banking industry wanted to only take the innovation out of bitcoin without its disruptive aspect on the economic and financial world and therefore would only mention the word blockchain. The blockchain itself is just one of many components of bitcoin and would be worthless without the decentralization aspect, rendering it a glorified, high-availability database. After all, if decentralization in a system is not necessary, any existing databases would be more of value than a blockchain for the purpose of rapidly storing and updating information. Because the term blockchain was hijacked by the banking industry, some in the bitcoin world now refer to blockchain as a "timechain." This reminds me of the socialists in the early 1900s hijacking the terms liberal and liberalism, forcing the original liberals to rebrand themselves as classical liberal or libertarian.

Another hot topic of debate regards the volatility of the altcoin market. It might come as a surprise to you, that bitcoiners could use volatility as an argument against altcoins, considering bitcoin itself is quite volatile; however, altcoins are even more so. One main reason is the size of their markets. Because bitcoin's market cap is quite large compared to other coins, its price fluctuation is not as violent. In fact, bitcoin's volatility today is quite mild compared to its early days. One of the first bitcoin crashes saw its price going from $23 all the way down to $1, a 95% crash in value. Today, bitcoin corrections are still notable but never drop more than 80%. Even then, the drop is only for a short time, until it stabilizes at a 60% below its most recent all-time high. We will cover more on this later.

An additional point raised by bitcoiners distinguishing bitcoin from altcoins regards the numerous projects launched by the altcoin's early-adoption speculators. These speculators run elaborate marketing schemes composed of elegant but faulty narratives designed to defraud uneducated and unsuspecting new investors. Unfortunately, these tactics have been pervasive, and the sad part is that when unsophisticated investors are burned in this way, they stay away from bitcoin as well. I have heard of a story of a bitcoiner trying to influence his friend to invest in bitcoin and a few months later, the friend came back and told him he lost nearly all in "crypto" and was sad he listened to him. After more conversation, the bitcoiner realized his friend invested in some ridiculous altcoin rather than bitcoin, even though his suggestion was strictly about bitcoin. Unfortunately, fraud exists and will always exist. The good thing is, not all altcoins are fraudulent. Some are legitimate projects with sound teams behind them with legit intentions and desire. Whether they are competent might be another story.

To distinguish bitcoin even further, bitcoiners often point to the regulations promulgated and enforced by the United States Securities and Exchange Commission (SEC). I'm amazed that some bitcoiners are almost joyful that the SEC is suing some altcoins. Two of the well-known projects the SEC has targeted are LBRY.com and Ripple, the company behind the currency XRP. First of all, to state that they are violating the law regarding securities doesn't make it any more justifiable than the Federal Reserve who's currently allowed to print dollars out of thin air and charge interest on it. The stated reason for SEC's existence is to protect the public. How can this work when the SEC's civil lawsuits are filed several years after the currency is launched and traded and, importantly, while none of the users are complaining. We will cover fraud later, but we will also cover more about the issues related to government regulations.

One final major argument advanced by bitcoiners can be expressed with a quote from Ramirez, the character played by Sean Connery in the movie Highlander: "There can be only one." When it comes to money, bitcoiners do not see the need for more than one digital currency, and the existence of others only adds to market's confusion, slows adoption and dilutes economic energy. I agree that when it comes to the combination of store of value and medium of exchange, an ecosystem tends to gravitate towards one currency. To me, bitcoin is the existing currency most likely to grow its adoption towards a tipping point – the point where it becomes the predominant cryptocurrency on the planet, irrespective of whether the central bankers of the world agree. That being said, does it mean private tokens required to get on a ride at the local fair will cease to exist? Unlikely. These tokens were created as a convenience for ride operators and their customers; they no longer deal constantly with accepting payments and giving back change. This type of localized "currency" and its original purpose will be explored in a later chapter.

Rather than plainly describing all these cryptocurrencies and what they try to resolve, in this book I intend to provide you with a perspective on how solid they are from a decentralization point of view, and what you should consider before you invest. Note that this is not financial advice, and you should consult your financial advisor for any actual decision. I'm merely trying to share with you the tip of the information iceberg in this battle of ideas – like Proof of Stake or Proof of Work and so on. There are so many perspectives and controversial topics in the cryptocurrency space, as well as in finance, in general, or even other topics like health and food. Take the carnivore diet for example. This way of eating in itself is a controversial topic for the mainstream point of view but even within this realm, an internal debate among doctors exists about whether it is important to include organ meat or is muscle alone sufficient. Similarly, the concept of a cryptocurrency harbors intense debates, particularly because it is so new. Thus, it is worth reading content that strives to be neutral and unbiased, while sharing different perspectives as much as possible. This is my goal: To provide an overview of the situation while trying not to be all too partisan. I desire to always question myself on topics like, "Am I missing an angle in the analysis that prevents me from looking at the bigger picture?" With this book, I will share many perspectives along with the reasoning for these positions, while providing you with enough information to decide on your own.

To provide a solid overview, we need to go survey Proof of Work, along with the major criticism against it. But to make a proper comparison, we also need to look at the implementation of Proof of Stake. Too many bitcoin "maximalists" do not understand how exactly Proof of Stake works, they just know the elevator pitch – which is the right to mine a block is linked to how many existing coins you have at stake. Some critics may not know about the requirement about putting coins in bonds that can be lost if they act badly.

Proof of Work relies on incentives alone while Proof of Stake uses a combination of both punishment for undesired behavior and incentives.

Another aspect we will cover is in what ways the banking cartel has dealt with bitcoin and cryptocurrencies. I will share some personal speculation, but to be clear, there is nothing definitive in what I posit. I will also run some theories of what I think are the different scenarios the banking cartel might have devised to circumvent bitcoin's potential to usurp its current power status it enjoys via central banking and fiat currencies.

In the early years of bitcoin, most bitcoin holders were hard-core libertarians and anarcho-capitalists (from the root "anarchy" meaning "no rulers" existing in a capitalistic environment). They understood that bitcoin was more than just an investment but rather it embodied the possibility of challenging central bank currency, particularly when its debt-based system leads to an inevitable currency crisis. As bitcoin grew, it embraced many other political views, and as the years passed, particularly around 2013 and 2014, various groups became interested in it. Today, bitcoin's advocates come from all walks of life; a common ground for libertarians and, surprisingly (or some say suspiciously) progressives alike.

> One of the major benefits of bitcoin has been the education about sound money, with a currency having a hard limit on its supply. It would not be surprising if central bankers feared the education bitcoin has brought to the general public more than bitcoin itself.

On that note, I have often said that one of the major benefits of bitcoin has been the education about our financial system it brings to the masses about our financial system. I believe central bankers are more afraid of this enlightenment effect ushered in by understanding bitcoin than bitcoin itself. Now that bitcoin, as a concept and technology, is out in the open and the public is gaining a deeper understanding of both bitcoin and the fiat financial system, the public's awakening has become irreversible. An additional benefit of studying bitcoin is the exposure to the principles of the Austrian School of Economics, which is rarely taught in school today. In fact, students educated in most university economic programs today study the Keynesian school of economics. Based on central planning rather than understanding human action, a study of Keynesian economics often generates opposing views in people (students) than those who study the Austrian School. Thus, not everyone approaches bitcoin from the same initial perspective and background. I came to bitcoin from a gold/silver investor mindset having read extensively about the Austrian School of Economics. My main task was to understand how bitcoin's design allows it to have a status equivalent to an "electronic gold." As we have seen with Peter Schiff, a gold promoter since at least the early 2000s, not everyone from this background will make that jump. Considering my professional background is in software engineering, it was quite easy for me to grasp the concept behind bitcoin, as opposed to a person who has limited knowledge in this space.

When we were on a gold standard, ordinary folks could easily save and plan for their futures because gold kept its value throughout their life. Not so today. Consider this: If someone 30 years old earns $100,000 per year today and wants to retire in 30 years with this same income in today's value by accumulating enough cash, how many millions will this person need to accumulate? We can estimate, but it all depends on what we expect the value of the dollar to be in 30 years. If one uses the inflation metric of the past 30 years, which is claimed to be below 4%, one might face a major surprise with just this past year where we experienced above 8% inflation, if not more. In fact, it's likely much higher, but the government hides true inflation with accounting tricks so that it can boast a lower official inflation rate. The point is, we really have no way of predicting the inflation rate year after year. Under a gold currency standard (a currency backed by gold like we had in the 1800s where the supply is tied to that of gold), however, that calculation would be much easier. Funding a lifestyle at $100,000 per year today would require about $100,000 per year in 30 years, with the added benefits of new technology likely creating deflation.

With that in mind, knowing you can safely store your wealth in a certain asset with the assurance it will still be there in 10 years is important. Accountants, CPAs, and actuaries today must estimate this uncertain value in future inflation. Unsurprisingly most defined benefit retirement plans began disappearing in the 1970s when we officially went off the gold standard. With the gold standard decimated, accountants and actuaries were forced to guesstimate how future inflation might impact a worker's monthly payout under a defined benefit plan for the next 10, 20, or 30 years. So instead, most companies switched to defined contribution plans; in the United States (US), this is administered under the 401K plan. With 401K, the worker sets how much he decides to contribute to his pension funds, but what this will lead to in terms of purchasing power at the time of retirement is anyone's guess. Under a gold standard, cowboys could just pile up gold coins under their mattresses as a way of savings, knowing that what one ounce of gold bought at the time it was tossed under the mattress would be about the same 40 years later when they needed it. Planning for the future did not require speculation about which mutual funds to invest in, hoping you have picked the right one. Neither did it require diversification into a multitude of stocks managed by some company that, more often than not, has performance worse than the S&P 500 index or the Dow Jones Industrial Index.

Personally, I see real estate as a better investment over the long term than the stock market. Obviously, real estate experiences periods where it is overvalued such as in 2007 and in 2021 due to the artificially low interest rate set by central bankers. But putting aside this phenomena, assuming the city where you invest maintains its attractive attributes over time, rent will follow inflation or catch up to it. If a house you bought as an investment brings you $2000 per month in income after taxes and insurance, and you bought it with a mortgage with a 20% down payment, in 20 or 30 years you have the full $2000 per month to yourself (mortgage being paid off), indexed for inflation. If you think you will need $4000 per month to live comfortably with today's cost of living, you know you need to invest in two such houses. And with a fiat based system, you have the additional artificial gain from the value of your loan being devalued through inflation. Great for investors but very sad for tenants. Even worse, it allows for another wonderful excuse for socialist governments to come to the rescue of these tenants by trying to fix the symptoms with rent control that only exacerbates the problem instead of working on the cause - the fiat currency system itself.

Gold has always been used as a long-term store of wealth, and every year bitcoin is rising as an alternative to gold. I will explain why I believe you should place bitcoin at the core of your portfolio when it comes to cryptocurrencies. Just like some are invested heavily in physical gold, they might also own stocks of mining companies for more speculative purposes. As such, you may decide to invest in other cryptocurrencies that you have studied, so long as you are aware of the heavy speculative risk of placing that bet. A rule of thumb is the smaller the cryptocurrency in terms of market capitalization, the more speculative it is.

Some podcasts and youtubers believe "gold bugs" hate bitcoin. Interestingly, bitcoiners and gold bugs do have at least one point in common, we know the current central banking system is flawed. It runs on "Proof of Debt," where more debt must be created constantly to pay the interest on the current debt. Therefore, Washington D.C. has to constantly set up a new debt *target* (they wrongly call it a debt ceiling), otherwise the system collapses on itself. Since 1960, the debt "ceiling" has been raised 78 times. Of course, this unstable system has a multitude of booms and busts built in. It's like we are witnessing a drunk driver at the wheel of a three-trailer road train (which is an exceptionally long truck used in Australia) on a meandering road.

In the next chapter, we will detail the blockchain war, beginning with a perspective of bitcoin versus gold. Then, we will discuss the rise of altcoins. This sequence will give you a better historical context prior to exploring the arguments of each camp, that is those against Proof of Work and bitcoin, and those against Proof of Stake and so on.

But before we do, it is important to mention that the goal of this book is to give you an overview of the major debates, not to march through every cryptocurrency. My goal is to give you insight into the general landscape and debates, specifically addressing whether the existence of a plethora of altcoins is good or bad. Covering the dynamic field of hundreds of altcoins would make little sense. For the purpose of clarity, however, particularly when it comes to Proof of Stake, we will use some as an example.

2

BACKGROUND ON THE BLOCKCHAIN WAR

If you are new to the "cryptocurrency world," you will discover that people in this space hold a wide variety of perspectives about the proper weighting of bitcoin in one's asset portfolio. At one end of the spectrum, sit "bitcoin maximalists." As mentioned in the prior chapter, a "bitcoin maximalist" is one who advocates for bitcoin and bitcoin only. Maximalists believe people should store their savings in bitcoin (they prefer the term savings over investing) and shun all other coins or blockchain projects, provocatively calling those "shitcoins." Others see this position as a bit radical but agree that newbies should only invest in bitcoin, ignoring anything else. Still, others recommend that people should keep most of their investment in bitcoin and only invest a small portion in other coins for speculation and trading with the sole purpose of accumulating more bit-coins.

Moving along this spectrum, we find another set of bitcoin fans who support a few other cryptocurrency projects but also firmly believe that bitcoin should and will be the electronic gold standard where people keep the bulk of their investment. For simplicity, let's refer to the groups I have just described as "bitcoiners." In direct opposition to bitcoin maximalists, sit a group who rejects bitcoin and instead invests in one or more other cryptocurrencies. Ironically, some even call bitcoin a "boomer coin," as they see it as old and outdated. quite ironic indeed considering bitcoin has only been around since 2009.

To stay current, I follow many twitter accounts and watch many Youtu-bers, and it is interesting to see how the public perceives cryptocurren-cies in general. Bitcoiners, like gold investors, believe the dollar is on its deathbed. They believe central bankers everywhere prop up national currencies through manipulation of public perception to ensure that the public's ongoing faith in the value of these currencies remains strong, or at least minimize its decline. I am part of this group. We believe the cur-rent system is unsustainable. We anticipate a major dollar devaluation and with it, an attempt by the banking cartel to impose some new world reserve currency. The exact structure of this new currency is irrelevant, as long as it remains under their control, benefiting the central bankers and nefarious political cartels. To that end, many central banks are pushing for Central Bank Digital Currency (CBDC), which they believe would give them a better control of both the free and black markets.

Because central banks lack control over bitcoin's supply and move-ment, they are certainly not fans of its proliferation. On the other hand, others believe central banking, as we know it today, will continue to ex-ist, even though the system may evolve and operate differently over time. Still others believe some countries will return to a gold-backed standard or national currency. In the great marketplace of world ideas, it will be inter-esting to watch countries develop, as some, like El Salvador, adopt bitcoin as currency while others pursue more conventional monetary solutions.

The looming currency war will involve CBDC but governments know a decentralized cryptocurrency such as bitcoin is akin to digital gold, a currency that does not require guns and taxes to support it. To maintain control, central banks employ two major tools: income tax, including capital gains tax, and debt. Both nefarious, a tax siphons off a portion of the economy's productivity, while debt allows central bankers to inflate and deflate the currency by manipulating interest rates and the credit market. Fiat currencies are born out of debt and are destroyed when such debt is paid back. This system, however, is unworkable because the increase in debt will always outpace the ability to pay it due to accrued interest.

The commercial banking sector is responsible for a large amount of this debt creation, and when the economy is running too hot, where asset prices are rising too fast leading to price inflation, central bankers react by raising interest rates, plunging the economy into a recession. A recession forces repayment of some of the debt, leading to deflation. Only those who prepare by having a good amount of currency on hand can step in and buy these assets at a bargain price. This is what occurred in 2008 and more acutely in the 1930s. *The Big Short,* a 2015 Oscar-winning film adaptation of author Michael Lewis's best-selling book of the same name, depicted the build-up and subsequent collapse of the 2008 United States housing bubble.

To maintain the status quo, the powerful will enlist the many tools at their disposal, including movies, tv shows, mainstream media just to name a few. It is well recognized by veteran traders that, for decades, the price of gold and silver has been manipulated with the use of paper contracts. By comparison, storing bitcoins is a lot cheaper and easier than gold, hence, they have to rely on other tricks such as threats of regulations or facilitating bubbles, which can more easily lead to crashes.

To deal with bitcoin, central bankers may also seek to divide and conquer the competition. Although some cryptocurrency projects might have value, from the central banker's perspective, perpetuating a great number of cryptocurrency projects is somewhat beneficial for them. So, let's go over the details of this blockchain war.

WE LIVE IN AN ELECTRONIC WORLD

Congressman Ron Paul had a sign on his desk that read: "Don't steal! The government hates competition." Well, the government and central banks certainly hated anything that could compete against Federal Reserve Notes[4], that is the US dollar in its current form. From 1998 to 2007, a private organization called Liberty Services minted silver coins marked as American Liberty Dollar (ALD). They were also issuing paper certificates that could be redeemed for these coins, which were stored at Sunshine Minting in Idaho for their buyers. In November 2007, the Federal Bureau of Investigations (FBI) and US Secret Service raided Sunshine Minting, seized gold, silver and copper, and charged its operators with violation of federal laws. The federal government asserted that ALD coins were too similar to those of the US Mint; thus Sunshine Minting was accused of counterfeiting. Would the federal agencies have left Sunshine Minting alone if its coins had no resemblance to the US Mint's coins? I do not know, but I'm guessing Satoshi Nakamoto didn't want to learn, first hand, the scope of the government's interest in private currency, and it may have been one of the reasons he maintained his anonymity.

Finding the best currency for a society is tricky. Any currency that maintains its value such as gold would be better than government fiat, and paper currency is more convenient than gold coins for exchange, particularly with any large amount or over a long distance. Electronic currency is even more convenient. Central bankers are quite aware that any hard money currency (currency not devalued at their whim) would easily compete against their inflatable faith-based fiat currency. And if that hard money currency could take electronic form, the threat would be even greater.

The electronic aspect, or portability, of a currency is the key feature that gold bugs fail to grasp about bitcoin. Ironically, I've heard many of them praising the blockchain and seeing it as a great way to exchange

---

[4]Personally, I prefer to call them "Fraudulent Reserve Notes."

gold or to back a currency by gold. It seems difficult to explain to them how marking hard assets like gold to a "blockchain" doesn't prevent the secret service from seizing physical gold stored in vaults, leaving their blockchain currency backed by nothing. The central banking cartel is very resourceful when it comes to justifying their actions. It cites protecting consumers from money laundering, fraud, terrorism, anything where they can obfuscate their real intention - shutting down competition. Of course, the government might propose a blockchain approved by the government and backed by its gold, but we are circling back to the initial problem that will lead to unbacked fiat currencies inflated at will.

> "Trust us, we have your gold in our vault!" said the bankers.

More than 99% of financial transactions are done electronically - on-line shopping, wire transfers, credit card payments, etc . . . If gold were the currency of choice today, monetary processes would be unwieldy. We would be forced to have a third party to verify our gold's authenticity, hold it for us in a vault, and electronically track its ownership. Moreover, any third party could be attacked and shut down by the cartel. We also must ask: Who is that third party? How can it be trusted? If an audit must be done, how much can we trust the auditors? And to underscore the importance of trustworth auditors, I highly suggest the movie *The Big Short*, where credit rating agencies hand out triple A ratings to junk bonds so as to not lose the bank's business.

Does this mean you shouldn't own gold and silver? Not at all. Consider a major event where the Internet or electricity is unavailable either in your part of the country or even the entire world for a short or long period of time. Gold and silver coins will likely reign supreme. What's the probability of this happening in your lifetime? I do not know, but I would not put it at 0.

One thing I'm sure about, we live in an electronic world, and the central banking cartel is more scared of bitcoin than it is of gold. Whatever concerns people have with bitcoin, such as transaction speed and the lack of privacy, developers and entrepreneurs are constantly researching and developing solutions to mitigate those concerns. Back in 2008, few would have believed a decentralized cryptocurrency was possible. Yet, a year later, bitcoin proved it possible. The lightning network is already achieving high transaction speeds, and there is more to come, as hinted by the white paper for CoinPool[5].

Development does not stop at the bitcoin protocol itself. A lot of bitcoin utility can be derived by tools and services in development, such as Impervious browser[6]. In essence, gold investors who discard bitcoin see it simply as a mere accounting of nothing, of air since it is not tangible. It's odd because I consider gold investors sharp, and yet, their arguments are often ridiculous. Some arguments I've heard in podcasts include:

- *There are thousands of cryptocurrencies, so bitcoin is not rare.*

They are omitting the importance of the network effect (Metcalfe's law[7]). Each cryptocurrencies is like a different phone network system (or social media platform), where the more people on the same network, the more valuable the system. Cryptocurrencies barely used or known by anyone are not worth much and have little chance of displacing the well-recognized bitcoin.

- *Everything is hackable, as we have seen on many websites.*

There is a significant difference between a website containing private source code versus an open-source software, which anyone can verify. Additionally, bitcoin has been running for over a decade, relying on primitives such as SHA256 and elliptic curve cryptography. Any flaws in those would send the entire electronic financial world tumbling. Interestingly, there is even a bounty for the best hackers to find any flaw in the open

---

[5] Just like the lightning network, CoinPool is a layer 2 mechanism. We discuss CoinPool in more detail in a later chapter.

[6] See, http://www.impervious.ai/

[7] https://en.wikipedia.org/wiki/Metcalfe%27s_law

source code of bitcoin. The point being, as soon as a flaw is discovered, a fix can be issued before a catastrophic failure ensues.

- *Peter Schiff, a prominent gold investor, sees bitcoin as a pyramid scheme where buyers are holding in the hopes of selling to a greater fool.*

That's an odd assertion coming from a prominent gold investor because I've heard the same argument used against gold. The reasoning he provides for this distinction is that gold has utility as jewelry and in electronics, and for something to be considered money, it must have utility. Strangely, Peter Schiff declares himself a follower of the Austrian School of Economics, which does not require utility for an object or concept to become money. Ludwig von Mises, himself, one of the early economists in this school of thought, stated that exchange stems from value and time. People are willing to part with an object they value in exchange for this form of money because they expect that money to retain its purchasing power tomorrow. That's because they remember its purchasing power yesterday and the day before. So, it is the expectation of retaining its purchasing power, rather than whether said item has any utility.

It appears Schiff is stuck on Carl Menger's origin of money. Carl Menger is known as the first Austrian economist to propose that in a state of barter, goods have different degrees of saleability (marketability or liquidity). The more saleable a good, the easier it is for an owner to exchange it. At some point, one type of good gets recognized as the most marketable and becomes universally accepted, even by those who have no need of its utility. But, at the time of Menger's observation, the Austrian School of Economics was at its infancy. As Ludwig von Mises stated later, money is recognized more from an item's known purchasing power maintained from yesterday to today or from a year ago to this year, than whether it has utility for a specific group.

In short, it is bitcoin's perceived lack of utility that pushes gold bugs away from bitcoin. Satoshi himself put it well:

As a thought experiment, imagine there was a base metal as scarce as gold but with the following properties:

- Noring grey colour

- Not a good conductor of electricity

- Not particularly strong, but not ductile or easily malleable either

- Not useful for any practical or ornamental purpose

And one special magical property:

- Can be transported over a communication channel[8]

When we think about it, the ability to transport a scarce item over long distances without the intervention of a third party who might decide to censor your financial transactions for whatever reason, appears to me to be extremely useful.

I strongly believe that in the cryptocurrency debate there are many who have skewed and biased perspectives that lead them to make flawed and sometimes even nonsensical arguments about each other. Whether it be gold bugs, bitcoiners, or altcoiners, anyone can suffer from these kinds of bad arguments when trying to fix things to their biases. I have not been immune to this myself.

Perma-bitcoin-bears, that is people who believe bitcoin will die, of which many are gold bugs, look at the bitcoin chart, constantly predicting its demise. When it goes up, it's in a bubble. When it goes down, the bubble has burst, and it is heading towards zero. Repeat ad-nauseam. But regarding trading, bitcoin's blockchain offers something new. Something unavailable to gold, or the stock markets: blockchain analysis. For example, bitcoin price analysts have observed a corresponding trend regarding how many bitcoins are in cold storage (private keys held by individuals rather than exchanges) versus the price. Another interesting metric is the

---

[8]See, The Book of Satoshi, p282

Coin Destroyed Days (CDD), which is calculated for any transaction by taking the number of bitcoins in a transaction and multiplying it by the number of days since these bitcoins last moved. Some fascinating correlation exists between these metrics and the price of bitcoin. Analysts have noted that the price of bitcoin is about to stop correcting downward when a high number of bitcoins are *taken off* exchanges. Conversely, the price of bitcoin is about to top when a high number of bitcoins are *moved onto* exchanges. Equivalently, CDD is low when the price of bitcoin makes a low, and CDD is high when the price is high - when bitcoins previously held for a long time are moved to the exchange to capture new all-time highs.

CENTRAL BANKER'S PROOF OF DEBT

In the first few years after bitcoin's creation, most people involved were libertarian and anarcho-capitalist, like me, who believed central banking and fiat currency should be abolished. At these early bitcoin meetups, advocates of the existing system shared their insights and preference for central banking policies, but also asked questions about bitcoin. Today, however, many adherents to the current system own bitcoin (or other altcoins) as an investment mainly because bitcoin has evolved from a highly speculative project with high volatility to a stable project with high volatility. Considering this, it is important to include an analysis of central banking's flawed system, what I called a Proof of Debt (PoD).

Bitcoin uses Proof of Work to establish consensus on a protocol that dictates a gradually diminishing rate of inflation (minting new bitcoins). Comparatively, central banking and fractional reserve banking run on Proof of Debt. For simplicity, let's imagine an island with a single bank, Acme Bank, where all residents conduct business. Bob wants to borrow from Acme Bank to purchase a new car from Carl, the local car dealer. Through the "wonder" of fractional reserve banking, to fund those loans

Acme Bank can use up to 90% of the currency it holds from depositors, including money sitting in checking accounts. After the purchase, Carl deposits the loan check in his Acme Bank account. Now Acme Bank can use 90% of the car dealer's funds to again make new loans. But since all these currencies can be withdrawn or spent at any time by all the depositors, Acme just increased the total supply of currency on the island.

To further illustrate: Say, another depositor, Dean, buys a new car without a loan and makes a payment directly to the car dealer from his Acme checking account, technically reusing the same currency that Acme used to fund Bob's car loan. So, the same currency has been used by two different people to make two separate purchases. Additionally, when Bob decides to pay off the loan, both the debt he owes and the currency he paid it off with disappear. Thus, the same way the currency was created through the loan process, an accounting gimmick, is the same way it will be destroyed.

Let's simplify it a bit. As long as this new currency never goes above 90% of the amount held by depositors, the bank can create money out of thin air to make loans. Residents who take loans to purchase houses or make investments that increase in value will get richer than those who don't take loans. Does this feel familiar? It's the same systemic pattern generated between 2003 to 2007 in the run up to the great financial collapse of 2008 or in the early 2020, when artificially low interest rates were implemented to fight the economic impact from the lockdowns. As we experienced, when interest rates were pushed lower and lower, borrowers raced to outbid each other because loan payments correspondingly decreased.

On the island and in our society, fractionalized lending increases the supply of currency, but as much as increased money supply sounds enticing, the problem is that it comes with a matching amount in debt and interest payments must be made. Even though we might have started with $100 million on the island, loans may have grown the money supply to $250 million with $150 million of it matched by a corresponding debt. Loans taken in a currency with a fixed supply, increases the debt in the economy. Therefore, at some point, borrowers will have to save more than they spend to pay the interest. This activity generates a boom in spending followed by a savings frenzy, creating a mild recession due to the dramatic reduction in economic activity. This whole process is exponentially aggravated when a central bank, with an unrestricted fiat currency supply, allows for unlimited government spending to fuel the base of this inverse debt-growth pyramid.

Knowing how fractional reserve banking works, makes it easier to understand bank runs. During the gold standard era, like the panic of 1907, when bank customers deposited gold coins and currency into their accounts and the bank turned around made a loan using 85% of it, if the next day, all these customers were asking to withdraw their gold coins and currency, the bank would not have but only 15%. The 15% was born from the idea that, typically, customers ask to withdraw no more than 15% of their funds at any one time.[9]

In 2020 the minimum reserve requirement was reduced to 0%. No need for any backing to make a loan. Of course, if everyone was on digital cash or CBDC, banks with actually no deposit would be fine. It is not unheard of that big account holders in small regional banks must justify their withdrawal requests. In fact, any bank could technically be subject to a bank run, though in the US its depositors are insured by the Federal Deposit Insurance Corporation (FDIC).

On the other hand, if bank loans were restricted to the amount locked in Certificates of Deposit (which under a fiat system should be called Certificate of Depreciation) or where the bank sells notes backed by these loans, the money supply and loan issuance would be restricted. In such an environment, Dean the depositor whose funds are locked in a certificate of deposit would not be able to compete with Bob the borrower in bidding for a car or a house. When less funding is available, the market would naturally increase interest rates, attracting a greater number of depositors who agree to keep their funds unavailable for a certain period in exchange for higher returns.

---

[9]https://www.federalreserve.gov/monetarypolicy/0693lead.pdf p. 573

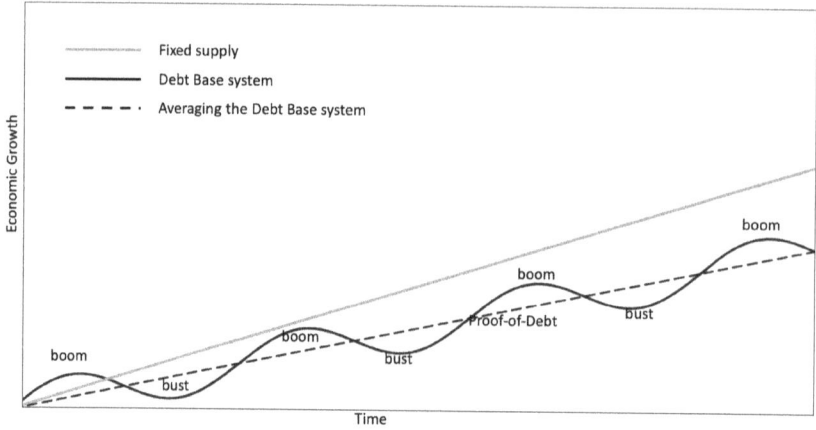

Figure 1: Economic growth with or without PoD.

The figure above contrasts the economic growth of a fixed supply and a debt supply system over the course of several decades. Economic growth and technological progress would be experienced under both systems. In our debt-based system we have witnessed great improvements over the past 150 years. Today, we have cars, airplanes, radios, television, and so much more that have increased our living standard. This growth was experienced under central banking and its proof-of-debt system. Consider the swing between the remarkable booms that occur when interest rates are lower and economic activity is induced from loans in the commercial banking sector, to the inevitable busts that occur when the interest rates are increased, as the commercial banks are at the limit of this pyramid scheme of deposits recycled into new loans.

The fact we have central banking and a fiat currency magnifies the extent of these booms and busts, which, otherwise, would have been milder and likely more localized. Indeed, localization of asynchronous booms and busts was the norm in the United States prior to the formation of the Federal Reserve. Central bank might buffer these busts and extend the duration of the cycle, but they make them worse in the long run. Isn't it ironic that the Federal Reserve was established with the promise of instituting economic stability and avoiding bank runs that occurred when some banks went too far in issuing loans?

Banks in the 1907 panic had stretched the pyramid scheme too far inducing a bust; their debt burden had grown too large for them to handle. Some have even speculated that the powerful banking cartel may have aggravated or induced the 1907 collapse to justify the creation of the Federal Reserve.[10] Think about the panic of 1907 and the subsequent creation of the Federal Reserve in 1913. Yet, only seven years later the Forgotten Depression of 1920-1921 gripped the American economy, followed by the decadent and money-flush Roaring Twenties, only to be bookended by the Great Depression of the 1930s. Even then, the Federal Reserve failed its intended purpose.

The "fixed supply" (see Figure 1) illustrates what I think would have been experienced if bankers refrained from fractional reserve banking. Society would still experience some variations (wave curve) but the flux would be quite moderate in comparison to fractional reserve banking, particularly under a central bank inflatable fiat currency regime. In addition, the average rate of growth is lower with fractional reserve banking, as artificial booms likely fuel malinvestment or go towards projects with a low potential. When currency and funding is easier to access, people compete for returns, and the frenzy leads to malinvestments. Wasting valuable resources through malinvestments is the primary reason this system provides, on average, a lower rate of growth (the dashed line) compared to a non-fractional reserve banking system (the light gray line).

Figure 2 on the next page, from goldchartsrus.com, presents the value of the Dow Jones Industrial Average priced in gold since 1800. Because the DJIA was created in 1882, a surrogate index was constructed for the first 82 years. The graph depicts a marked difference in the degree of fluctuation shortly after 1913, when the Federal Reserve was established. Prior to 1913, obvious variations track with the Civil War and other notable events such as the 1840 banking crisis in England, which had a central bank, that affected the world. But nothing compares to the post 1913 booms and busts. The first cycle occurs after World War I, during which

---

[10]Read The Creature from Jekyll Island by G. Edward Griffin.

Figure 2: Dow/Gold Ratio.

mass quantities of Federal Reserve Notes were created to fund the war. Next we see the impact of artificially low interest rates set in the 1920s, which led to the infamous 1929 crash and subsequent Great Depression. Yes, artificially low interest rate, just like before 2008 and recently in 2020.

Figure 2 presents a continuous average growth rate before and after 1913, which might indicate a distinction from my hypothesis. I believe a more accurate depiction of the growth rate would have been to draw two different average lines, one before 1913 and one after, which would show the slowdown in the actual rate of growth.

Since the "Nixon shock" of 1971, when we abandoned the semi-gold standard, fiat currencies have fluctuated against one another. But what I find amusing is how economists often compare these currencies against each other as a barometer of a currency's overall health. Typically, the US dollar index is used as the benchmark, but since all currencies are devaluing, bragging that your national currency is not sinking as fast as the others misses the point. At certain times, the US dollar will gain against all others, particularly when the Federal Reserve is increasing interest rates, but this strength is temporary as eventually the dollar catches up to the others.

Fiat currencies have exacerbated rather than alleviated poverty. This system benefits the wealthy, who own large apartment complexes and commercial real estate that is partially financed by debt that depreciates over time. Price inflation leads to higher salaries, which lead to higher rents while mortgage payments remain fixed. This is the first argument I raise with socialists who favor a fiat system to fund social programs. Most are unaware that depreciation of the dollar raises the cost of living and that the poor and lower-middle class are most affected by this hidden tax we know as inflation. Again, this is one of the core reasons bitcoiners believe bitcoin is well positioned to replace the entire fiat-based system.

I use the term Proof of Debt because, under the current central banking system, every dollar in existence is backed by someone owing that same amount. It makes no difference whether the debt is owed by the Federal Government, a state, a municipality, a corporate bond or even a home mortgage, a credit card, or a car loan. Regardless of the holder, all debt fuels our Proof of Debt system, leaving today's system far more dysfunctional than when the bankers pretended to back the dollar with gold. This is the reason the Federal government keeps raising the debt ceiling; clearly, it should be renamed a debt *target*, as it is obvious to anyone that once the government reaches the new ceiling, it will simply raise it to another level - again and again. If they stop doing so, the entire system implodes because the federal government is forced to issue new debt, which generates new money to reflate the commercial banking sector's pyramid scheme, enabling it to issue more loans.

To further illustrate: inflation and debt work together. Debt creates an artificial need for fiat currency to repay the loans, instilling a fear of deflation. Hollywood creations, such as *The Big Short* movie reminded the masses of this event, while also serving as a reminder that it may be unwise to go all in on competing currency since when deflation collapse happens, the debt takes over the inflation, giving the central banker even more power. Hence why Proof of Debt is so much a sick system compared to Proof of Work or any other for that matter.

A debt-based central banking system must be continually replenished with new debt, otherwise it will implode. This new debt, and the currency it creates, is primarily generated by the commercial banking sector in the form of personal or corporate expansion loans. Artificially low interest rates accelerate this process to a point where debt saturates the markets, just like in 2008, and exceedingly so in 1929. What follows is a recession or depression, along with a contraction of the money supply. During this time, government revenue from income tax is reduced because fewer peo-ple are making money, hence there is less income taxes. And, unless the government cuts spending, its deficit increases.

Rather than have the government cut spending, central bankers prefer that the government increase its spending to reflate the base of this in-verse pyramid of debt, allowing more currency to flood the commercial banking sector through support for new projects or new social programs. This newly minted currency then gives the banking sector the ability to make new loans and restart the process. Nevermind that while many in the private sector are suffering from the effects of a recession or depression, those closest to government spending benefit greatly, including govern-ment contractors often armed with excellent lobbyists and contacts. It's no wonder Roosevelt went on a spending spree, constructing many projects, implementing new social programs, and installing new regulations that ul-timately prolonged the depression.

The great depression of 1921 (yes, I did say 1921, not 1929) was short lived, only 18 months. The government cut spending, and the Federal Reserve let the interest rate be pushed higher by the market. At the time, the economy was backed by a strong gold currency. This action forced the dollar to keep its value against gold and other commodities - quite the opposite of Roosevelt's decision to devalue the dollar against gold by 40% and reflate the base with government spending. Today, the system is so full of derivatives and debt that it would implode if the Federal Reserve stopped the printing press.

Now that we have a full picture of the current fiat system, it lays the foundation for why Satoshi Nakamoto had a motivation in creating bit-coin. Although bitcoin might sound complicated to the uninitiated, once you understand a few core concepts like the Hash Algorithm, it gets much easier from there.

HASH ALGORITHM

Before diving into the comparison between bitcoin and altcoins, let's explore the key algorithm securing bitcoin's Proof of Work - the hash algorithm. A hash function is a mathematical algorithm that can be viewed as a one-way cryptographic function that creates a "fingerprint" of a document or text of any arbitrary length. The output generated by a hash always has a fixed size and is the hash value or message digest. For example, I could hash the entire content of this book using the SHA256 hash algorithm – which is the same one used by bitcoin – to get a hash output. If you do the same, we both will end up with the exact same hash output.

SHA-2 (or SHA256) stands for Secure Hash Algorithm which generates a fixed size output of 256 bits, or 32 bytes. The following is the output of a SHA256:

754ba38b7c62e1a09c7785cb35b5f3696c899fc63b59b412cf9e9ad42b6a344d

It was generated from this text:

This is the text I am using to show the output of a hash function

Just looking at a hash output, one has no way to know what originally generated it, and certainly one could not guess its size. Similarly, no one could have accurately guessed what the output of my text would look like until after I ran the SHA256. If I were to change a single character in my original text, I would end up with a completely different SHA256 output. You can try it yourself by searching on the web for SHA256 online generators. I used this link for this test:

https://emn178.github.io/online-tools/sha256.html

To win a block, a bitcoin miner must generate a hash output of his version of the block, which contains the bitcoin transactions he selected and which credits him with transaction fees and the newly created bitcoin as part of the block rewards. This hash output also must be lower than a certain value, meaning the hash output must contain a certain number of leading zeros. To achieve this, miners must increment a specific number in their block until the hash output reaches a specific attribute. This means a lot of calls to the SHA256 function must be made until one lucky miner is the first to discover such a hash output. As an example, the hash output below was for bitcoin block number 750464. The hash output discovered was:

0000000000000000009bf7fa29635b5d638d46c27bac1ab554fdc4ae9fadb7f

In essence, this miner must dedicate enormous effort to generate these millions of hash calculations, yet it is easy for anyone to verify with a single calculation. This is what constitutes Proof of Work (PoW). As applied, PoW secures the bitcoin network, and it also touches another topic, energy usage, that we will discuss later.

THE IMPORTANCE OF DECENTRALIZATION

Decentralization of the bitcoin network is so integral to its success that it warrants further discussion. Recall the story of the FBI's raid of coins and certificate paper at Sunshine Minting. The record shows that the FBI never returned the silver and certificates to those rightful owners, sending a clear message to anyone who might be interested in investing in a similar program in the future. More recently, in March of 2022, Western governments began seizing yachts of rich Russians, just for being Russian, regardless of their relationship with the Russian government itself. Meanwhile, services like YouTube, Airbnb, and Upwork barred anyone from Russia from receiving revenue streams, even though not all Russian banks were banned from the SWIFT (Society for Worldwide Interbank Financial Telecommunications) system. And of course, some cryptocurrency exchanges indiscriminately blocked accounts of Russian citizens.

Russians were not the only group to suffer a recent government crackdown on monetary freedom. In February 2022, the Canadian government ordered banks to freeze accounts of Freedom convoy truckers and even some of those who donated to their cause. The Canadian government also ordered all regulated financial firms to block any transactions from 34 bitcoin addresses that held donations to the truckers in the Freedom convoy.

In times of "crisis," most governments will increase surveillance and control, revealing their true nature. Governments that want to go after economic freedom will, among other things, clamp down on centralized exchanges, the regulated on and off ramps for US dollar and bitcoin trades. Know-Your-Customer (KYC) and Anti-Money Laundering (AML) regulations require customers to provide information to prove that the customer is who he says he is. That information can easily tie each customer to a bitcoin address when the bitcoin is first withdrawn from an exchange. But what happens when a cryptocurrency network is not decentralized enough? Most bitcoin maximalists view decentralization as a 1 or 0, meaning it is either decentralized, like bitcoin, or it is not. I disagree with this assessment. To me, decentralization is a matter of degree. Consider: How much crazy "1984" style government activity, or rather, how much government planetary worldwide coordination, would be required to block a cryptocurrency? In other words, what if all worldwide governments went full authoritarian mode and made it illegal for anyone to operate a cryptocurrency network, or if they are permitted to operate, nodes must follow KYC/AML regulations.

If the entire planet were blanketed by such a ruling, no cryptocurrency could flourish. Sure, you could run a bitcoin node on a boat in the middle of the Pacific with a satellite link[11] to avoid these regulations, but all the other nodes would reject your blocks for containing blacklisted addresses. What is the current possibility of such a scenario? Very low, right now, but perhaps not as much in some (I hope) far distant dystopian future where we have another 9/11 style attack justifying war on terrorism, forcing countries to participate in an Orwellian program.

What about a partial version of this? What if, say, all European countries and the United States and Canada forced bitcoin miners within their jurisdiction to only include transactions containing whitelisted bitcoin addresses in their blocks? Since, in aggregate, these miners would have more than 51% of the current hash power, blocks mined in other countries allowing blacklisted addresses would be rejected by miners located in these Euro-North American countries. Because the Euro-North American miners comprise the majority of the hash power, the longest chain would always be the one following the whitelisted ruling, breaking the fungibility of bitcoin. Is there a way around this? Probably. Due to economic pressures, these miners will likely close shop and move their equipment to another country outside the whitelist-only jurisdictions, hence increasing the hash power of miners external to the Euro-North American blockade.

Predatory governments could always pass laws that require seizure of mining equipment if the owners attempted to move them out of the whitelist blockade. Of course, in the long run, mining companies subject to these oppressive, ridiculous regulations would stop investing in equip-

---

[11] https://blockstream.com/satellite/

ment and start investing in territories friendly to mining endeavors. It is also possible that the bitcoin code is modified so as to induce a fork (soft or hard) where miners outside of the blockade disregard miners operating in them. This example I just mentioned is to illustrate what type of cold war like scenario might be played out, but what I really want to show is how decentralization is a polarized concept. Thus, I don't think it is as simple as bitcoin maximalists assert. If one argues that only a decentralized blockchain makes sense, then the Liquid Network, made by a group of bitcoin maximalists, doesn't make sense. To best understand, we need to look at this from a probability perspective, with the worst scenario being a complete ban of bitcoin by all governments of the world. I do want to point out, however, that I believe bitcoin is the most decentralized of all cryptocurrencies.

By now, decentralization's importance to the bitcoin network is clear, particularly when it comes to preserving fungibility. Certainly, decentralization would prevent any other form of attacks or manipulation by bad actors. For example, they could be rewriting transaction history where they recover prior payments they have done, or they get an artificial benefit in mining blocks. Fungibility is where one bitcoin is the same as any other bitcoin, but if a government puts my bitcoin address and its content in a blacklist where I cannot spend it, it breaks the fungibility. The more decentralized a coin and its blockchain is, the less chances of this to happen.

The more computer nodes are running bitcoin and keeping a copy of its blockchain, the more resilient and secure it becomes and which in term increases its attraction as a secure store of value which in terms attracts more nodes to join, therefore a positive feedback loop increasing its network effect.

One of the main points to consider when evaluating various cryptocurrencies and consensus mechanisms is each currency's degree of decentralization. For some, it might be acceptable to have a less decentralized currency playground if the amount of wealth involved is lower and proportional to its risk. Other than a few drug lords, no one carries hundreds of thousands of dollars in his pocket because the risk of loss is great should you be attacked by a mugger or arrested by a police officer who exercises the power of civil asset forfeiture laws.[12] The same would apply to your wealth on a blockchain. In this case, most of it should be in the most secure form, which I argue is bitcoin, and, to a much lesser degree, other suitable blockchains, should you choose that path.

So, if we agree that decentralization is important and that among the key elements to achieve this is to have a lot of computer nodes carrying a copy of the blockchain, then this set of requirements will be among the top we will consider. Granted, other considerations might compensate for a lack of nodes, but these factors must be explored.

Because there are always some dependencies somewhere, decentralization is a shade of gray or a gradient. As for bitcoin, its main dependency rests with physical mining nodes relying on electricity and the fact miners are the one deciding which transactions will go in the next block. Consider if the IMF-World bank imposed a planetary-wide ban on bitcoin mining. Another dependency is procuring specialized chips for bitcoin mining, which are manufactured exclusively in a handful of countries and require specialized licensing, patents, and more. Even in the land of the free, President F.D. Roosevelt outlawed gold ownership in 1933. But, I believe an action this extreme relating to bitcoin is quite improbable in the foreseeable future.

If decentralization is so vital, why isn't it the primary focus and then the controversy would be settled? The issue is that decentralization comes at the expense of something else. A blockchain design must prioritize three properties: decentralization, scalability, and security.

Decentralization is where you have a system that is not controlled by one or a few organizations. Scalable is where the system can handle a high volume of transactions. Finally, security is when the system is resilient to attacks or hacks. The trilemma comes from the general idea that

---

[12] In the United States, this does not require conviction or even criminal charges, and most forfeitures are related to "suspected" illicit drug activities. For a detailed review, search the Internet for "police seize cash from motorists."

compromises must be made on one of the 3 properties in order to satisfy the other 2. Recognizing this trade-off, Vitalik Buterin, one of Ethereum's co-founders, coined the phrase "blockchain trilemma" to describe the challenge developers must confront when attempting to create a blockchain with all three qualities. This is often depicted as a triangle as illustrated here:

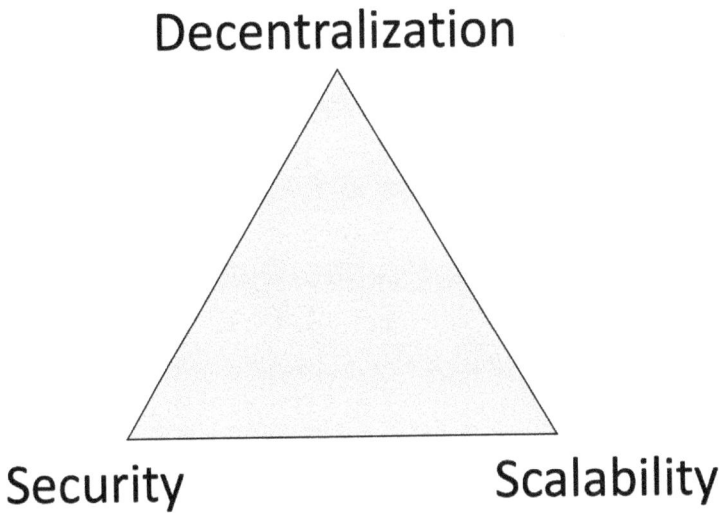

Decentralization

Security   Scalability

Figure 3: The 3 ultimate attributes of a blockchain.

As you might be aware, bitcoin has focused heavily on decentralization and security, which, for a long-term store of wealth, would be the primary attribute of importance. Scalability, however, has not been neglected and can still be achieved with layer-2 mechanisms such as the lightning network. Notably, layer-2 mechanisms are not an integral part of the blockchain's activity, but in the end does it matter? We will go over this in more detail in a later chapter.

THE RISE OF ALTCOINS

Satoshi Nakamoto opened a flood gate of discoveries advancing decentralization and cryptography when he revealed to the world a decentralized digital currency with a finite supply that prevented double spending. At the beginning, skepticism was rampant but as bitcoin proved itself, criticism took over. Once bitcoin gained in popularity, some complained that bitcoin mining was largely performed by GPU (Graphic Processing Unit), raising concerns that mining had a high barrier of entry. This led to the creation of the first altcoin project called Tenebrix (TBX), which replaced SHA256 with the *scrypt algorithm*, which does not make it economically feasible for ASIC (Application Specific Integrated Circuit) hardware. At launch, the developers intended to credit themselves (with pre-mine coins) a total of 7.7 million TBX. This move was heavily criticized, and the project did not take off. Soon after, Charlie Lee, a then employee of Google, recycled this idea, launching Litecoin (LTC) in October 2011. Using bitcoin's source code, he made the following minor modifications:

- Total supply set at 84 million maximum coins - 4 times larger than bitcoin's 21 million maximum supply;

- Time between block is 2.5 minutes, 4 times smaller at than bitcoin's 10 minutes average block time; and

- Scrypt is used rather than SHA256 as the hash algorithm for miners.

Litecoin didn't add much innovation, and many would claim not much value either. It offers nothing new, and it is no more a utility blockchain than bitcoin is. Users gain no value in having multiple currencies, it creates an overhead by having to exchange between and incurs a cost in the exchange rate. Sure, Litecoin blocks are 4 times faster, 2.5-minute intervals, but the corresponding lower difficulty level requires four times more blocks to get the same level of confirmation as bitcoin. Many regarded Litecoin as an annoying project shifting the limelight from bitcoin. But since its market cap was a fraction of bitcoin's, most bitcoiners dismissed it as a threat. Because the price of Litecoin is quite a bit more volatile than bitcoin, traders are among the happiest about its existence. This important point illustrates why I believe bitcoin should function as the gold standard in an investment portfolio. Review this chart of Litecoin priced in US dollars. At first glance, it seems Litecoin investors have been doing quite well.

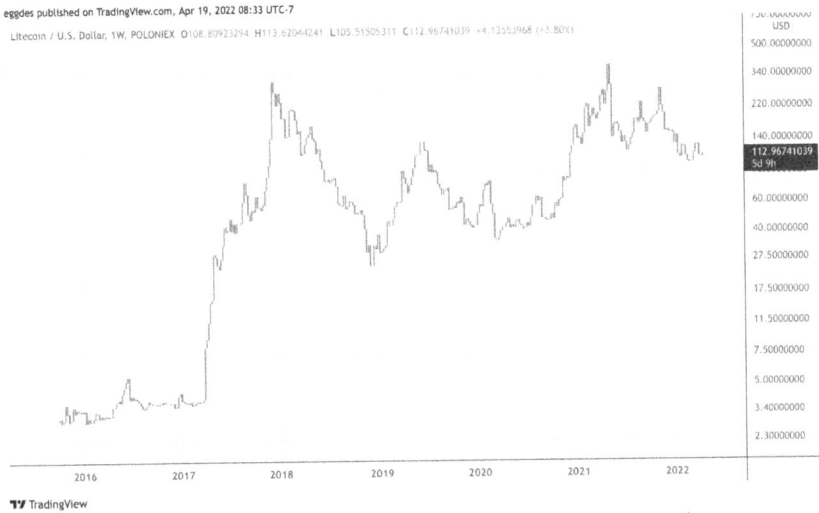

Figure 4: Litecoin priced in USD.

This chart goes back to 2015. Particularly in 2017, the price of Litecoin jumped from about $3.50 to about $330, almost a factor of 100 in the year. Then, it corrected all the way down to $25, and as I am writing this today in April 2023, it is around $98. So, since 2015, it looks strong, but if you are interested in investing in a cryptocurrency, you might as well compare it against others. Your question is: which of these options would have performed the best? And importantly, what can you expect in the future?

Pricing a cryptocurrency against the USD and/or your respective national currency is an important analysis. But, to form a more complete picture, you should also compare it against bitcoin. eg., What does the chart of Litecoin look like when priced in bitcoin instead? The Figure 5 depicts this pairing on the Poloniex exchange all the way back to 2014.

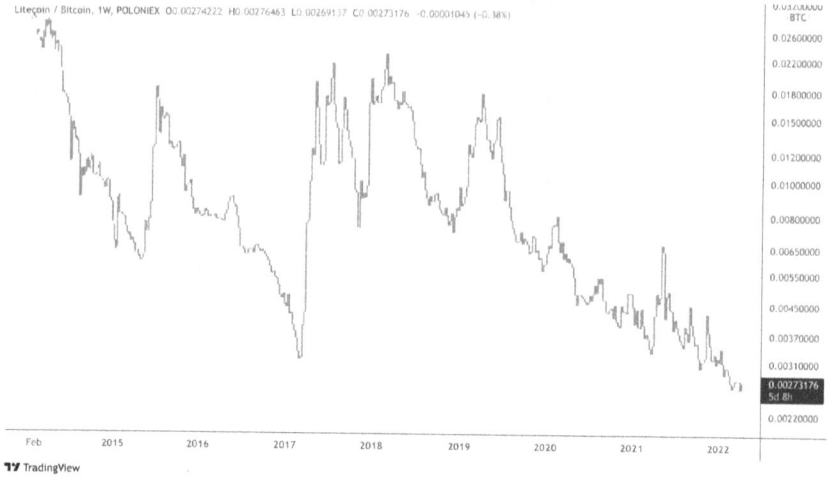

Figure 5: Litecoin priced in bitcoin.

This figure shows that bitcoin has outperformed Litecoin since its peak in 2014. Yet, it is possible that Litecoin could catch up to bitcoin's highs during what cryptocurrency traders call the altcoin season. If your intention is to be a trader, then this chart will undoubtedly excite you as you see trading potential from its inherent volatility. Unfortunately, many non-trader newbie investors will jump into the frenzy when Litecoin goes up and buy at the top (priced in bitcoin) exactly when the experienced traders are selling. It's also worth noting that Litecoin has been in a bear market (when priced in bitcoin) since 2018 and not made a new high when priced in dollars (still true in 2023).

So Litecoin's performance is not that impressive compared to bitcoin, but what about with other cryptocurrencies? For this comparison, you can research several websites, coingecko.com and coinmarketcap.com are two of the most popular. These sites rank cryptocurrencies by market capitalization. When visiting https://coinmarketcap.com/historical, you can view a historical snapshot showing past rankings. The table on the next page shows the rankings on February 9, 2014. Given that Litecoin was the second cryptocurrency created, it enjoyed a relatively significant value compared to others in the beginning, with one twentieth the size of bitcoin.

Rank	Name	Symbol	Market Cap	Price
1	Bitcoin	BTC	$8,451,229,252.14	$682.90
2	Litecoin	LTC	$465,932,119.29	$18.22
3	XRP	XRP	$135,951,310.04	$0.01739
4	Peercoin	PPC	$98,911,679.93	$4.68
5	Dogecoin	DOGE	$60,542,522.21	$0.001291
6	Nxt	NXT	$48,927,824.73	$0.04893
7	Omni	OMNI	$38,623,691.43	$62.35
8	Namecoin	NMC	$34,226,581.98	$4.28
9	Quark	QRK	$19,774,657.92	$0.07989
10	BitShares PTS	PTS	$16,778,316.76	$11.60

Table 1: Coinmarketcap.com Feb 9th, 2014[13]

When most altcoins are compared against BTC, a vast majority are marching to the graveyard.

Consider Populous (PPT) which on January 30th, 2018, was ranked #21 on coinmarketcap.com and was valued at 0.0068 BTC, or 680,000 satoshis per PPT. (Note: 1 satoshi is 10-8 BTC). Today, it is ranked #1025 and valued at 0.00000354 BTC or 354 satoshis, which is only a fraction (about 1/2000) of its prior value. This story has been told before and will be told again - different coin, same plotline. Many hardened bitcoin maximalists today were once invested in altcoins but ultimately lost a significant amount of money in them, which has steeled their resolve to only own bitcoins.

Interestingly, while there was still an intense debate in 2017 about updating bitcoin's code to include segregated witness ("segwit") and the battle about increasing the block size, Litecoin pushed through and introduced segwit in May 2017. Segregated witness was a soft fork change in the transaction format that removed transaction malleability from bitcoin, an undesirable property that hackers could exploit if exchanges and other op-

---

[13]https://coinmarketcap.com/historical/20140209/

erators were not vigilant. In fact, this is one of the reasons why hackers were able to steal funds from the infamous Mt. Gox bitcoin exchange in 2014. Implementation of Segwit was also required to develop the lightning network, a layer 2 protocol that allows bitcoin to transfer at a high throughput (many transactions per second) and with instant delivery. So, Litecoin was one of the first to introduce segwit it in May 2017, allowing for the lightning network to be used and tested live for the first time in a reasonably sized network. Some argued that Litecoin could then be viewed as a beta test of the segregated witness soft fork, although I'm sure Litecoin developers did not consider their work a beta network program.[14]

Just months before developers created Litecoin in October 2011, another group of developers launched Namecoin (NMC) in April of that same year. Hilariously Namecoin's concept had been discussed by Satoshi Nakamoto himself in a forum post where he described another blockchain and theoretical currency called BitDNS. (See, *The Book of Satoshi*, p. 314). The purpose of both BitDNS and Namecoin was to register domain names. What is fascinating, and crucial in terms of Proof of Work, is Satoshi's argument about how the hash power of the two blockchains, bitcoin and bitDNS could be merged to combine forces. Satoshi's forum post reads as follows:

> I think it would be possible for BitDNS to be a completely separate network and separate block chain, yet share CPU power with bitcoin. The only overlap is to make it so miners can search for Proof of Work for both networks simultaneously. The networks wouldn't need any coordination. Miners would subscribe to both networks in parallel. They would scan SHA such that if they get a hit, they potentially solve both at once. A solution may be for just one of the networks if one network has a lower difficulty. I think an external miner could call getwork on both programs and combine the work. Maybe

---

[14] A beta program is a pre-release of a new software product by software companies to certain customers willing to take a risk and try it out.

call bitcoin, get work from it, hand it to BitDNS getwork to combine into a combined work. Instead of fragmentation, networks share and augment each other's total CPU power. This would solve the problem that if there are multiple networks, they are a danger to each other if the available CPU power gangs up on one. Instead, all networks in the world would share combined CPU power, increasing the total strength. It would make it easier for small networks to get started by tapping into a ready base of miners.

This is an important issue to grasp because the amount of hash power is inextricably linked to the network's security. The challenge for altcoins is that they consistently have only a fragment of bitcoin's hash power, creating a perpetual threat of a 51% attack, an extremely low threat for bitcoin itself. We will cover hash power in greater detail in chapter three.

Because Namecoin had a specific utility – storing domain name – it wasn't wholly perceived as a useless altcoin. Remember, at the time, cryptocurrencies with smart contracts, like Ethereum, had not yet been developed. One of Namecoin's major flaws was that it failed to combine hash power with bitcoin, as Satoshi envisioned, which would have required a fork of bitcoin. Without this crucial tie to bitcoin, Namecoin remained subject to the 51% attack. Namecoin's fate imparts a critical lesson. Today, Namecoin's market capitalization is quite low, ranking 521 as of this writing, demonstrating the significance of bitcoin as a store of value, a theme that will be repeated often throughout this book.

Table 2 shows a partial list of the first cryptocurrencies introduced up through 2013. In this table, PoW stands for Proof of Work, PoS stands for Proof of Stake.

Additional cryptocurrencies were launched in 2014, even more in 2015, and quite a few more in 2016 and 2017, thus the ramping up of the "production" of altcoins. Although a few developers claimed to have a legitimate business strategy for their project, many were merely copycats. Until 2017, most people saw these altcoins as either a fresh concept, an

Year	Currency	Symbol	Hash algorithm	Consensus	Description
2009	Bitcoin	BTC	SHA-256	PoW	Genesis block created on January 3rd, 2009
2011	Litecoin	LTC	Scrypt	PoW	First to use Scrypt
2011	Namecoin	NMC	SHA-256	PoW	Decentralized Domain Name server
2012	Peercoin	PPC	SHA-256	PoW & PoS	First to use Proof of Stake
2013	Dogecoin	DOGE	Scrypt	PoW	Originally created as a joke from a meme
2013	Gridcoin	GRC	Scrypt	PoS	Another PoS variant. Currently ranked 1315 in market capitalization
2013	Primecoin	XPM	Cunningham Chain	PoW	Proof of Work with the practical use of searching for chains of prime numbers
2013	Ripple	XRP	ECDSA	Consensus	Settlement system and remittance and other uses. See Chapter on it

Table 2: Creation of the first cryptocurrencies

interesting experiment or dummy project, but none were seen as a threat to bitcoin's unrivaled supremacy. However, as Figure 6 illustrates, this changed radically in 2017. This chart depicts the percentage of bitcoin's market cap in relation to the total market cap of all cryptocurrencies. Before 2017, bitcoin dominated the market, accounting for 95% or more of the total market capitalization. Note, however, the introduction of a myriad of tiny, illiquid projects since 2016 has distorted bitcoin's genuine significance. For example, if 30% of the coins are held by founders who never moved their coins, it inflates their respective market cap as there is less liquidity.

Then, in 2017, with the rise of Ethereum and all of its tokens and smart contracts, as well as the bitcoin fork that resulted in the creation of Bitcoin

eggdes published on TradingView.com, Apr 12, 2022 11:54 UTC-7

Market Cap BTC Dominance, % (CALCULATED BY TRADINGVIEW), 1W, CRYPTOCAP O41.70% H41.89% L41.38% C41.57% -0.11% (-0.25%)

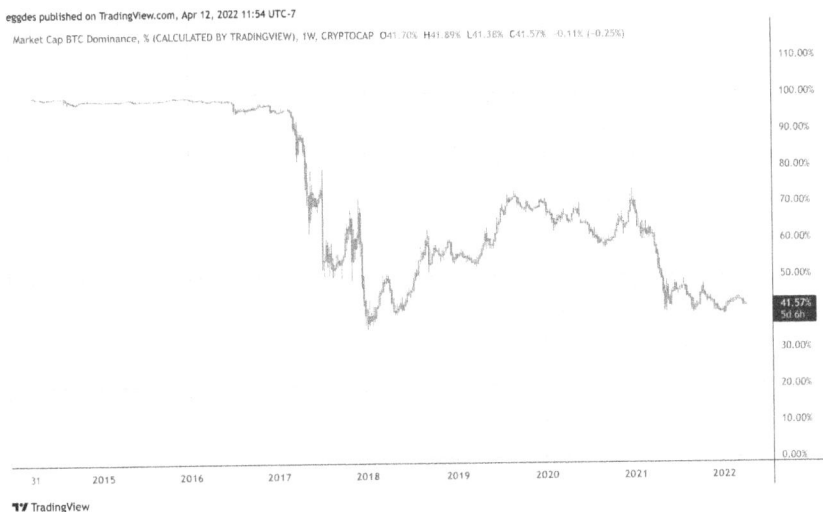

Figure 6: Bitcoin Dominance chart in %

Cash, bitcoin dominance fell significantly, reaching an all-time low of 35% of the overall market cap at the end of the bitcoin bull market in December 2017. Indeed, the data shows a dramatic decline from 66% to 35% in a couple of weeks.

During the bull market of 2017, many joined a speculative frenzy of investing in various "tokens," cryptocurrencies, and projects, and although some people won money, many others lost. (Tokens will be discussed in greater depth later.) It was at this time a bitcoin fork emerged from an intensive war of words including the big block-small block argument. Here is where two opposing visions of what bitcoin should look like coexisted, resulting in a split of the ledger history into two distinct blockchains, with the new one known as Bitcoin Cash emerging. This split produced a fork that increased the maximum block size from 1 Megabyte to 8 Megabyte. At that moment, all bitcoin holders also became owners of Bitcoin Cash. Before this historical twist, new cryptocurrencies would either duplicate the broad idea of bitcoin, or actually clone the complete code base and just make small adjustments, as Litecoin did, but begin anew, with a fresh blockchain. But this time, they not only shared the same code with small adjustments, in this case raising the block size, but they also shared the same blockchain up to that divergent point.

Figure 7 depicts the various histories of bitcoin, Litecoin, and Bitcoin Cash. Because Litecoin began with a new blockchain history, Litecoin history is isolated from what happened on bitcoin's blockchain. They do, however, have a shared background with Bitcoin Cash. People who possessed bitcoins before the Bitcoin Cash schism ended up having the same amount of both bitcoin and Bitcoin Cash. Some did nothing, while others sold their Bitcoin Cash and traded it for bitcoin or, to a lesser extent, vice versa. After the fork, people had to choose whose blockchain history (which currency between bitcoin and Bitcoin Cash) they would buy, just as they had done with Litecoin from the start.

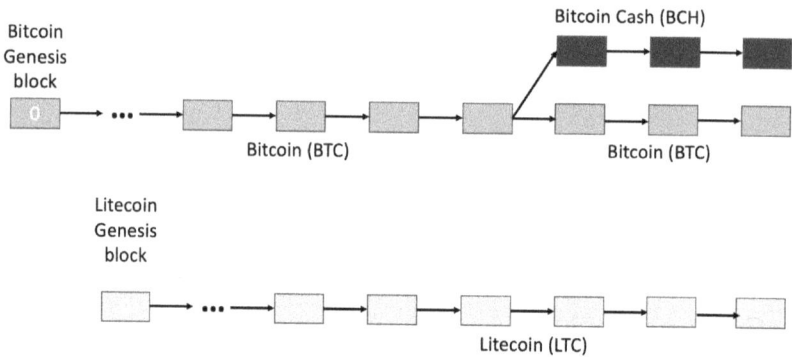

Figure 7: Bitcoin, Litecoin and Bitcoin Cash

This schism abruptly divided bitcoiners into multiple camps, and many users were unsure where to go. Additional issues emerged, such as whether the user should retain both and do nothing, or whether the user should sell the Bitcoin Cash and acquire more bitcoins, or vice versa. And which one should people who desire to amass more bitcoin choose? After all, the advocates of Bitcoin Cash framed it as the "right bitcoin," so how could the average person seeking to get into this not be perplexed? Although the word "shitcoin" was initially mentioned on the BitcoinTalk forum in 2010, it rose in popularity after the Bitcoin Cash fork on August 1, 2017. Before the hard fork and for some time thereafter, the transaction fees on bitcoin were quite high, reaching as much as $100 per transaction. Naturally, this fueled Bitcoin Cash promoters' claim that they were correct and that their blockchain should be recognized as the one true bitcoin.

In reality, though, Bitcoin Cash never challenged bitcoin. Bitcoin Cash's peak price was about 25% that of bitcoin, trailing Ethereum in price. As of this writing, in April 2023, Bitcoin Cash is ranked 27th in market capitalization. I believe developers botched the Bitcoin Cash fork as it should have included a new bitcoin address format to distinguish between the two. At the time, bitcoin addresses began with a 1, as in "1ah5j...", and Bitcoin Cash initially followed the same pattern. Numerous users who attempted to move bitcoins to or from an exchange sent them to an address on the opposite blockchain, resulting in the loss of their bitcoins. It was not until January 2018 that Bitcoin Cash developers looked into the issue and remedied it with a new format. This makes sense; after all, it was Bitcoin Cash developers who altered the code that created the hard fork, therefore it was their obligation to change the address format.

The year 2017 heralded the start of a new era in cryptocurrency investing. Before, most people had only heard of bitcoin, but by now they had become familiar with Ethereum and perhaps a few others. New investors flooded into this market, sometimes skipping the market leader, bitcoin, and diving directly into altcoins. Then, as today, people avoided bitcoin due to negative feedback from friends and relatives. Bitcoin has been criticized in the following ways:

- Proof of Work wastes energy;

- Transactions are slow, with only 7 per second; and

- Bitcoin is useless and has no purpose.

Some of these are appropriate concerns to address, but before we can fully address each of them, we must first answer the proper fundamental questions.

- Why was bitcoin created?

- How important decentralization is and why would it be?

- How can a cryptocurrency network and its blockchain be made resilient to interference by any kind of cartel?

- What should be the primary focus – transactions throughput or decentralization or something else?

I'll explain later why I view these as the essential issues we must first answer before moving on to the three concerns outlined above, but first let's work through these four questions.

Returning to today, we can divide the current state of thought into several groups. Bitcoiners regard speculation in "shitcoins" as disastrous for newbies who invest in coins that will inevitably go through the pump and dump cycle. They also express concern that these altcoins pull the spotlight away from bitcoin. According to them, if the goal is to get rid of central banking, bitcoin must be widely adopted, and the more time and money spent on other initiatives, the longer it will take for bitcoin to supplant the present defective central banking system. Conversely, those involved in altcoins either see bitcoin as inefficient or believe that other complementary projects can bring added value such as new, decentralized economic activity to avoid the requirement of third parties. Consider smart contracts, which enable the exchange of stable coins for bitcoin or Ether on the blockchain without centralized exchanges.

VARIANTS FROM PROOF OF WORK

In the several years after bitcoin was introduced to the world, altcoins began to proliferate and some devised methods to guarantee consensus with some degree of decentralization. To be truly decentralized and secure, a network must defend against a Sybil attack. In other words, it must be Sybil resistant. The name "Sybil" is inspired from the title of a 1973 book chronicling the actual tale of Shirley Ardell Mason, who wrote under the pen name Sybil Dorsett while suffering from multiple personality disorder. A Sybil attack is an exploit against a network in which a small number of bad actors attempt to take control of the network by leveraging multiple accounts, entities, nodes, or computers. In such an attack, the bad actors create what are called Sybil identities to out-vote honest nodes. These same bad actors would also aim to operate numerous Sybil identities to influence the network by denying transactions, disrupting the network, or even attempting to rewrite history, as with the 51% assault in Proof of Work. Both Proof of Work and Proof of Stake rely on economic deterrents against Sybil attacks by requiring users to spend either energy or collateral in the currency linked to the blockchain's value to participate in network operation and maintenance. The table on the next page lists and describes the various ways cryptocurrencies employ consensus mechanisms today.

In this book, we will cover the three most popular consensus methods: Proof of Work, Proof of Stake, and Proof of Authority. What's noteworthy about those top three is how hard-core supporters of each believe their approach is the only one that's genuine. The most contentious of the three is Proof of Authority, with criticism focusing on how centralized it is.

BITCOIN HATERS

Bitcoin's unifying principle, as articulated in the white paper, opens the door to a new type of shared database, with its consensus process allowing everyone to affirm its most recent state in a decentralized manner. And yet, detractors remain. Of course, gold bugs have their reasons, but individuals, too, have concerns with user experience, throughput, speedy confirmation, but are not so concerned with security issues, like the prospect of a cartel attacking or taking over a network.

Most computer scientists and professionals in cryptography and

---

[15]For more information about this unique consensus method, see, https://filecoin.io /filecoin.pdf.

[16]For more information about PoET: https://www.investopedia.com/terms/p/proof-elapsed-time-cryptocurrency.asp

Mechanism	Description
Proof of Work (PoW)	Computational work to be the first to solve a cryptographic puzzle (hash of block with specific attribute). Any proposed block not respecting this will be rejected and hence a waste of time and energy.
Proof of Stake (PoS)	Impose a financial stake by forcing consensus participants to lock up funds in the digital currency. The protocol would penalize any participants performing invalid operations. Cardano is one well known.
Proof of Authority (PoA)	This is based on reputation where a consortium of players chooses who can participate. See, for example, XRP and the bitcoin Liquid network.
Proof of Space (or space-time) (PoST)	Participants must allocate disk space to solve challenges; they earn rewards in return. Filecoin[15]is the most well-known cryptocurrency using it.
Proof of Elapsed Time[16](PoET)	Used to decide on mining rights by permissioned blockchain networks which are a type of network that require any would-be participant to identify itself before it is permitted to join. PoETs are typically not publicly accessible. Hyperledger Sawtooth by Intel is an example.
Proof of Burn (PoB)	Miners must burn coins to earn the right to create blocks and be rewarded. Invalid blocks would get rejected and this would mean burning coins as a complete loss, hence a penalty.

Table 3: Various consensus mechanisms employed by different cryptocurrencies

networking focus on important theoretical concerns like probability, game theory, and other components that the uninitiated will be unaware of, which is why this distinction exists. Let's look at a few youtubers and influencers engaged with XRP and its primary company, Ripple. These influencers consider bitcoin and its Proof of Work system as "nonfunctional" because they believe it is sluggish and consumes too much energy. They also assert it offers no use but that XRP does. Their idea is that XRP will replace the antiquated SWIFT system while also enabling smart contracts like Ethereum. Conversely, bitcoiners, like myself, find XRP insufficiently decentralized, if at all, leaving it open to subjugation by governments and nefarious cartels. XRP supporters highlight that it can process 1500 transactions per second, while confirming them in a matter of seconds. These individuals, as well as many others pushing high throughput cryptocurrency schemes, are primarily concerned with scalability, yet still claim that XRP is sufficiently decentralized. XRP supporters also point to the time it takes for a bitcoin transaction to be confirmed. The average time between blocks is 10 minutes and a transaction must wait up to three to six blocks before it can be fully confirmed with great confidence. To them, anything faster is seen as a vastly superior, more enhanced cryptocurrency, regardless of its other deficiencies.

Sometimes I ponder what if bitcoin's network and consensus had been designed with high scalability but a weak form of decentralization. Would the Secret Service or another agency have raided the homes of the few dozens of early network node operators? Or perhaps a government would have captured the nascent bitcoin mining community when it consisted of just a handful of miners running software on personal computers. Notably, neither happened. One reason bitcoin was ignored by governments and big business is that the banking cartel saw it as just a funny experiment unlikely to succeed. After all, the majority of banking and government leaders had been (and still are) indoctrinated by Keynesian economics and they could not conceive that a currency could thrive without being backed by guns, taxes or some form of utility commodity, like gold. It is easy to imagine that if a libertarian gold bug like Peter Schiff dismissed it, others would have as well. Perhaps we can even speculate that past periodic bitcoin price crashes may have fueled their belief that bitcoin's short-lived success had run its course, while under the radar, bitcoin accumulated more hash power and a larger number of nodes, surreptitiously growing more resilient over time. So, if bitcoin's decentralization is vital to its longevity, many would ask why not have hundreds of currencies for different purposes.

THERE CAN BE ONLY ONE

Why is there such a heated argument in one asset class that is not present in others, such as stocks? No investor in Apple (AAPL) would publicly criticize shareholders of competitors, as is the case with bitcoin and many other cryptocurrencies. One important factor is the network effect. Individuals who have invested in XRP or Bitcoin Cash will argue that bitcoin is inefficient and slow and that their preferred currency should be the one gaining network effect and be used as the main currency. Similarly, bitcoin maximalists believe that bitcoin will eventually become the world currency, and that any promotion of rival cryptocurrencies merely delays its adoption and harms those who have invested in the losing currencies, as they will never replace bitcoin. This tweet from Saifedean Ammous, author of *The Bitcoin Standard*, illustrates this point.

Saifedean.com
@saifedean
...

Bitcoiners and shitcoiners are not on the same team. They couldn't be more different.

Bitcoiners see a once-in-a-millennium chance for the total eradication of seigniorage & monetary parasites.

Shitcoiners just see an opportunity for them to become the monetary parasites.

1:34 AM · Oct 24, 2021 · Twitter Web App

This entire episode, which heightened in 2017 when bitcoin's market dominance was dramatically diminished, has fueled bitcoiners' animosity toward all other projects. Bitcoin is unlikely to relinquish its top spot, but it is worth further discussion as it may be part of the banking cartel's plan B. Those who advocate for Ethereum, XRP, or any other Proof of Stake currencies find this type of message divisive and demeaning. They regard bitcoin as inefficient, sluggish, and expensive, despite the fact that the lightning network, a layer 2 network built on top of bitcoin, addresses the majority of these use cases. One thing I like to remind people of is that prior to the publication of the bitcoin white paper, everyone claimed there was no way to develop a decentralized cryptocurrency. Yet it happened. The lightning network white paper, published a few years after bitcoin's establishment in February 2015, addressed the need for faster, less expensive transaction fees - and further enhancements are on the way.

Back in the early 2010s, many bitcoiners, myself included, saw alternative cryptocurrencies such as Litecoin as nuisance projects. What was the point? The "Bitcoin is gold and Litecoin is silver" mantra was, in my opinion, a silly analogy given that bitcoin solves gold's portability problem. It's just as easy to pay 0.0001 BTC as it is to pay 0.1 BTC, while the distinction between paying either 1 gram or 1 ton of gold is obvious; further gold could never transact in micro payments where just 1 atom would be transacted, unless done so electronically.

But we must not forget that government fiat currency continues to dominate. This frenzy is fueled by a low-interest-rate environment that allows for reckless speculation in all asset classes, including stocks and real estate. Nothing will change this unless the central banking train fully derails. When I say that the existing central banking system relies on proof-of-debt, I mean it. With every dollar in existence, someone is in debt that exact amount and more due to interest payments. Plus, there is always more debt than government currency to pay it, which is why the US Congress is continually forced to set a new debt target. In my opinion, they wrongly call it raising the debt ceiling since, clearly, they never have the intention to respect it. In reality, you can't stop a debt system from issuing additional debt; otherwise, it will implode.

The vast majority of dollars are generated in the commercial banking sector when customers borrow to buy a house, a vehicle, or any other financial item that is financed. When the federal government needs to borrow, central banks are always eager to lend; yet, in private banking, customers eventually run out of gas, resulting in a crash. As a result, these booms and busts continue. Many are calling for a major market crash, which probably will start with a bond market problem. I am writing this in late 2022 so by the time you read this, circumstances may be different and a debt crisis may be underway already. Because of the immense amount of debt in the commercial sector, when there is a recession/depression, people become frightened and pay off some of their debt. Because dollars and debt are like matter and antimatter, when these dollars pay off that debt, they are destroyed just like this debt. Fractional reserve banking works in reverse when the debt is paid, which creates a deflationary trend, unless the central bank compensates with heavy printing. When this occurs, all assets will be hit. At some point during the deflationary trend, we should expect a major intervention by central bankers, just as we have seen in the past. The argument is that, in times of uncertainty, investors steer away from specialized cryptocurrencies, but will seek shelter in proven, good investments that provide a rational alternative to the under-pressure bond market.

Conversely, during times of heavy price inflation or even hyperinflation, all cryptocurrencies as well as gold and silver will skyrocket. When the dollar is sinking like the Titanic, everything that floats, even if barely, may look like a lifeboat. This same type of collapse occurred in Weimar Germany in 1922-1923, a time when hyperinflation raged. Indeed, a wheelbarrow was thought to be more precious than the amount of Deutsche Marks it held. All the while, the value of the wheelbarrow, real estate, and every other good was crashing in relation to gold, the most prominent and well-known currency. It is said, one ounce of gold was enough to purchase a beautiful home in central Berlin! So, keep that story in mind.

Many cryptocurrencies will go up but not in the same way. Some altcoins will go up in value compared to bitcoin only to crash later. Their high volatility will make bitcoin appear more attractive and less speculative. During periods of intense price inflation, speculation goes into overdrive, resulting in unprecedented volatility. When gold was priced in Deutsche Marks during Weimar Germany's hyperinflation period, it might climb by 300% in three days before falling by 40% the next day, only to rise again the next day.

Central banking and fiat currency are both horrible, and our best hope is to replace them with a sound currency like bitcoin. Many agree that the sooner we get there, the better. On this topic, Saifedeen Ammous, author of *The Bitcoin Standard* (and of the before referenced tweet), makes an interesting point. Does it really matter if other cryptocurrencies exist? How would things be different if bitcoin had been the sole cryptocurrency up and running since 2009? Would a greater number of individuals have invested in cryptocurrency - specifically bitcoin - than we have today? Did the non-fungible token (NFT) mania on smart contract blockchains truly raise interest in cryptocurrencies pushing people to grow intrigued by and read books about bitcoin? When I survey the types of books covering cryptocurrencies, the majority focus exclusively on bitcoin, with the second most frequently discussed subject being cryptocurrency trading, while only a few books cover Ethereum and other altcoins. Those who begin consuming bitcoin material are quickly exposed to a multitude of topics, including the pillars of the Austrian School of Economics, as well as the bitcoin network and all its related developments. True, some who are interested in bitcoin shun the reading material and are only interested in making a quick buck, hoping to invest in the next Dogecoin and score a capital gain of 50x in under 2 months. But, unless they sell near the top, which is typically only a small minority, they will lose most of that gain soon after the bubble pops.

Returning to the main argument - although bitcoin maximalists describe altcoins in pejorative terms like shitcoins, they are (well, for the most part, I assume) in favor of a free market, allowing each person to decide rather than imposing a prohibition against trading altcoins, which is how governments operate. The question, then, is what might the free market decide? What attributes would be valued for the primary store of value and medium of exchange? Or, alternatively, might one cryptocurrency be designated as a store of value and another as a means of exchange? We have been living in a world where the currency we use is imposed by our separate national governments. Since 1944 when the Bretton Woods system was agreed upon by allies in Bretton Woods, New Hampshire, every country has had to guarantee convertibility of its currencies into the US dollar to within a 1% fixed parity rate. Meanwhile, the US dollar was convertible to gold bullion at a fixed rate of $35 per troy ounce for foreign governments and central banks. Note that from 1933 to 1974, Americans were restricted from owning gold, whereas citizens of almost all other non-communist countries have been permitted to do so.[17]

What an irony considering Article 1 Section 10 Clause 1 of the US Constitution states:

> **No State shall enter into any Treaty, Alliance, or Confederation; grant Letters of Marque and Reprisal; coin Money; emit Bills of Credit; <u>make any Thing but gold and silver Coin a Tender in Payment of Debts</u>; pass any Bill of Attainder, ex post facto Law, or Law impairing the Obligation of Contracts, or grant any Title of Nobility. (Emphasis added.)**

That's right, "make any Thing but gold and silver Coin a Tender in Payment of Debts" is clear, and no amendments to the US constitution alter this specific rule. It's pretty difficult for residents of any US state to respect this rule if they are restricted from owning gold coins. Anyway, this demonstrates how the banking cartel and control freak politicians can veer away from a directive, even the U.S. Constitution. For more historical context, check out *The Creature from Jekyll Island* (1994), by G. Edward Griffin. The beauty of bitcoin is that, unlike a government whose ruling is forced on all its residents, no one truly controls bitcoin. This explains why modifications to the protocol thus far have been very conservative, and one should anticipate this restrained approach to continue. I am confident that if the US Constitution had been interpreted in a similar manner, that is, with a decentralized Proof of Work styled consensus, we would still be on a gold and silver currency standard.

Granted, the electronic form of these commodities would be the dominant medium in our current society, but the ability to convert them to physical gold and silver coins would have been a prerequisite to transition

---

[17]The EO specifically forbids "the hoarding of gold coin, gold bullion, and gold certificates within the continental United States." https://en.wikipedia.org/wiki/Executive_Order_6102

to electronic transactions. If you allow me to fantasize, I believe that if bitcoin had existed at the time of the writing of the US Constitution and that phrase instead had been "make any Thing but bitcoin a tender in payment of Debts," the banking cartel and big government politicians would have found it extremely difficult to justify the creation of a central bank and paper currency. In truth, fractional reserve banking would have been far more difficult to implement and certainly not to the extent it exists today. Returning to today's national currencies, if you travel to other nations, you must use the local money, albeit they may take US dollars in some situations. Prices are marked in local money; it is legal tender, thus merchants must take it.

Analyzing what the free market would choose as money when we have been living under regulations that have imposed a specific legal tender, makes it quite challenging to know what could have been. Thus, such consideration is more of a theoretical question than a practical one, as we cannot know if or when a populace will be free to embrace the currency of its choosing. Well to be fair, merchants are free to accept any currency of their choosing in addition to the one that is legal tender, and capital gain taxes complicate this decision for the consumer. Despite their centralization, credit cards and debit cards have made one thing convenient - processing of exchange rates. Exchange rates are calculated automatically, which means the merchant can accept only UK pounds while you pull out your American credit card. With technology, this is a straightforward and simple transaction for the consumer, where he must only remember the conversion rate to estimate the price.

Despite our modern world conveniences, the network effect thrives, bringing strong attraction to the few major currencies. Similarly, when it comes to social networks, even if Facebook or Twitter were open source and uncensored, people would still use those platforms rather than switch to a bunch of copycats because that is where their friends and family are. Suppose that, tomorrow, all governments lifted prohibitions and capital gains taxes on cryptocurrencies, and all legal tender currencies laws were abolished. Let us further imagine a popular payment app that nearly all retailers and service providers use. This app is special because it allows businesses to accept any of the top 500 hundred cryptocurrencies or national currencies. With this software, merchants could select the final currency (or currencies) they want to receive, independent of the currency the customer chooses to pay in, and any conversion fees will be borne by the consumer. If adopted, I believe two main criteria would influence consumers' selection of a payment cryptocurrency. In order of importance to the customer, the two factors are:

1. Short confirmation time - Confirmation time for the merchant must be brief. The customer does not want to be kept waiting for an hour before he can collect his purchases and leave the store.

2. Low price volatility - If the merchant does not accept the customer's preferred payment currency, he will default to a cryptocurrency with a large volume of transactions so that the bid/ask spread is modest, resulting in the cheapest exchange rate fee possible. If the merchant only accepts bitcoin, then the transaction incurs no exchange rate costs. The only fees that might apply would be minimal and significantly smaller than the 3% current rate credit card companies charge in the United States. The greater the cryptocurrency's market capitalization, the less the volatility in its purchasing power. A leading cryptocurrency will have a more stable price and the market will tend to perceive it as secure, as well. Plus, merchants are more likely to choose it as a store of value to then make future purchases to restock their inventory. Thus further advancing the cryptocurrency's domination in the marketplace.

Although the customer convenience embedded in the first factor is critical, the second factor is the most important, because developers have devised a solution to the first. Let me explain. The lightning network enables small, fast, inexpensive bitcoin transactions. Without it, all bitcoin transactions would occur on-chain and for merchants and customers to do business, bitcoin would have to be kept on exchanges or other similar services that could interact with each other. Basically, acting like the banking system we have today. With the lightning network operating the payment rails of a secure, decentralized, and dominant blockchain, bitcoin rises as the top contender for merchant-consumer transactions. But, because we are on a fiat system with capital gain taxes imposed on consumers, the interest in using cryptocurrencies is limited, unless you live in El Salvador or the Central African Republic, both of which have made bitcoin legal tender.

Does this mean there would be only one cryptocurrency? Personally, I doubt it since altcoins are playgrounds for new experiments and ideas. Bitcoin is and will likely remain the primary store of value, due to its conservative approach to protocol changes. With bitcoin secure, developments on Layer 2 can flourish. When it comes to payments and storing value, the network effect is the most crucial component, and I don't see how bitcoin could be displaced, even if another cryptocurrency offers tons of transactions per second. Bitcoin's layer 2 network provides the transactional means while the Proof of Work and network effect provides the security required to store large amounts of wealth. This characteristic is essential to major merchants because they have a significant cash flow, money accumulation, and a need to manage inventory. This dynamic solidifies a self-perpetuating feedback loop as it leads to a higher market capitalization for the cryptocurrency which translates to a higher network effect.

What if the fiat system collapsed and cryptocurrencies emerged as the free-market choice to be used as money, would there be only one cryptocurrency? Or perhaps two or three main currencies and fragments of others? From the analysis presented above, it is likely that bitcoin will emerge as the premiere cryptocurrency, but it is also likely that other cryptocurrencies and their associated blockchains will continue to exist. Unfortunately, as long as we persist under the spell of government fiat currencies, cryptocurrency speculation will be rampant, particularly as the fiat system crumbles and we suffer under extreme price inflation. Fundamentally and for practicality and safety purposes, the largest monetary asset will be sought after since it will be more stable than the others. As the instability in the banking sector grows, the market will hunt for a safe, robust store of value. For millennia, gold filled this role, but given that more than 99% of all modern transactions are electronic, bitcoin can steal its thunder and overtake gold's market capitalization and become the main store of value and currency. The banking cartel made certain to quash a gold-backed electronic currency, since it would necessitate that a third party store the gold, which could easily be shut down by the government agencies with any of their usual excuses. No one, however, anticipated the emergence of a decentralized digital currency.

At this point you might ask, isn't there some utility and value in other blockchain projects? Does it mean all altcoins should be discarded? My personal view is that a number of legitimate altcoin projects serve as an experimental sandbox to explore new features and ideas, some of which could coexist with bitcoin as utility-based projects. Their store of value capacity would be miniscule compared to bitcoin's, more on par with shares of a company. Regardless of what I or anybody else believes about the future of altcoin projects, we desire a free market. Therefore, we must give bitcoin time to prove that it will triumph. If you are not yet convinced about bitcoin's potential, you might think I am overstating its future. With nations like El Salvador not only adopting bitcoin but also implementing security measures to enhance its acceptance and the Central African Republic following a year later bitcoin's horizon is coming into focus. Granted, these are small countries, but that's how you start a trend[18].

As mentioned earlier, people in the 1800s did not have to speculate to ensure their financial stability, as they were operating on a gold standard. Simply by adding more gold coins to their stack people could save for the future and eventually buy a farm or a house. Today, saving in dollars is a losing venture and everyone either consciously or unconsciously knows about this. Everyone understands they must speculate out of the dollar into something that increases faster than it loses value. This high-

---

[18]https://www.youtube.com/watch?v=V74AxCqOTvg

risk mindset promotes consumerism for those who forego investing. In the 1800s and early 1900s, speculation looked different, people invested their limited amounts of gold in companies, ventures, and community projects. They understood this speculation was into or toward a project that could improve the overall standard of living, while simultaneously increasing their wealth. I see this in the altcoin market, as well. Take smart contracts for example. Bitcoin does not compete directly with this, but shifts smart contracts to the bitcoin Liquid Network, which is about as centralized as XRP. Sure, at least the folks at Liquid Network don't claim to be decentralized, but that doesn't make it any safer. Regardless, I think the Liquid Network is a plus for the bitcoin ecosystem and believe it was influenced by many of the other crypto projects.

To me, other crypto projects offer a glimpse into how we might decentralize many aspects of our existing infrastructure. For example, one might look at Ethereum, where countless projects are germinating, unfortunately many fraudulent, but others fascinating. Ethereum, itself, faces serious challenges; I don't know how this will end and feel more people should be concerned about its flaws. Nothing would boost the confidence of the banking cartel more than watching a major project like Ethereum crash and burn. Another possibility is the cartel uses an existing altcoin as a Trojan horse of some kind by claiming how much more convenient and better it is than bitcoin. A heavy machine, Ethereum labors to correct flaws, including a fork to rewind the blockchain history after a hacker exploited a defect in a smart contract. Such exploits shine light on bitcoin's virtuous conservatism and the inherent restraint imposed on developers. Exciting new projects like Monero and Zcash are lauded for their ability to improve privacy. Tezos, with its unique built-in governance mechanism, allows for scheduled upgrades by the entire network, hence avoiding any hard fork. Tezos also supports smart contracts written with a functional programming language and formal verification, and Cardano also uses a functional programming language. But I will remind you that often, these currencies are losing value against bitcoin over the long term.

My point is, altcoin developments parallel the 1800s where you would have the ability to invest your gold in companies providing new services. Today, you can invest your funds into these other blockchain projects. Of course, there is a distinction in the sense that investing in a company does not involve using shares of that company as a currency. Rather, investing in altcoins is akin to going to an amusement park where you need tokens to get into rides, the price in tokens of each ride is fixed, but the token's value in $ fluctuates. It is a closed system where the currency is mostly used within that ecosystem. In practice, bitcoin would operate as the main currency in the economy, but specific tokens would be required to engage in smart contracts in specific blockchain ecosystems. As this concept becomes more widely understood, the speculation frenzy will decrease because the low interest rate mania no longer presents favorable conditions. Additionally, it implies that bitcoin should always be used as your primary asset and store of wealth because all other options involve more risk and speculative activity.

Recall that when the price of a coin with a small market cap starts to soar, astute traders and speculators will take advantage of newcomers entering the frenzy. It is entirely possible that because we invest or speculate on "currencies" or tokens as opposed to shares of a company where profit expectations are tied to a product or service, speculation in cryptocurrency might be even more irrational. Think of the late 1920s, it resembles what we saw in the 2017 altcoin market. When companies strive to reach the pinnacle, they base their heights within the framework of their specific industry. When cryptocurrencies attempt to maximize their market share, many imagine them matching or surpassing bitcoin.

Bitcoin should always be regarded as a main store of value of wealth, while anything else involves higher speculation and risk.

Similar to the outgrowth of projects on Ethereum, I also envision the possibility that Layer 2 (Lightning) or sidechain (Liquid) developments will expand the bitcoin ecosystem. We obviously do not want bitcoin side chains to rely on Proof of Work as a consensus mechanism for two main reasons: 1) we want the bulk of the computing hash power to remain on bitcoin's blockchain, and 2) we want to avoid the situation where that sidechain would be subject to 51% attack because its hash power would be much weaker. One alternative is something in line with what Satoshi Nakamoto suggested when talking about BitDNS, where miners suddenly apply their mining power to both bitcoin's blockchain and to its side chain.

Another alternative, and this might come as a surprise to some, is where the side chain uses Proof of Stake, where validators are strictly rewarded from the transaction fees. Obviously, no new bitcoins would be created there, such creation is only done on the current bitcoin blockchain with its existing supply unaltered. People could then stake their bitcoins on the sidechain. Astute readers will understand bitcoin cannot co-exist or freely move on both the main chain and the sidechain. It is only once the bitcoins on the main chain are frozen in some way – via a special smart contract – that a representation of them can be created on the side chain. And only once a user returns their bitcoins to the mainchain will the sidechain representation of bitcoin be destroyed, with the corresponding bitcoins on the main chain unfrozen via that smart contract.

Remember that before bitcoin's white paper, it was believed impossible to create a decentralized digital currency where double spending would be prevented. Although scams and misconceptions are prevalent in the altcoin marketplace, the development and research done in the whole space will be overall beneficial to all cryptocurrencies, including bitcoin. We will go over more examples later. But in the end, regarding a store of value and major dominant crypto-currencies, bitcoin is well placed to retain its preeminence , so long as its fundamentals and Proof of Work remain the most reliable and strongest in the cryptocurrency marketplace.

EXPERIMENT OR SCAM?

Sadly, many new to the cryptocurrency world invest in a variety of tokens without knowing much about them. The recommendation of pretty much every bitcoin maximalist is to only invest in bitcoin. Unless you rigorously study other projects, and you are aware of the high speculation risk involved, it is a perilous venture. Jameson Lopp said it best with this tweet:

Jameson Lopp ✅
@lopp

Maximalism vs multicoinism is a tale as old as time. Do you spread your focus a mile wide and an inch deep?
Or do you go a mile deep at an inch width?

5:59 AM · Jan 10, 2022 · Twitter Web App

Of course, there are valid projects out there with interesting concepts that could eventually be partially included in one form or another into bit-coin as a side chain as a layer 2 component. Also, if you are a day trader and your specialty is chart reading and short-term trading, that is another story. Humans will be humans and market dynamics will remain at play. As such, no matter what anyone's perspective is about these myriads of projects, we must expect a variety of them, including silly ones. As long as these projects are not outright scams, where it is provable in court that the promoter's intention was to deceive investors, they will continue to exist in a free market. U.S. courts have adjudicated scams since the late 1700s, and, therefore, the United States Security and Exchange Cartel, sorry I mean Commission (SEC), is duplicative and was never required.

To sufficiently understand a cryptocurrency does not mean you have to be an absolute mile deep expert - like knowing the details of its imple-mentations – just as you don't need to understand how your transmission works to be able to drive your car. But you do need to understand its funda-mentals, what issues it solves, and how it compares to its competition. All cryptocurrencies share many similarities such as open source software and multiple nodes running the blockchain protocol, with a consensus mechanism to ensure that all nodes agree on the latest state. Bitcoin, in a nutshell, functions as digital gold and silver. Both silver and gold work here, because historically speaking, gold coins were used for storing large wealth or to make important transactions, while silver was typically used for everyday purchases. Bitcoin's dual role renders any other cryptocurrencies as more of a playground for new, decentralized functionality on a blockchain.

But just as gold investors benefit by understanding the current flaws of the existing fiat central banking system, so too a bitcoin investor understands these same flaws and perceives how bitcoin actually offers solutions to problems encountered in today's digital world. If your intention is to invest in any token or cryptocurrencies, you better understand its fundamentals. Still, when friends ask for advice, I recommend that they first learn and invest the bulk of their money in bitcoin. It is dominant for a reason. After learning and investing in bitcoin, an investor should only speculate on the other coins after having done due diligence. Projects early in their life cycle have inherent risks, like undiscovered bugs, just as bitcoin did in its early years. Now, after successfully running without major issues for more than a decade, bitcoin is showing the world it is a gold standard. Initially, it had its share of bugs like the inflation bug, but developers fixed and released the repair, and after the majority of nodes had upgraded, the issue was officially made public.[19] The same delayed public notification strategy was also employed to resolve a major flaw in Domain Name Resolution (DNS), the system relied on to translate domain names into IP addresses.

On a final note, complexity brings potential for hacking. Bitcoin has very little complexity beyond the cryptographic primitive function calls it uses (SHA256, Elliptic Curve Cryptography ...), while other blockchains or smart contracts employ complex machinery to handle the movement of their currency. One only has to look at websites like https://rekt.news to be convinced.

---

[19]https://cointelegraph.com/news/inflation-bug-still-a-danger-to-more-than-half-of-all-bitcoin-full-nodes

SEC & ICO AND REGULATIONS

Examining relevant laws and SEC regulations and actions is important when analyzing how these projects could be affected, regardless of whether fraud, deception and or incompetence is involved.

Bitcoin's design poses a significant challenge for governments and officials who seek to regulate it. The main vectors of attack are the energy consumption associated with Proof of Work (which will be explained later) and the possibility of illicit activities such as criminal usage. The SEC, a U.S. government agency with regulatory authority over securities and possibly many cryptocurrencies, was established in the aftermath of the 1929 crash to "protect" investors from fraud and maintain fairness and efficiency of the U.S. market. To accomplish this, the SEC requires organizations engaged in specific activities to register, proactively, with the commission. This registration process is expensive and time-consuming.

In recent years, the SEC has expanded its jurisdiction into cryptocurrencies and has filed enforcement actions in limited circumstances. Prior to the SEC, cases involving fraud and deception were settled privately and through the judicial system.

It is ironic that while anyone can gamble their savings away in Las Vegas playing roulette or blackjack, elite and private investment opportunities are only accessible to a select few. These individuals are classified as accredited investors by the SEC and must have a net worth above 1 million dollars (excluding their primary residence) or earn over $250,000 per year. Interestingly, these eligibility requirements have remained unchanged since the 1930s, a time when 1 million dollars had significantly more value than it does today. It is my belief that these requirements are a means of restricting the number of investors who can participate in potentially lucrative early investment opportunities.

Consider a scenario where only accredited investors had the opportunity to invest in or mine bitcoin until it was approved for public use by the SEC. Conversely, imagine a situation where Facebook shares were accessible to anyone just a few days after its launch, instead of being restricted to privileged, connected investors. In both cases, the early investors would have enjoyed substantial returns after holding onto their investments for 10 years or more. Admittedly, there have been more failures than successes, but it is worth noting that similar lopsided odds are available to gamblers in Las Vegas without any objection from authorities.

In reality, I believe that the SEC, with its supposed regulations and role as a watchdog, has done more harm than good since it gives many investors a false sense of security. Investors often mistakenly assume that investments have been thoroughly vetted by regulators since they are offered to investors under SEC regulations. This seems to not always be the case. The Bernie Madoff Ponzi scheme meltdown serves as a prime example. One might ask, "If blatant fraud were involved, surely the SEC would have intervened sooner, right?" But, it wasn't until the scheme collapsed due to a lack of funds, in December 2008, that the fraud was exposed. Would the outcome have been worse if the SEC was not involved? After all, it can't catch everything. No, I do not believe so. Investors were less likely to be suspicious of fraud because they believed the SEC was their watchdog.

Interestingly, in 1999, financial analyst Harry Markopolos alerted the SEC that his investigation of Madoff's numbers didn't add up and concluded that the gains achieved were mathematically impossible.[20] Despite the warning nine years earlier, the SEC declined to take any action until the scheme collapsed and authorities finally intervened. If the SEC had only missed the Madoff scandal, the oversight would not have seemed so glaring. But there were others. And its failure to take action has contributed to the belief held by many that the agency is more aligned with big banks on Wall Street than with serving the public interest. Indeed, the Enron scandal, which resulted in the company's bankruptcy in December 2001, further eroded trust in the SEC. Enron's financial statements were convoluted and contained accounting loopholes that should have been cause for concern. Even a Wall Street Journal article published in September 2000

---

[20]https://en.wikipedia.org/wiki/Bernie_Madoff#Investment_scandal

pointed to the prevalence of mark-to-market accounting within the energy industry based on unverifiable assumptions. Despite further investigations by other parties, it took until February 20, 2001, when Fortune magazine reported on Enron's hidden debt, for the SEC to take any action. Even then, the SEC did not launch an inquiry into Enron's finances until October 19, 2001, just two months before the company's bankruptcy. Given that Enron was a highly visible, publicly traded company, it is perplexing that such questionable accounting practices were allowed to persist for so long. And, once again, it was the private sector that first raised concerns about Enron's finances.

If the SEC's exclusive role were to be an effective watchdog, it wouldn't be as bad as I'm sure there are important cases where it timely intervened and protected investors from fraud. But unfortunately, the pain goes the other way as well. Back in the 1800s, anyone could start a business and promote in any way to any would-be investors to invest in their venture. Although there was inevitably fraud, this era allowed people to learn valuable lessons by experiencing the consequences of investing in bad ventures and losing their money.

> Freedom comes with responsibility, outsourcing your responsibility and decision comes with the risk of abuse by those managing this role for you as well as the loss of freedom to make your own choices.

Many people prefer the sense of security that comes from entrusting decision-making to appointed bureaucrats, regardless of whether they voted for the politicians who appointed the regulators. What I found inspiring about bitcoin was that it established a new assets class, and due to the lack of pre-existing regulations, it thrived in a relatively unregulated market, particularly during its early years. It took several years for various branches and agencies of the US government to issue statements about how bitcoin should be treated. As is typical with a five-headed monster dealing with a complex topic, each agency had its own perspective on how to classify bitcoin. For instance, while the Internal Revenue

Service (IRS) labeled it as a commodity, the Commodity Futures Trading Commission (CFTC) defined it as a virtual currency. One consequence of this lack of regulation was the emergence of fundraising efforts to create new cryptocurrencies. Unlike bitcoin, which was created and then made available to the public, other projects sought funding before or during the development process.

These fundraising efforts, commonly referred to as Initial Coin Offerings or ICOs, drew inspiration from the term Initial Public Offering (IPO) used for stocks going public. Unfortunately, many questionable projects received funding through ICOs, and even more disappointing, some fraudsters took advantage of ICOs to deceive investors and steal their money. In my experience, almost all ICOs, including those that require payment in bitcoin, eventually return to their original ICO price or even lower once they become available on cryptocurrency exchanges. Ethereum, however, was an exception. It was initially offered for a price of 2000 ETH for 1 BTC, or 0.0005 BTC per ETH. The lowest price at which ETH was traded on exchange was at 0.0016 per BTC, which was about three months after the launch of the Ethereum blockchain in mid 2015. Today (early 2023), it is around 0.07 BTC per ETH. There are only a few successes like this.

Is it necessary to have so many blockchain projects? I seriously doubt it, but it is not my place to make that decision, the market will. Although they are abundant, many projects support valuable explorations into forms of distributed payment systems linked to blockchains. Since bitcoin cannot support this by itself, perhaps these projects should be launched until there are ways to integrate bitcoins and satoshis into the payment method? I find it unreasonable to delay innovation in the name of stifling currency competition, because "there can be only one." Many of these decentralized innovations require an embedded currency as part of their protocol, similar to the creation of tokens for a ride on the merry-go-round at a fair. It is currently necessary to involve a third party to peg an altcoin currency to bitcoin, but there is nothing stopping it from being done.

In Chapter 1, we compared altcoin tokens to tokens used at fairs and exhibitions, which were created to avoid the hassle of making change.

Similarly, an embedded currency is required for the proper function of a blockchain that supports smart contracts, content delivery, decentralized VPN, or Tor network. Many blockchain projects aim to provide these functionalities in a decentralized way. These projects will require their own currencies, controlled and managed by their respective protocols, regardless of whether they are pegged to bitcoin, although ideally they would be pegged to reduce volatility and dilution of economic interest. Economic rewards are necessary to incentivize mining, even if only by fees, which requires a currency for payment. The transfer of ownership of that currency must also be accounted for, thus, a currency is required, just like what we have with bitcoin.

One may question whether an ICO was necessary to fund these projects. After all, bitcoin was funded solely by Satoshi Nakamoto's time and capital, and many other Proof of Work coins were funded in a similar way. It's a valid question since the work involved mostly consists of research and coding to create what becomes an open-source code that can be distributed freely. And if the project is sound, the founders have the automatic benefit of being early adopters. But this is for the market to decide, not you, not I and certainly not bureaucrats.

I do, in fact, understand some projects may require significant funding to get off the ground and continue operating long term. Proof of Stake blockchains require some form of initial distribution so you can actually have stakeholders. This is not required with Proof of Work, as all early miners receive the initial distribution. Typically, the Proof of Stake project will have a "[Insert Coin Name] Foundation" that will manage the ICO where interested parties send bitcoins (and in some cases ETH) to an address in exchange for a pre-allocated number of the future coins once the blockchain is live and operational.

Assuming the blockchain goes live, the foundation will act as the sole validator during the initial phase, which could last for several days or weeks. Once this phase is completed, nodes, operated by individual miners, can take over using their active and available pre-allocated coins from the ICO. The involvement of these foundations reduces the level of decentralization in these projects, as they can exert significant influence over important decisions. Although some foundations choose to stay neutral, the bitcoins they received as funding are often used for coin promotions and development, which could indirectly impact other areas.

In my earnest opinion, there is a better strategy for Proof of Stake projects to achieve stronger decentralization. The foundation for a Proof of Stake coin could, shortly after the blockchain has been released and is traded on exchanges, start slowly buying back the coins distributed during the ICO, using the received bitcoins, minus perhaps operation costs required to process and manage the ICO. Anything besides this framework, lends credence to bitcoin maximalists' claims that it is the equivalent of a pre-mine Proof of Work coin. Then, once the pre-mine coins (the ones received in exchange for bitcoin) trade on exchanges, the foundation should burn the project's ICO coin allotment, thus reducing the coin's overall supply. Then, the foundation should close up shop. These steps would bring the project closer to the decentralized nature that Proof of Work coins enjoy. It's certainly possible for eager coin holders to create new foundations, just as we've seen with the bitcoin Foundation and other similar organizations that lack power or authority over bitcoin itself. One might wonder whether buying up all the coins would exhaust the supply, leaving none on the market for anyone else. This concern is mitigated by the fact that mining rewards will continue to create new coins, and any buyback program would likely be gradual and publicly announced. As demand outstrips supply, prices are likely to rise, and the foundation would only need to purchase a fraction of the total existing supply. The main scenario in which this plan could fail is if the blockchain is operated poorly, creating no demand for the coins. Individuals who invest in ICOs should be cautious because the market is rife with fraudulent schemes and dubious proposals, making it a high-risk venture. Ultimately, investors must exercise prudence and discernment, as there are many more dubious ideas out there than solid ones.

Paradoxically, I believe that the presence of security regulations has led to a greater number of cryptocurrencies and tokens being funded through

ICOs than if such laws did not exist. Although some blockchain projects necessitate the creation of a native currency or token, this is not always the case. Due to existing laws and regulations, however, entrepreneurs and developers are unable to promote their business for funding using traditional methods such as issuing shares. Therefore, cryptocurrencies and more particularly tokens have emerged as an attractive means of acquiring public funding for their projects, as was the case with Ethereum, which has managed to sidestep SEC regulations. Thus far, Ethereum appears to have avoided any regulatory obstacles.

Contrary to what many think, Ethereum's ICO did not go unnoticed, as the SEC was fully aware of its launch. The ICO took place in 2014, after which it took a year for the developer to release it. By 2016-2017, with the crypto frenzy raging, the SEC had still not taken action against Ethereum, despite it having been publicly funded with a promise of receiving allocated coins once the project was completed. Unlike the issuance of actual shares and because it involved distribution of future tokens that would be utilized as currency, Ethereum's offering was not a clear-cut textbook case of a security-based investment. Naturally, the SEC's inaction in response to this high-profile offering by the Ethereum Foundation opened the floodgates for others to follow suit.

The federal law forcing entrepreneurs to register the sales of securities with the SEC is in my opinion horrible and a waste, and perhaps it might not even be constitutional. All too frequently, the SEC sues companies and individuals for the crime of not registering even when there is no fraud involved and no complaints from the investors. In fact, in some cases the investors are happy campers getting an excellent return. But of course, there are legitimate cases like in the case of a South African named Eran Eyal who was charged and convicted for taking $40 million dollars from investors via an ICO for the token "Shopin."[21] Although the charges cited a lack of registration as a security, the charges also included fraudulent claims and misappropriation of funds for his personal use. Eyal fooled

---

[21] https://www.reuters.com/article/us-shopin-eyal-idINKBN1YG22F

Shopin investors by promising that the money would be used to create a "Universal Shopper Profiles" that would track customer purchases from online retailers, with the end goal to make tailored product recommendations. He also falsely claimed that the platform had been successfully tested at Bed Bath & Beyond and that he had lined up partnerships with other retailers. Unfortunately for the investors, only 3,105 Ether (the currency part of the Ethereum blockchain) was left. This is significantly less than the about 74,000 Ether it received at the end of the ICO in April 2018. You might think the investors were naïve, but Eyal used an elaborate and sophisticated social strategy visible on the @shopinapp twitter account,[22] where we can see him interviewed by prominent media companies at different events, including the 2018 Bitcoin Conference in Miami. In other words, smart investors do not rely on the SEC to vet or even intervene in scams or fraudulent projects. Rather, they do their own research, or better yet, unless they are very confident, they do the safe thing and just stick to bitcoin.

On the flip side, some projects have founders with good intentions and boast satisfied investors. Yet, despite their positive qualities, the SEC has sued them for violating security-selling regulations. In two prominent lawsuits, defendants challenged these accusations in court. The first case involves Ripple, Inc., the company associated with the XRP cryptocurrency. The SEC filed suit against Ripple in December 2020, and a month later, all US exchanges halted trading of XRP. The announcement caused the price to plummet by 60%, as Americans rushed to sell their XRP before trading came to a complete stop.

According to the SEC, XRP should be classified as a security rather than a cryptocurrency that was used to finance the Ripple company. The other lawsuit involves LBRY, a Proof of Work coin that intends to do for the publishing world what bitcoin did for money.

To gain a better understanding, let's take a closer look at XRP's story. Ripple's[23] origins date back to 2004, predating the release of Satoshi's

---

[22]https://twitter.com/shopinapp/status/954483289674235904
[23]https://coinmarketcap.com/alexandria/article/xrp-a-history

white paper. Ryan Fugger created the first version of Ripple and dubbed it RipplePay. Unlike blockchain-based systems, RipplePay was a credit-based digital monetary system that relied on a network of trusted individuals to extend credit and exchange debt. For example, Bob trusts Alice, and Charlie trusts Bob; therefore, Alice can promise to pay Charlie based on her relationship with Bob. This system formed a chain of trust between individuals, allowing transactions to occur between parties who trusted each other. The key difference is that the bitcoin blockchain provides the foundational trust, and the lightning network is based on actual bitcoin rather than credit/debt.

Then, in 2011, influenced by the recent arrival of bitcoin, Jed McCaleb, David Schwartz, and Arthur Britto developed a digital currency system called XRP Ledger (XRPL) where transactions were verified by a consensus among members of a network. In 2012, McCaleb hired Chris Larsen and the two approached Ryan Fugger who subsequently entrusted his Ripple project to them.

In June of 2012, the XRP currency was created with a fixed supply of 100 billion and no mining. Superficially, it looked great. A closer inspection, however, revealed that 100% of the coins were premined. Eighty percent of the total supply was ultimately credited to Ripple Labs, and the rest was distributed among the founders, individuals, and companies through gifts and giveaways.[24]

Later that same year, OpenCoin, co-founded by Larsen and McCaleb and later renamed Ripple Labs, began developing the Ripple protocol and payment network, and the XRP ledger went live in December. Larsen Ripple Labs received private funding from investors like Andreessen Horowitz, Google Ventures, and Accenture in 2013. As a result, it seems that most of the initial supply of XRP acquired by the public was purchased on crypto exchanges when Ripple Labs, founders, and other pre-mine recipients sold their holdings.

---

[24]https://www.coindesk.com/company/ripple-labs/

Of the approximately 20 million bitcoin currently in circulation, Satoshi Nakamoto, the creator of bitcoin, is believed to still hold around one million coins mined at bitcoin's inception. This has been criticized by some who are against bitcoin, including XRP holders, which is rather ironic as XRP's creators hold a much more significant portion of its total supply.

Returning to SEC, interestingly, the SEC filed its suit against XRP in December 2020, on the very last day of Chair Jay Clayton tenure. About two weeks before the suit against Ripple was filed, former SEC Commissioner Joseph Grundfest sent Chair Clayton a letter recommending that he not bring an action against Ripple. Grundfest pointed out there was no urgency, considering XRP has been trading for seven years and that the SEC could not make any material distinction between XRP and Ether. He also warned civil action would drastically impact innocent holders of XRP:

> **But simply initiating the action will impose substantial harm on innocent holders of XRP, regardless of the ultimate resolution. ... Upon learning of the proceeding, intermediaries will cease transacting in XRP because of the associated legal risk. The resulting reduction in liquidity will cause XRP's value to decline.**

The question to be resolved by a court is whether XRP is a security or a currency. The fact XRP was created before the company existed and it possesses all the attributes of a currency, makes it challenging for the SEC to claim it is a security. Could I buy a cup of coffee with a share of a company? Theoretically, I could, if I find someone interested in owning/investing in that company. A share's value is tied to its company's viability. And here is where it gets tricky. What would happen to the market value of XRP if Ripple were to go bankrupt or cease operations? While XRP's value would experience a significant crash, it would not necessarily drop to zero since XRP can technically operate without Ripple, at least on paper. (We will delve into this later.) Notably, Ripple owns the patent related to the XRP's network functionality, which, according to supporters, could potentially replace the SWIFT system.

Ripple was funded by its investors with existing XRP. This is analogous to a scenario in which an entrepreneur, who owns forest land, incorporates a company and then transfers the land to the company. Then later, the company sells the woods. I am not defending this pre-mining, but it's incredible that the market did not punish them as happened with Tenebrix (TBX).[25] TBX, a Proof of Work coin, faltered because the founders pre-mined and credited to themselves 10% of the total coin supply.

Proof of Work consensus requires no pre-mining, but XRP uses a different consensus mechanism where no coins are created, so all coins had to be pre-mined. This is also the case with Proof of Stake, where a mechanism is required to create original coins that will kick start the process. So, what is the solution? In a subsequent chapter on Proof of Stake, I will propose a potential solution. Nonetheless, there may be instances where funding is necessary to support a valid infrastructure.

In my view, the SEC's case lacks merit, much like it would against the lumber company. Emerging technologies often introduce new systems and concepts that render existing regulations obsolete, yet some regulators are thirsty for action. The SEC's actions, or lack thereof, foment a lack of clarity in the regulatory environment. It is perplexing that the SEC filed civil suits several years after the currency had launched and traded, particularly in the two major ongoing cases that have proceeded to court instead of settlement. By delaying action and then suspending trading and initiating civil action, the SEC has inflicted greater harm on investors than the supposed sellers of these securities ever did. What's more, the SEC's lawsuits usually end with a settlement agreement where the project owners are required to pay a fee to the SEC. This fee, of course, is then utilized to finance the agency's pursuit of other projects. Plus, these projects must also cover their own legal expenses. As a result, investors who did not file a complaint and were not defrauded (or do not consider themselves as

---

[25] https://www.coinopsy.com/dead-coins/tenebrix/

such) are left with a cryptocurrency that has lost value in the marketplace, while a sizable portion of their initial investment has been allocated towards paying the SEC, rather than improving the project. It is ironic that the SEC, which is meant to support the "little guy," inflicts more harm than good.

Unfortunately, the lack of clarity does not end here. During the 2018 Fintech Week conference, then SEC Director William Hinman stated that the sale of ETH did not fall under the category of "securities transactions." It is important to note that Ethereum was initially a Proof of Work coin and the developers employed an ICO to finance their development efforts. Following the successful completion of the ICO, Ethereum was created and launched one year later, with investors who contributed to the ICO receiving ETH as credit. In essence, Ethereum was also pre-mined, but the recipients were the original ICO contributors as well as developers, insiders and other organizations.

If Hinman considered Ethereum's ICO to not be a securities transaction, then it is reasonable to assume that any other ICO would not be classified as such, especially in the case of Ripple since they never launched an ICO but instead secured private funding through the typical Silicon Valley means. The SEC has been attempting to have Hinman's speech excluded from evidence in the court case, but this legal saga highlights how absurd, irrational, and, at times, inconsistent the SEC's actions have been. Numerous legal scholars anticipate a settlement in Ripple's favor, or if it goes to trial, a triumph for Ripple.

LBRY, a Proof of Work coin, was established using pre-mining, with some of the coins awarded to the LBRY organization immediately after the first block was created. This structure allowed the organization to finance its early operations. LBRY is a two-layered, decentralized system, consisting of the LBRY blockchain and LBRYNet. LBRYNet enables various hosts to manage the provision of different blocks of data, much like on the Tor Network. The blockchain holds ownership of LBC coins (LBRY credits), as well as metadata information associated with an identifying key. To gain control of the value connected with such a key, a user must conduct a transaction on the blockchain, similar to a DNS system. LBRYNet enables various hosts to manage the provision of different blocks of data, much like on the Tor Network. Once received, the end user client can recreate the original content. You can find out more at https://lbry.com/what.

Now the interesting story involving the SEC's involvement with LBRY began when it reached out to the LBRY team to inquire about their operations. After providing information about their pre-mined currency, LBRY Credits (LBC), and asking if there were any concerns, the SEC did not provide any feedback. A few months later, however, it filed a lawsuit against LBRY. Despite being pre-mined, LBC functions as a decentralized currency for purchasing content access, registering keys, and other features. The LBRY foundation has also been utilized to fund the project's development. During a conversation with Jeremy Kauffman, the CEO of LBRY, he revealed to me that LBRY had been seeking clarity from the SEC about its operations from the outset, but the agency never provided a clear answer. It's as if entrepreneurs and businessmen must be sued before they can find out if they are doing something wrong. Absurd! This lack of clarity raises questions about whether it is intentional, given that part of the SEC's stated role is to launch lawsuits against con men and businessmen. LBRY has around a million users per day, and many of them are obtaining LBC coins for their utility, rather than speculation. In a recent hearing regarding this case, the judge asked the SEC if it would still be considered a security if only 25% of buyers of LBC were speculators while 75% were buying it for its utility in the network. The SEC replied, "Yes." This discrepancy highlights the ambiguous and punitive impact of current legislation, which has not kept pace with technological advancements.

To me, what is particularly odd is that lawyers, who previously worked at the SEC, are often hired by companies being sued by the SEC. These lawyers have intricate knowledge of how the SEC operates and also maintain relationships with their former colleagues. And of course, these lawyers can earn much more in the private sector. The entire system seems to incentivize the SEC to sue as many entities as possible, so they can either win or settle and collect fees to fund their operations, while simultaneously creating job opportunities for former SEC lawyers who now defend these companies. Meanwhile, it's worth noting that anyone can go to Las Vegas and gamble heavily on roulette or blackjack, yet we still rely on the SEC to protect investors from risky investments. Although bitcoin maximalists may be pleased with the SEC's actions, as bitcoin has no CEO or foundation created with an initial ICO, in my case, I believe that the SEC should be abolished. As long as Las Vegas casinos are open, the need for a company to register as a security, which is a costly operation, should not be required. But could this be Plan B for the banking cartel?

BANKING CARTEL'S PLAN B?

For centuries, banking cartels have fought for control. Over time, they developed elaborate techniques to influence politicians and manipulate a large portion of the public towards their goal. The book *"The Creature From Jekyll Island"* by G. Edward Griffin, provides an alternative historical perspective that has not been taught in school nor discussed in mainstream publications. Ironically, the sophisticated scheme used by a group of bankers to pass the Federal Reserve Act, which Griffin exposes in his book, is well-documented in publications in books and newspapers of the 1930s and beyond. Once firmly established in the American financial system, these bankers boasted about colluding to create the Federal Reserve, despite knowing that the American public opposed a centralized banking system, particularly one controlled by private bankers. While I will not delve into the specifics of this scheme, it is worth noting that they understood and acknowledged the public's skepticism of their efforts.

It's incredible how different the collective mindset of the 19th and early 20th century Americans were compared to their descendants today. Those early Americans would all be considered hard core libertarians or conservatives today. When H.R. 7387, the bill that would benefit major bankers, was proposed, banks publicly criticized it, claiming it would harm their businesses. This created the public perception that if the bankers opposed it, then it must be good for them. Exploiting this contrived mindset, the large banking institutions managed to pass the bill, which was signed into law in late December 1913, while most of the congressmen who opposed it had gone on a Christmas break. The Federal Reserve System, composed of 12 regional Federal Reserve private banks, is chaired by an appointee of the U.S. President. These banks are authorized to print and lend U.S. dollars, with a portion of the interest income distributed as dividends to their private shareholders. And yes, I did say private banks. The Federal Reserve system is not federal and does not have reserves; it essentially creates money out of thin air.

Imagine if I had been given the power to have Congress accept my printed "Phil's Reserve Notes" whenever the federal government needed to purchase federal debt to fund the US government, which then becomes the established currency used by citizens. The government requires its citizens to use this Phil's Reserve Notes as it is the only currency accepted for tax payments. In this case, I wouldn't need to save currency before lending to the government, and I could directly lend with minimal effort and collect interest payments. With ease and minimal work, I could lend directly by just typing keys on the keyboard and then collect a portion of the interest payments. Notice how the income tax system plays an integral role in this scheme by artificially creating a demand for this currency. Citizens must acquire this currency to pay their taxes, which creates a need for it. And, if you were to choose another more stable currency, such as gold or bitcoin, exchanging it for goods or services incurs a taxable event, penalizing the use of other currencies while, again, maintaining the artificial demand. It's no coincidence that the 16th amendment to the U.S. Constitution allowing Congress to levy an income tax was passed in the same year as the Federal Reserve Act, 1913. Remember, the keyword here is deception!

So, what does this mean for bitcoin and altcoins? In 2015 and 2016, skeptics, including mainstream media financial articles, speculated that the government would ban bitcoin and altcoins. At the time, only a small portion of the population had invested in these cryptocurrencies, so such claims were not completely irrelevant. Today, however, too many people and institutions are involved for a ban to be effective. Their window of opportunity might have been in the early years, say in 2010 or 2011. But even if the U.S. government managed to ban cryptocurrencies, the cat was already out of the bag. By waiting, the idea had already spread, and governments worldwide would have had to act quickly and in cooperation to ban it.

Once released by Satoshi Nakamoto, the white paper and original source code became free and available to anyone. Any attempt to intervene by the government would have been suspicious, especially since so few people were involved at the time. Even then, tracking down and confiscating each operating node at every individual house would have been prohibitive. And remember, in the beginning, most economists, particularly Keynesian economists, dismissed it as a silly experiment doomed to fail as it was not backed by governments, guns, and jails.

So, what other options does the banking cartel have? Let's don our Al Capone hat and place ourselves in the mind of the devil. Of course, this is pure speculation on my part. Let's start with one of the major arguments that gold bugs assert when criticizing bitcoin: there are more than 10,000 entries on coinmarketcap.com, of which at least several hundred are running their own blockchain and protocol, hence cryptocurrencies are not rare. Obviously, this argument is missing the point since one doge – the cryptocurrency of Dogecoin - has nothing to do with one bitcoin. And there is the network effect to consider, as space where bitcoin excels, as you can easily find a merchant who accepts bitcoin but rarely one who accepts Dogecoin. The banking cartel is aware of this and could attempt to disrupt bitcoin by artificially inflating the value of another cryptocurrency (that they could more easily control) to temporarily surpass bitcoin's market capitalization. Nonetheless, this would only slow down bitcoin's adoption temporarily.

Before the advent of bitcoin, the US government would not have permitted the existence of any centralized digital currency. Bitcoin has withstood government attacks due to its highly decentralized nature. Now that bitcoin is established and cannot be directly attacked, it is wiser to permit the existence of all kinds of cryptocurrencies, regardless of their level of decentralization. Attempting to attack the network of a "less decentralized" cryptocurrency would only draw more attention to bitcoin's robust decentralization feature.

Consider the implications if bitcoin were to lose its dominant position, even if only for a short period of time. Bankers would whisper amongst themselves: "Divide and conquer! Divide the public across multiple cryptocurrencies so that none becomes dominant, and our Central Bank Digital Currencies have a chance to shine." Bankers would also quietly accumulate positions in bitcoin so they could manipulate its price later. This fragmentation, however, would be temporary. Despite existing factions within the crypto space, such as those invested in XRP who criticize bitcoin's slow transaction times, the overall financial environment is currently relatively stable.

As the central bank's flawed proof-of-debt system becomes increasingly unstable, people will begin to prioritize security over functionality or utility. At that point, bitcoin's decentralized structure will make it the most appealing cryptocurrency. In times of high inflation or hyperinflation, anything that floats will be attractive and most cryptocurrencies will experience extreme volatility and fluctuation. During such periods, bitcoin and gold will grow more attractive as safe havens, while other options will be cast aside as speculative assets.

Caution: Unless you have an established history of proven success investing in a wildly volatile market, it is advisable to stick with bitcoin. Additionally, if more people start borrowing using their bitcoins as collateral during these boom times, it could contribute to bitcoin's eventual crash. It's important to remember that borrowing dollars using bitcoin as collateral is essentially betting long on bitcoin and short on the US dollar using leverage. So when the price of bitcoin drops, borrowers may need to sell some or all of their bitcoins to cover for the loss.

Looking at the recent FTX bankruptcy nightmare, where fraud was evident, we can see another way that the central banking cartel could manipulate the cryptocurrency market. If they can prop up a few top 20 altcoins then let them crash due to fraud, malfunctions, or even a generic pump and dump scheme, they can create a sense of "crypto fatigue" among the public, causing many to stay away from due to the market's perceived volatility and prominent exchanges going bankrupt. Moreover, if they can tempt people into borrowing against their bitcoin during boom times, they can accelerate a crash in bitcoin's price. These fraudulent activities could also be exploited as an opportunity to push for more government regulations, despite the fact that existing laws were already violated by the CEO of FTX. Such regulations would only serve to control the crypto space and favor cronies in Washington D.C.

If all of this can happen while turning a cold shower on bitcoin while subtly orchestrating increased control for the banking cartel, all the better. Nevertheless, it's worth noting that many people learn valuable lessons from pump-and-dump schemes and chaos of market volatility, and once they do, they opt to only invest in the most stable cryptocurrency available - bitcoin. Stealing the show from bitcoin is one scenario I expect the government and their friends in the central banking cartel to try. Perhaps it has already happened by the time you read this book. Ask yourself, what do you think will happen if, suddenly, you see a more easily controllable and subvertable cryptocurrency sitting in the number one spot in market capitalization? The gold bugs argument would be fulfilled, well, momentarily as I don't expect this to last. Gold bugs do not anticipate that copper or zinc will eclipsed gold's market cap. Gold is gold, with unique, specific physical properties that no other metal can duplicate. Being the first and best has its advantages, but for the man on the street, if bitcoin is displaced it would shatter the notion that it is wise to blindly invest in bitcoin rather than explore flashy altcoins. The concept of sound money is supposed to mean you can invest in it and never look back for 20, 30, 40 or 50 years. That has been the case for gold, and Peter Schiff, a prominent gold bug who hates bitcoin would have his day if bitcoin is displaced, even if just a few hours.

As previously mentioned, bitcoin's high level of decentralization ensures that the majority of individuals in the free market will recognize its financial benefits. Those who previously speculated in altcoins and captured meteoric gains will eventually see those coins move back down the ranks and return to bitcoin as a secure investment. Ultimately, the truth regarding bitcoin's superiority will prevail, and we will delve into this further in upcoming chapters. In the end, the truth always wins. What is the truth you might ask? How can someone accurately select bitcoin as the winner? Well, we have other chapters ahead.

In addition, there is the Central Bank Digital Currency (CBDC) that they are also planning on. This is no better than the current system they are feeding us with, and likely worse as they can track every transaction and potentially penalize dissidents. The main obstacle to the success of a CBDC is the growing awareness of bitcoin's benefits among the general public.

With each passing day, more people are learning about the value of decentralized digital currency and the importance of sound money. The ongoing weakening of the dollar and the problem of price inflation, which has worsened since 2020, serve as free advertising for bitcoin. These factors are all converging towards an acceleration in the adoption of bitcoin, and this decade promises to be very interesting indeed. Had CBDCs been the prevalent currency during the Freedom convoy in downtown Ottawa, Prime Minister Trudeau could have easily frozen any accounts linked to or supporting it. With CBDC, the government can impose conditions that restrict spending, rendering CBDC holders powerless. Without paper currency in circulation that can be exchanged anonymously, the government's ability to monitor and control the population could easily be cranked up.

What about the energy used by bitcoin? That's another argument the banking cartel and some politicians have already been using for several years. In early 2022, the European Union attempted to pass legislation that would prohibit bitcoin mining, but the proposal was unsuccessful. While it is true that bitcoin mining consumes energy, much of this energy was unavailable for commercial or residential use due to the remote location of the energy source. Take the case of an unused hydro-electric dam in a ghost town located in Eastern Europe that was previously supplying power to a now-defunct industry now powers a bitcoin mining operation. A similar story happened in Costa Rica when a hydroelectric power plant was forced to shut down due to the government's cessation of electricity purchases during the COVID-19 pandemic. To prevent revenue loss from their infrastructure, the plant's owner opted to repurpose it for bitcoin mining. Oil and gas giant Exxon has begun mining bitcoin by redirecting methane gas from on-site gas flares to power gas converters to power miners. During oil drilling, both liquid hydrocarbons and natural gas are extracted, but in locations where the infrastructure for storage, transportation, and marketing of natural gas is inadequate, it is more profitable for companies to flare the gas instead of selling it at a financial loss. And now thanks to bitcoin, these isolated places only require an internet connection (satellite if need be) and because bitcoin's blocks are small enough, the bandwidth requirement is very reasonable.

Additionally, an interesting recent research study out of the University of Cambridge revealed that the energy wasted in devices left idle by US residents uses 4 times more energy than the entire bitcoin network. So yes, bitcoin does use energy but so do all the televisions, computers, and other plugged in but inactive devices.

Bitcoin mining is being woven into the energy sector in creative ways. It is my expectation that in the near future, more and more infrastructure will be developed in cold-climate areas to mine bitcoin, warming houses during the winter season and heating water tanks, pools, or anything that requires heat. If locations are already using electricity for heating, then the transition to bitcoin mining would not be controversial. Currently, a French company, wisemining.io, is already offering water heaters, and I anticipate further development in this area will optimize the process. There is also the BTU project in Quebec, which aims to heat a church using bitcoin mining.[26]

In El Salvador, where bitcoin has been made legal tender, investors have been building power plants that mine bitcoin by harnessing energy

---

[26]https://montreal.ctvnews.ca/this-is-how-an-eastern-townships-artist-is-using-bitcoin-to-heat-his-multimedia-studio-1.5299600

from inactive volcanoes. An expansion of green energy bitcoin is expected to come onboard so even if one government in Europe or the entire European Union were to ban bitcoin mining, as China did, bitcoin mining will still prosper in other jurisdictions like El Salvador. And more is coming. Just like we saw with the war on plants (marijuana), banning mining bitcoin would only send it to the black market along with the use of VPN, resulting in a sizable loss of tax revenue in the process.

3

SMART CONTRACTS AND BEYOND

In this chapter, we will discuss the latest developments in the bitcoin and altcoin ecosystems. While there are many frivolous projects, some are developing interesting features that may, one day, be introduced into bitcoin. Others are less likely to be adopted.

One significant development is elaborate smart contracts with state management, which were introduced with Ethereum. Today, multiple cryptocurrencies offer similar smart contracts. Bitcoin also supports them, but they are much simpler. For a given input, bitcoin can perform conditional checks that may create alternative outputs. In contrast, Ethereum smart contracts may contain variables to keep states. Another important development is privacy coins. Bitcoin's transactions are transparent, meaning anyone can see the actual transactions, even though they may not know who owns the bitcoin addresses involved in those transactions. However, when these transactions reach cryptocurrency exchanges where people are required to undergo Know-Your-Customer (KYC) procedures, the exchange knows who performed all associated transactions.

A PRIMER ON SMART CONTRACTS

The term "smart contract" was first conceived by Nick Szabo, one of the early libertarian crypto experts called cypherpunks. A smart contract is a set of instructions that can be executed to perform a contractual term or obligation. For example, a smart contract might be invoked when a specific transaction occurs, in which case another transaction will be executed in response.

Besides a list of operations, smart contracts can also contain a storage section where specific information is stored and associated with one or more owners or keys. This storage allows for the creation and management of tokens and non-fungible tokens (NFTs). For NFTs, the storage includes ownership attribution and the hash of a digital object such as a JPG (but not the actual object itself).

One smart contract can also perform operations involving other smart contracts. These smart contracts are open source and stored on the blockchain; their code and associated storage are visible. The storage, which can be used as a database with key-value pairs, sometimes contains a coin address (such as an Ethereum or Tezos address) for which a right or ownership is credited.

While there are many possibilities associated with smart contracts, there is also potential for devastating bugs. This was certainly the case with Ethereum. On November 7th, 2017, a bug was discovered in the Parity Ethereum Wallet that handled multi-signature addresses through smart contracts. A multi-signature contract allows for more than one signature to authorize the spending of the ether linked to the contract, in effect mimicking multi-signature addresses in bitcoin.

In the Parity Wallet case, the bug was a simple error in the smart contract that failed to prevent users from resetting the signatory addresses. As a result, an attacker could easily change the addresses in the contract to ones they own and control. Since many companies conducting ICOs were using that specific multi-signature contract to receive funding, up to $170 million USD was stolen.

COINS, SMART-CONTRACT TOKENS AND NFTS

With the advent of Ethereum, it is now possible to create new tokens whose ownership is tracked through smart contracts on Ethereum's blockchain. Therefore, these tokens leverage Ethereum's blockchain instead of developing their own chains, eliminating the requirement to develop their own protocols and infrastructure. Token smart contracts keep track of which Ethereum addresses own and control these tokens, and they may contain additional code that provides instructions. The smart contract code allows for the transfer of a certain number of tokens from one Ethereum address to another. Both the code and the storage element of the smart contract are stored on the blockchain.

Compared to bitcoin, which has an upper limit of 1 MB per block, Ethereum uses significantly more disk space. Ethereum node operators may use *pruning* and other techniques to reduce the size of the stored chain, which also causes the node to lose the history of previous transfers. Therefore, the minimum storage space required to run an Ethereum node is just twice that of bitcoin, despite bitcoin running six years longer than Ethereum. Pruning[27] ensures that current balances are recorded, but all preceding transactions are no longer stored.

---

[27] https://www.trustnodes.com/2022/07/22/vitalik-puts-pruning-on-ethereums-roadmap

On Ethereum, most tokens use a standard contract called ERC-20. This means you will often hear them referred to as ERC-20 tokens. Since these tokens run on Ethereum, one Ethereum address can own both ethers (Ethereum's native currency) and tokens associated with a specific smart contract, typically ERC-20.

The source code and storage of each smart contract can be viewed by using an Ethereum blockchain explorer to look up the address associated with that contract. For example, you can view the details of the GateChain token (randomly chosen) by following the link below:

https://etherscan.io/token/0xe66747a101bff2dba3697199dcce5b743b454759 #balances

The "Transfers" tab displays all smart contract transfers, which are events that occur when one token owner (indicated in the database-storage section of the contract) transfers some tokens to another address. When this happens, a transaction is executed on the Ethereum blockchain that invokes a specific function of the smart contract. Only tokens are transferred, not ethers, although ethers are required to pay the gas fees. Gas fees are the cost paid by the sender of the transaction to compensate miners for spending resources to run the smart contract. The link below shows a transaction example:

https://etherscan.io/tx/0x18250f2afe0728ec0c6500f49a10cfa58811e91df3d 889239e17e92065058e31

The following figure shows the functions that are part of the ERC-20 smart contract.

Most smart contract functions interact with the content in the storage section of their database. Since each contract can be copied as desired, it's no surprise that there are many of them. The only practical restriction on copying contracts is the requirement to pay gas fees. There are over 10,000 cryptocurrencies listed on popular coin-tracking websites, but the vast majority are smart-contract tokens running on Ethereum or another smart-contract-enabled blockchain. This nuance may be obscure and con-

```
pragma solidity ^0.6.0;

interface IERC20 {

    function totalSupply() external view returns (uint256);
    function balanceOf(address account) external view returns (uint256);
    function allowance(address owner, address spender) external view returns (uint256);

    function transfer(address recipient, uint256 amount) external returns (bool);
    function approve(address spender, uint256 amount) external returns (bool);
    function transferFrom(address sender, address recipient, uint256 amount) external returns (bool);

    event Transfer(address indexed from, address indexed to, uint256 value);
    event Approval(address indexed owner, address indexed spender, uint256 value);
}
```

Figure 8: ERC-20 smart contract.

fusing for newcomers who might assume that each coin runs on its own blockchain.

The considerable number of "crypto assets" resulting from the creation of tokens is often cited by gold bugs as a reason to denigrate bitcoin. They argue that the sheer number of "cryptos" makes cryptocurrencies a diluted soup. However, the network effect is what really matters. Even if a million new cryptocurrencies were created tomorrow, bitcoin's relative importance would remain unchanged.

Many tokens have a specific purpose attached to their smart contract, differing from traditional currencies such as bitcoin, litecoin, and ether. However, these tokens still require ether to be transferred on the Ethereum blockchain. Therefore, the creation of more tokens on Ethereum is beneficial for Ethereum itself, as it increases its network effect and the demand for ether.

Ethereum has grown faster than its capacity to handle traffic, and transaction fees on Ethereum were $100 or more on several occasions. Smart-contract transactions are costlier than regular transactions (where only ether is exchanged from one address to another) as they require additional processing, depending on the size and complexity of the smart-contract instruction.

Some smart contracts involve trading, and to facilitate this process, certain groups and organizations have created wrapped bitcoins. These tokens are tied to an Ethereum smart contract, representing actual bitcoins held in custody by the organization. In exchange for the bitcoins, these organizations issue so-called "wrapped" BTC in tokens such as wBTC. Wrapped bitcoins introduce third-party risk compared to holding one's own keys. The organization holding the bitcoins must be trusted in the hope that there will be no hacks or fraudulent activity. The Ethereum blockchain must also be trusted to function correctly. Rather than a single dependency on your bitcoin investment and only worrying about the health of bitcoin's network, there is an additional dependency on Ethereum's network and the safety of the third-party organization. While any risk may be low, it is still higher than simply holding bitcoin. However, most people involved with wBTC and other variants use them in conjunction with smart contracts for trading and other financial activities like lending.

Other cryptocurrency blockchains have also introduced smart contracts, supporting tokens and their trading. Tezos, for example, has tzBTC on its blockchain which represents bitcoin, as well as US dollar tokens such as USDtz. This is where central bankers felt cheated on, as these decentralized systems suddenly allow for a digital representation of their fiat currency.

In addition to ERC-20 smart-contract tokens, Non-Fungible Tokens (NFTs) have risen to fame in 2020 and 2021. Fungibility means each unit of a currency or asset has the same value and can be exchanged equally. Artwork is non-fungible because each piece is unique and cannot be exchanged for another piece of equal value. NFTs can be used to represent non-fungible assets, such as collectibles, access keys, lottery tickets, or even specific seats at a concert or sporting event. Like fungible tokens, there is a standard smart contract for NFTs called ERC-721.

https://eips.ethereum.org/EIPS/eip-721

To ensure uniqueness, each NFT is assigned a unique integer number. The combination of this number and the smart-contract address creates a globally unique identifier for a specific asset on the Ethereum blockchain. Like regular tokens, ownership of NFTs can be transferred to another

Ethereum address. Whoever possesses the private keys associated with the address has control over its ownership and can transfer it to a new address.

Just like with anything new, it doesn't take long before a frenzy brews and overtakes rational thought. This is obviously what happened with NFTs. While many artists have benefited from this new asset technology, there was also abuse. Plus a giant bubble loomed on the horizon. Certain tools enabled NFT creators to generate hundreds of derivatives of a cartoon animal and sell each as an NFT. But many of these NFTs are now selling for fractions of their original purchase prices.

Although NFTs have mostly been concentrated in digital art, there are some conversations about using them for real estate, as described by Forbes.[28]

Many have tried to make money by speculating in NFTs, but they would have been better off just investing in bitcoin. There is potential value, however, for several use cases such as concerts or sporting events where the ticket system could be managed by the blockchain. If the smart contract is well-written and bug-free, it would be more secure than a ticketing system run by a centralized firm.

Ethereum's extreme fees often make it less practical to use. Polygon and other second layer solutions on top of Ethereum resolve the issue of fees somewhat. However, we could expect NFTs to be used on another smart-contract platform.

> Data on the blockchain survives if the blockchain does, but a company or organization might not. Using a decentralized blockchain as a database allows users to be more confident on the reliability and persistence of the data. The organization providing convenience of access might fail, but another organization can replace the previous one in that situation.

[28] https://www.forbes.com/sites/forbesbusinesscouncil/2022/08/04/guide-to-using-nfts-in-real-estate/?sh=3d76996b5e8a

NFTs and similar concepts are not limited to the art world. Car manufacturers, such as BMW, have chosen Tezos[29] to track and authenticate their manufacturing parts. Why would they use a blockchain from a cryptocurrency instead of a simple database administered by a third party? One benefit is that the information is stored on the blockchain, even if the third party goes out of business. One example of this is hicetnunc.xtz, an NFT platform that tracked, managed, and auctioned NFTs stored on Tezos. At one point, it was the largest NFT platform in the world. The website was closed by its creator, leaving all NFT users behind. Fortunately, because the data was open source and all relevant information was stored on the blockchain, a group of users managed to recreate the website in less than an hour.

DECENTRALIZED EXCHANGE CONTRACTS

Two parties who wish to trade one asset for another or for a currency are always required to do this in person or with a third party to facilitate the exchange. The requirement for a third party is even more relevant when it comes to trading digitally. Exchanges require traders to trust them as custodians of the assets and/or currency they are holding on your behalf. The first official cryptocurrency exchange was the infamous Mt Gox which ended up being hacked. There is always a risk as nobody knows how secure they might be.

Vitalik Buterin, one of the founders of Ethereum, wrote an article a few years back suggesting a smart contract could allow for trading assets. The principle of the idea came to life in a smart contract named Uniswap.[30] As opposed to what exchanges offer with an order book, limit order and stop losses, the trading smart contract is more rudimentary as all transactions are at the market price according to the smart contract. Although simple, the advantage is it doesn't rely on a custodian running a website with its network configuration and source code kept private for security purposes.

---

[29] https://cryptonews.net/news/altcoins/317465/
[30] https://uniswap.org/whitepaper-v3.pdf

Instead, everybody can inspect the smart-contract code to evaluate any flaws. Another advantage is the benefit of avoiding exchange with KYC (which can be used to track how many bitcoins you hold once withdrawn from the exchanges). In this way, hackers could obtain this information and resell it. This is the equivalent of indicating that someone owns half a million dollars in gold and stores it in a vault in his house.

As for the principles of smart contracts, there are some minor differences between some of these smart contracts for trading, but they run on the same main principle. As mentioned earlier, a smart contract can contain both instructions for miners as well as data storage to track ownership of tokens (or other items). How does this decentralized smart-contract exchange work? The smart contract (let's use Uniswap for simplicity) contains a data store portion holding two pools, each containing one of the assets being traded. Let's say we are looking at an ETH to wBTC Uniswap smart contract. Wrapped bitcoins are tokens that are pegged to bitcoin, but not in a decentralized way, meaning you rely on a custodian to store the actual bitcoins these wBTC represent. So, in one case it is the native ETH currency, while the other is the wBTC token, which is operated and tracked by its own smart contract.

Let's assume Tom the trader wants to exchange some of his ether for wrapped bitcoins. Tom has an ETH address holding the ether and he sees that for the current price of ETH to BTC, he will get 1 wBTC for every 20 ETH. Next, he sends 20 ETH in payment to the ETH address associated with the smart contract and in return, the smart contract will transfer one of the wBTCs it contains in its pool to his ETH address. This will be seen on Ethereum blockchain as one single transaction involving three ETH addresses:

1. Tom's ETH address which initially has 20 ETH and will receive the 1 wBTC

2. The Uniswap smart contract ETH address

3. The smart-contract wBTC token.

Such Decentralized Finance (DeFi) smart contracts contain two pools. One of them contains ETH while the other contains wBTC; hence, this smart contract depends on another one — the ERC-20 smart contract for wBTC. The way the DeFi smart contract establishes the exchange rate between wBTC and ETH depends on the ratio of the quantity in each of these two pools. For Tom to receive 1 wBTC when transferring 20 ETH, this means that there is approximately 20 times more ETH in the DeFi ETH pool than there is wBTC. We will go over the reason for saying "approximately" twenty times, but let us first look at the smart-contract fundamentals in Figure 9.

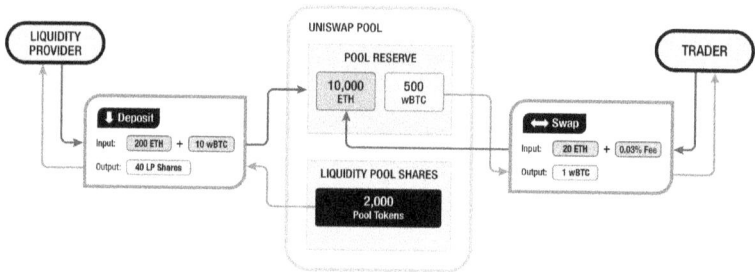

Figure 9: Uniswap.

Obviously, those two pools need to be funded somehow and this is accomplished by "liquidity providers". These providers contribute to the pool by adding an arbitrary number of tokens. Anyone can become a provider by contributing to the pool. These providers are using a dedicated website with an interface that calculates the correct ratio of one token versus the other that matches the current existing ratio in the pool. This ratio dictates what the market price is, and in the example in the figure with 10,000 ETH and 500 wBTC, this gives a pricing of 20 ETH per wBTC. To track their respective ownership, Liquidity pool tokens are created and credited to the liquidity providers that contribute to the pool. Continuing with the example, the liquidity provider here sent 200 ETH and 10 wBTC. In return for this contribution, the provider is credited with 40 LP (Liquidity Pool) tokens out of the total of 2000 LP tokens, meaning this provider owns 2% of the total pool content (both pools). These LP tokens are just like other tokens using ERC-20 smart contracts and are assigned to the ETH address of the provider. In addition the ownership of these tokens can be transferred to any other ETH address if desired. For offering this liquidity, these providers get the revenue from the fees charged for each trade. Liquidity providers can decide to redeem these LP tokens at any time. Similarly, a liquidity provider can decide to withdraw funds from the pool where LP tokens deposited to the contract are then burned. In this case, the corresponding ETH and wBTC are transferred to the provider.

The fees involved relate to the very reason for this smart contract — the trade. The right side of Figure 9 illustrates the action when a trader wants to exchange ETH for wBTC. In the example, the trader is sending 20 ETH using a dedicated website that invokes the proper smart contract functions with correct arguments the function expects. Although the use of a website may not seem decentralized, these websites are there to facilitate the use of these smart contracts and many of them can interact with these same contracts. Any tech-savvy individual can also operate directly on the blockchain with the proper calls or by copying the information from these websites. Part of the transaction includes a fee that will be retained by the pool owners. As a result of receiving 20 ETH (as well as the proper fee via a specific function call of the smart contract), it will return 1 wBTC to the corresponding ETH address that sent the ETH. In other words, one transaction leads to another in reaction. In this case, this smart contract interacts with the ERC-20 smart contract that handles wBTC, but it can interact with any other contract. In fact, just as anyone can create a new ERC-20 token, anyone can create a new trading smart contract pair (e.g., ETH/myToken) that includes it.

The mechanics of the trade are more complicated as the results are highly dependent on the amount in the pool. For instance, if the pool only has 10,000 ETH and 500 wBTC, it certainly couldn't accommodate a trade of 20,000 ETH for 1,000 wBTC. However, focusing on a smaller trade, such as 20 ETH for 1 wBTC or vice versa will allow us to understand the process better. The pair in a pool acts as an automated market maker, where one token is automatically exchanged for the other token so long as the "constant product" is preserved. This constant product (referred to as "k") is simply expressed as the product of the number of one token multiplied by the number of the other tokens. Say we have x ETH and y wBTC in the pool, then x * y = k. After a trade, k remains the same as it was before. In the example we have the factor of 10,000 and 500 giving a k of 5,000,000. Note that the smart contract applies a fee to the trades which ends up being added to the reserve, thus increasing k slightly every time to the benefit of liquidity providers. If the smart contract in the example had a lower deposit amount in the pool, the variation or "slippage" in a trade would be greater. The following section will explain how the trade is made, before expanding on the terms 'liquidity' and 'slippage'.

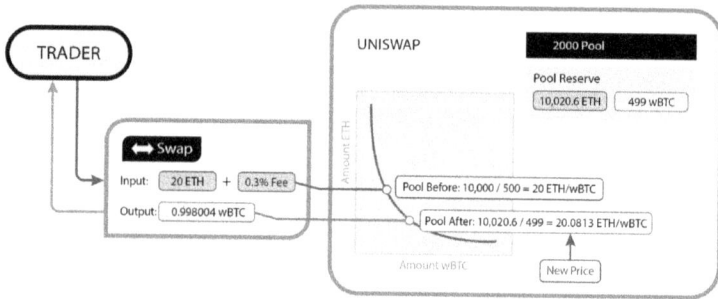

Figure 10: Uniswap trade.

Figure 10 shows a Uniswap trade, where 20 ETH are traded for 1 wBTC. The balance of the pool is changed correspondingly, changing the price in the pool to a new one. However, the exact amount received is not 1 wBTC, but slightly less: 0.998004 wBTC (producing a slightly higher price of 20.03999 ETH for 1 BTC). As stated earlier, the value of k must remain constant. If it was 5,000,000 before the trade, it must remain at 5,000,000 after the trade. Since the trader added 20 ETH to the ETH pool, then the new balance of ETH is 10,020, (10,020.06 with the 0.3% fee). In this case, the fees have been excluded for the sake of simplicity. Because this is a trade, wBTC must be sent to the trader and the number of wBTC to leave the pool must permit the value of k to stay at 5,000,000. This means the new wBTC balance in the pool after the trade is:

$$y = \frac{5,000,000}{10020} = 499.001996 \qquad (3.1)$$

Therefore, y is the new amount of wBTC in the pool. Because the transaction started with 500, the balance is what is sent to the trader to close the trade.

$$TraderwBTC = 500 - 499.001996 = 0.998004 \qquad (3.2)$$

The effective price the trader received for this trade is 20.0399 ETH/wBTC, not the 20 ETH/wBTC that the pool balance indicates. It is worth highlighting the importance of a larger liquidity pool to facilitate larger trades. If a significantly larger trade was to be placed, such as if 2,000 ETH were to be traded, then the trader would only get 83.3333 wBTC.

$$y = \frac{5,000,000}{12000} = 419.6667 \qquad (3.3)$$

As a result the loss of 83.3333 wBTC (500 − 419.6667) means a much higher price of 24 ETH/wBTC for this significantly larger trade. This is called 'slippage'. In Figure 11, we see a section of the curve representing the slippage. This area gets smaller with higher liquidity.

Since a trade is the only way to change the price, some investors have created tools that automatically monitor the price of ETH in BTC on centralized exchanges like Coinbase and Binance and perform arbitrage where they make a corresponding trade on the smart contract to bring the price

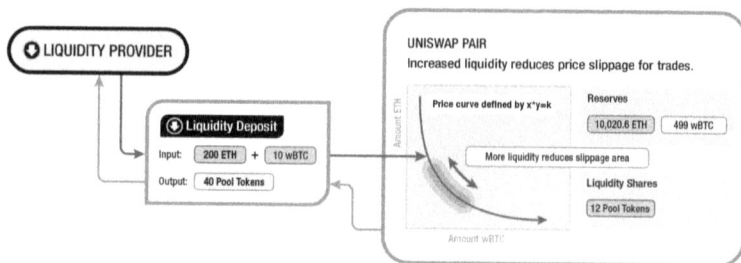

Figure 11: Adding Liquidity.

closer to current events on the exchange. Others will manually perform this arbitrage when they discover they can buy wBTC at a cheaper price on the smart contract than on an exchange.

In this way, these smart contracts for trade are somewhat basic, as one cannot place a buy order with a limit price "will buy 1 wBTC at the price of 20 ETH/wBTC or better" or any of the more sophisticated trades on centralized exchanges. This could be achieved, but the main point is that trading digitally has always required a third party service to facilitate the exchange where two parties trade one asset for a currency or to trade two different assets. More sophisticated smart-contracts may happen in the future that include stop losses, limit order, or perhaps even options.

Note that because Ethereum often has high fees, there has been an occurrence where such trading costs several hundreds of dollars in transaction fees. This is not the trading fee of 0.3% but rather the transaction fees paid to miners. When this involves NFT trading and transfer, the cost has been similar, so many people left Ethereum for other platforms such as Tezos (at some point the second most popular platform for NFTs in terms of transaction numbers). Although Tezos has a much smaller number of transactions in general compared to Ethereum, it has an equivalent to Uniswap called quipuswap.com, which works on the same principle described earlier. Uniswap has different versions of smart contracts with some variation in function, but the general idea is the same.

TRANSPARENCY AND PRIVACY USING ZERO-KNOWLEDGE PROOF

We have illustrated that the transparency of bitcoin transactions enables governments to track transactions on the blockchain itself, allowing for blacklisting on the exchange. Blacklisting reduces the fungibility aspect, although this is limited to the entry and exit point out of the blockchain. But what about Monero or Zcash? The cryptocurrency Monero uses ring signatures, zero-knowledge proofs, stealth addresses, and IP-address-obscuring methods to obscure transaction details, making it almost impossible for an observer to decipher the Monero addresses, transaction amounts, address balances and any transaction histories. All transactions in Monero benefit from this privacy. The major drawback of Monero is its relative difficulty of use as well as other issues such as the number of transactions (there are no layer 2 applications yet). In the case of Zcash, privacy is optional, but it also uses zero-knowledge proofs.

Zero-knowledge proof is a method by which one person (the "prover") can prove to another (the "verifier") that a given statement is true without having to convey any additional information apart from the fact the statement is indeed true. Obviously, it is easy to prove to someone else that you possess a piece of given information by revealing it, but it is more challenging to prove such possession without revealing the information itself or any additional information that could be used as a clue by the verifier to find it.

Certain abstract examples can help illustrate how zero-knowledge proof works. One often-used example is the Ali Baba cave, and was published in 1990 by Jean-Jacques Quisquater and others. In this story, Peggy (the prover) has discovered a secret key or password that opens a door within a cave. It's a special cave where once you have entered it, it will split into two paths that are linked to each other although separated by that locked door. Figure 12 illustrates the process. It shows an entrance to the cave and the two paths marked A and B. In the first image, Peggy enters and randomly picks a path while Victor (the verifier) waits outside, so he doesn't know which one she has picked. In the second image, Victor enters the cave up to the fork and randomly picks the path on which he expects Peggy to return. He then tells Peggy this path. In the final image, Victor should see Peggy coming back from that path he selected.

There are two possibilities here: either Peggy got lucky and did not need to unlock and use the door or either she was on the opposite path and had to unlock the door. So, Victor knows only with a 50% probability that she really possesses the secret password. To increase this probability, Peggy and Victor repeat the test with Victor again randomly choosing a path that Peggy must return on. After twenty of such tests, the chances of Peggy never having to unlock and use the door is two to the power of twenty or about one in a million. Consequently, Victor can safely assume with a 99.999904% degree of certainty that Peggy really knows the password or key. You might wonder why it is necessary to go through twenty tests when Victor would only need a single test if he saw, in the first image, which path Peggy picked (so he could pick the opposite). But this simple story is to represent what is essentially happening mathematically. In cryptography, the same principle is applied with mathematical equations which require multiple tests; hence, this story presenting the fundamentals has Victor not seeing which path Peggy initially picks. Typically, these mathematical proofs are complex with lots of calculation required for the prover while being simple to verify for the verifier.

Peggy randomly
choose path A or B
while Victor waits
outside.

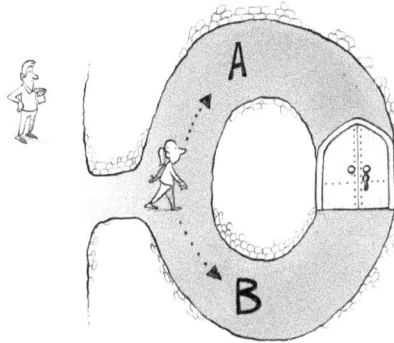

Victor enters and he
chooses a random path
for Peggy to return on.
He tells Peggy which
path to use.

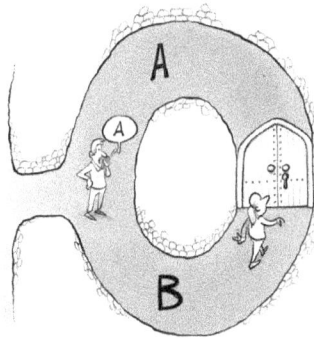

Peggy must reappear
on the designated path.

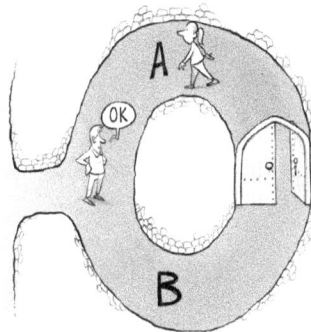

Figure 12: Zero Knowledge Proof with Ali Baba Cave.

Zero-knowledge proof is another astonishing discovery in the field of
modern cryptography, first discovered and published in 1985. Prior to the

era of computers, what is called "classic cryptography", it was simply the rearrangement and transpositions of letters, basically linguistic and lexicographic patterns. But in the 20th century, the focus has shifted towards extensive use of mathematics, information theory, abstract algebra, and number theory which led to the development of major breakthroughs. One such major development was asymmetric encryption revealed in November 1976 by Whitfield Diffie and Martin Hellman in which both a public key and private key are involved in the ciphering of a text. Before that, symmetric encryption was the only method in which both the sender and receiver share the same key that serves to encrypt and decrypt a message. The use of asymmetric encryption is a major factor in the dominance of bitcoin, where knowledge of the private key allows only the owner of a bitcoin address to spend it.

One criticism of bitcoin is the fact that all transactions are visible, and if you send some bitcoins to another person's bitcoin address over the bitcoin network, you will know when this person moves them out of that address. However, the lightning network itself does not have as much transparency, as only the initial opening of a channel is publicly visible. Any subsequent transactions on the lightning network are only known by the parties involved. Although Satoshi never publicly suggested a layer 2 mechanism such as the lightning network would come up as a solution to the throughput, there are other developments that will constantly improve bitcoin in astonishing ways. It may even be possible that zero-knowledge proof is integrated in some way with bitcoin – either at the base protocol or using a layer 2 – to provide powerful new functionality that would resolve some of the problems perceived with bitcoin today. With the very high interest that bitcoin and other cryptocurrencies have generated suddenly, there are more sharp minds studying and researching new and advanced concepts in the field of cryptography. It is likely that other fascinating discoveries await us. There is already a form of privacy for bitcoin with the lightning network as we will see later, but the study and possibilities that zero-knowledge proofs introduce, possibly combined with other tools, will be game changing. The central bankers will have to sweat some more.

GOVERNANCE

Off-chain discussions begin all proposed changes for all current crypto-currency blockchain and protocol. This can be via email, or through meetings among the experts, miners, or influencers. These changes can be backward compatible in the sense they can work with prior running versions, in which case they are called "soft fork". Soft fork does not create an alternative blockchain. Since other nodes that have not upgraded will not reject the blocks, they will just not process the new functionality which they simply disregard. On the other hand, if these changes are not backward compatible, then this creates a "hard fork" as the nodes that have not upgraded will reject the blocks submitted by the upgraded nodes, so the blockchain will split into two versions. Hard forks are avoided by the bitcoin developer community, although it does not mean it may never happen. For example, if there was a major flaw discovered that required a hard fork, it would immediately be created to fix the situation. Note that, in many cases, a soft fork might be sufficient — it all depends on the changes required. Regardless of the type of change, it starts with a proposal that once accepted, makes a new software available. Typically, the new functionality will only start to take effect at a certain block number to be mined in the very near future, allowing node operators the time to upgrade.

In 2014, Arthur Breitman published a white paper[31] for the Tezos blockchain under the pseudonym L.M. Goodman. The choice of this pseudonym is quite humorous as it is the name of the journalist that published an article in Newsweek magazine where she claimed to have found the creator of bitcoin, Satoshi Nakamoto. Her research was simple, she assumed it was not a pseudonym but his real name and hence started looking for any Satoshi Nakamoto residing in the United States. She found one who happened to be a software engineer, Dorian Satoshi Nakamoto, knocked on his door and asked him about bitcoin and the

---

[31] https://tezos.com/whitepaper.pdf

blockchain. He was confused as he thought she was asking about some government work he had done and simply said he couldn't talk about it[32]. From there, she went on to write an article claiming it was him. Long story short, Breitman likely wanted to be sarcastic. In this paper, there is a section called "amendment rules" (later called governance), where miners (called bakers in Tezos) vote on any proposal for changes to the protocol. This seems like quite a deviation from bitcoin where node operators and expert developers have the most influence on upgrades. Node operators might not be mining at all. However, as we will cover later, Tezos allows for the delegation of staking rights, as it is a Proof of Stake coin. Delegators choose who they delegate to so they are able to influence the decision by switching away from bakers who will not vote in the way they desire.

L.M. Goodman's white paper garnered interest when the Ethereum hard fork happened which split the blockchain and created two versions: Ethereum (which rewound the blockchain history before a hack of the DAO smart contract) and Ethereum Classic. This was an intense ideological war. In 2016, the DAO project had a major flaw in their smart contract that was running on Ethereum. It allowed a hacker to steal over 3.6 million Ether (or about $50 million at the time)[33]. The Ethereum Foundation and many influencers such as Vitalik Buterin decided to erase this hack by breaking an absolute principle of immutability of the blockchain: history should never be rewritten. They "manually" altered the blockchain by fixing the smart contract and returning the stolen Ether to the original owners. This became the main Ethereum blockchain (ETH) while the unaltered one became Ethereum Classic (ETC). And at about the same time, the debate about bitcoin's block size started to get more active, increasing the prospect of a future bitcoin hard fork to increase its size, potentially creating two versions. This, in fact, did happen with Bitcoin Cash. The prospect of having a built-in governance within the protocol started to make a lot more sense and the Tezos white paper got more traction then.

---

[32]https://news.bitcoin.com/many-facts-dorian-nakamoto-satoshi/
[33]https://www.gemini.com/cryptopedia/ethereum-classic-etc-vs-eth

The cryptocurrency Tezos has this governance process built in the protocol where miners (bakers) vote for a new software update proposal. When a new software update is to be proposed, the developers broadcast the proposal on the network, and it then goes through a vote by all bakers. This update may introduce small or significant changes to the Tezos protocol. Even if these changes induced a hard fork in other blockchains, Tezos, because the changes are decided on the blockchain itself, it does not create a hard fork; the protocol itself requires node operators to upgrade. If a proposal is accepted, all node operators must update the software so their node can switch to the new version at the time the protocol establishes it. In some way, it shares similarities with bitcoin where bitcoin node operators would load the new software which also contains a specific block number at which the features associated with this update become officially active. The difference for Tezos is that rather than having these decisions made off chain, the adoption is done through the protocol itself. In addition, software versions are stored in a directory identifying the protocol so that when the protocol dictates this is the new software version to use, the node accesses the correct software version from the proper directory.

One major criticism of the governance system is how bakers get to decide (through their vote) about the next upgrade. However, many of these bakers have delegates that can switch to bakers that have made their intention clear about which way they will vote, particularly when it is a controversial update. Coin holders can keep their coins in cold storage while they have delegated their staking rights to a specific baker who in exchange, typically returns 80% to 95% of their rewards back to them. The 5% to 20% fee is to pay them for the work of maintaining the node and for the bakers to have the burden of having their own coins put at risk in bond. Some bakers charged no fees during the beginning of their operation in the hope of attracting others. An advantage of this is that it provides an easy convenient way for a blockchain to go through upgrades very often, and Tezos has done this with several upgrades per year including a few major changes. Yet, this is also a potential drawback as it opens the door for impactful bugs to be introduced. Making use of a programming language not prone to bugs would be advantageous.

FUNCTIONAL PROGRAMMING

Both Cardano and Tezos have been built using functional programming languages — OCaml in the case of Tezos, and Haskell for Cardano. With the use of functional programming, a certain class of bug is avoided. For example, while traditional languages like C focus on the use of loops, functional programming focuses on recursion. When it comes to analyzing what a program is intended to perform, it gets much simpler and more conducive to the formal verification process when recursions are used. As an example, consider a function calculating Fibonacci numbers. Fibonacci numbers are a series of numbers starting with 1 that adds the 2 prior numbers to get the next one. These are Fibonacci numbers:

1, 1, 2, 3, 5, 8, 13, 21, 34, 55, 89, 144, ...

For the first and second number, we get 1, for the third we get 2 and for the fourth we get 3. In mathematical terms, the sequence Fn of Fibonacci numbers is defined by the recurrence relation:

$$F_n = F_{n-1} + F_{n-2} \tag{3.4}$$

With seed values:

$$F_0 = 0 \ and \ F_1 = 1 \tag{3.5}$$

If we were to create this function in a more traditional programming language like C, we would get something like what is on the left side of Figure 13, while in a functional programming language such as OCaml, it will look like the function on the right side. Note how the OCaml function is written, as it would be very inefficient as it would constantly recalculate the value of smaller Fibonacci numbers over and over and over.

Knowledgeable OCaml programmers would make use of cache which retains prior Fibonacci answers to avoid recomputing.

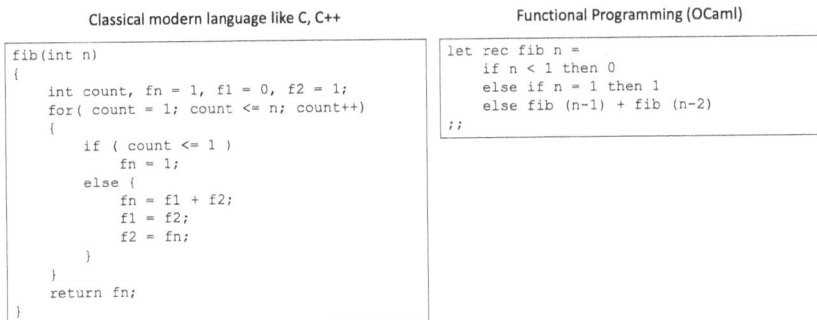

Classical modern language like C, C++

```
fib(int n)
{
    int count, fn = 1, f1 = 0, f2 = 1;
    for( count = 1; count <= n; count++)
    {
        if ( count <= 1 )
            fn = 1;
        else {
            fn = f1 + f2;
            f1 = f2;
            f2 = fn;
        }
    }
    return fn;
}
```

Functional Programming (OCaml)

```
let rec fib n =
    if n < 1 then 0
    else if n = 1 then 1
    else fib (n-1) + fib (n-2)
;;
```

Figure 13: Functional Programming comparison.

Here, the less efficient method was used to better illustrate the general concept in a simplified way. The use of cache is not necessary to understand the principle behind the language. Essentially, it is easy to verify the function is replicating the mathematical definition of Fibonacci numbers. Once past the first two Fibonacci numbers, the returned value is the sum of the prior two, exactly as the third line of the function states. Now, recursion is possible in traditional languages like C, but they are subject to what is called "busting the stack", which would happen for a very large value of n. The stack is what is used and grows every time a function call is taken within another function. Each function call without a return keeps growing the stack. In OCaml and Haskell, the language and the compiler provides a mechanism to avoid this issue.

As stated, recursion could also be used in C but it is often avoided because of its heavy use of the stack, which in some cases could bust it and crash the program. The stack is part of the memory in a program that stores arguments when a function call is made. In addition it stores the location of the instruction code for where to resume once the function call completes. If we were to use a large n number, at some point the program would run out of memory on the stack. With the use of variables and loops, the amount of memory used is fixed, regardless of how large the value of n is. In functional programming (FP), recursion does not bring up this memory stack issue as it is operating differently. Recursion is meant to be used without any restriction, just like the use of loops in the C language (except for the time and computation involved in running a large loop) or many recursions. Functional programming languages will use tail recursion which the compiler will effectively turn into an actual while loop which, just as in C, runs in a constant stack space. Although it might behave like a loop, from a programming perspective, humans can better analyze the code through the much easier recursion process.

OTHER INTERESTING PROJECTS

There have been many nonsensical projects, as well as some interesting concepts that will not gain any traction because they lack a clear competitive advantage that could take away from the network effect of bitcoin and even Ethereum. However, there are various projects that have brought valuable functionality. The problem for bitcoin maximalists is most of these projects will come with their own currency rather than using bitcoin/satoshis. Perhaps one day there will be a proper mechanism to peg bitcoins to another blockchain in a decentralized way so as to have another blockchain without the need to create new currencies every time. Pegging means using a derivative of bitcoin tied one to one with it. This will be discussed in a later chapter.

One of these projects, LBRY, was mentioned in an earlier section about the SEC. With the increasing censorship of content on YouTube and other social media, a solution like the one provided by LBRY is clearly valuable for sharing content. The founders of LBRY have no intention of replacing bitcoin. In fact, their motto is "LBRY does to publishing, what bitcoin did to money"[34]. I don't expect many people will store important wealth in LBRY tokens, but many need to use it. Bitcoin will very likely always be regarded as the long-term storage of wealth. Essentially, LBRY is a protocol allowing for the distribution of digital content across the globe using,

---

[34]https://lbry.com/

like bitcoin, a public permissionless run blockchain maintained by its protocol. The blockchain provides a single shared index of published content along with how to discover and pay for this content. This content includes books, music or movies and might only be accessible by paying a fee to the publisher or content creator. It has similar properties to BitTorrent in how it shares content but LBRY indexing allows for an easy way to track everything that is available[35].

Another project of interest is Theta, which attempts to offer a solution to streaming. Right now, any live broadcast made by an organization must be published from a limited number of distributed nodes relaying it to local users, each having their own connections. Typically, there is the original server where the stream starts from, which is then replicated to several nodes, who, in turn, distribute it. There might be a third layer of nodes so as to limit the impact. But the more resources deployed, the more costly this becomes, particularly if these resources are permanent. Theta acts as a way for anyone to insert their computer as an extra node that can serve other nodes. This is done 'on demand' and the user is paid back via the protocol. Perhaps, one day, ISPs will include themselves in the protocol, so that this way, whenever multiple subscribers are streaming the same live content, they only have to download a single stream from the provider. Before, each of the subscribers would download the same content, duplicating the same packet download. In some conditions, multicast is used as a way to broadcast to multiple nodes, but it is limited in some way. Theta however, a Samsung-backed project, makes this more feasible, and in addition, allows stream monetization. The ISP not only reduces the bandwidth usage from the source (since only one copy is downloaded), but by sharing this stream as part of the protocol, the ISP would be getting a Theta Fuel token as a source of additional revenue.

There are a variety of other projects that could be explored, but the point of this chapter is to offer a glimpse of what's going on in this dynamic and fast-changing field.

---

[35]https://lbry.tech/spec

4

BITCOIN AND PROOF OF WORK

In this chapter, I will cover the pros and cons of bitcoin and Proof of Work, which is the consensus used by the bitcoin network, as well as many others. I'll cover the different arguments and perspectives that have been shared by both proponents and antagonists of bitcoin. Many antagonists see Proof of Work as a failed system that chews up energy and is slow to achieve consensus. These individuals rank fast confirmations and the high number of transactions per second as the number one priority in a cryptocurrency. But to be truly functional, a cryptocurrency network must be sufficiently decentralized and resilient enough to withstand a cartel or government attack, which includes freezing coins linked to an address on the blockchain. A currency needs to be fungible, that is, interchangeable

— meaning that a dollar in your pocket holds the same value, or purchasing power, as a dollar in my pocket. This can only be truly achieved with a fully decentralized network. Therefore, decentralization assures that no one party has the ability to freeze transactions; decentralization should be the number one priority, at least for the most important cryptocurrency to be used as a long-term store of value. Sure, there could be some sort of side chain that is less decentralized, but then participants would be aware to hold a small amount of value in these accounts so as to limit their risk. The bitcoin Liquid network for example, is far less decentralized than bitcoin. It is, in fact, somewhat similar in nature to XRP, which we will review in more detail in chapter 7.

Even though bitcoin is limited in transactions per second as well as the time it takes to confirm the transaction, these problems are alleviated with the development of Layer 2 networks such as lightning network. Just as many previously believed that digital signatures were not possible before the discovery of asymmetric encryption in the 1970s, nor was a decentralized currency until the bitcoin white paper was published in 2008, whatever problem we see with bitcoin right now will likely be resolved in ways we haven't discovered yet. The lightning network was a breakthrough with its interesting use of hashed Timelock contracts and bi-directional payment channels. Although it has its limitations, a new system called CoinPool, inspired by Lightning, has already been proposed, which would provide a drastic improvement. We will cover this, too, in a later chapter.

PROOF OF WORK IN A NUTSHELL

Nearly all blockchains use the same principle. A long list of blocks (segments of data which, once added to the chain record, cannot be altered) are appended one after the other, forming a digital chain of blocks. When a new block is added, it specifies a set of new transactions which implies a change in the balance of existing accounts. Because this "append-only" database is not managed by a central authority, but rather a distributed set of interconnected computers scattered worldwide, there is a need for a consensus algorithm that enables all these computers to agree on what is the latest state of the blockchain. Proof of Work using what is called Nakamoto-style consensus (named after the pseudonym of the person or group behind bitcoin), is part of one such algorithm. Let's first recap how bitcoin, Proof of Work and the overall algorithm operate.

Bitcoin's blockchain provides a probabilistic finality in the sense that there is always the possibility that a block might be discarded, albeit the probability decreases as additional blocks are added, forming the longest chain. This concept can be described as a database that only allows new entries to be added and not modified, known as an append-only database. This database serves as a ledger that records the ownership of bitcoins held by various bitcoin addresses. Bitcoin miners engage in a competition to mine the next block that contains a fresh set of transactions. The miner that succeeds in mining the block is entitled to receive the associated block rewards and transaction fees paid by users to include their transactions in the block. Initially, the block reward was set at 50 bitcoins, scheduled to be cut in half about every four years. At this writing, the block reward is 6.25 BTC, scheduled to halve to 3.125 some time next year, continuing thusly until the year 2140, after which miners might only be rewarded from the transaction fees.

Essentially, the process of determining which participant has the right to create the next block and receive the associated rewards and fees involves establishing a clear winner among the competing miners. This is where Proof of Work comes into play, as it mandates that miners must include a unique hash value of the block header in their block. A hash function is a mathematical algorithm that maps any data of any size to a fixed-size output, referred to as a digest. This algorithm combines all the bytes of the data into a fixed-size value in an unpredictable manner, such that the resulting hash output for any given data cannot be determined until the hash algorithm is executed.Even if you start with an existing data where only a single byte is modified, the function must still be run to generate the new, completely different hash. A hash computation is somewhat costly, but rapid for modern computers; however, running thousands of hashes requires heavy computation. Bitcoin's PoW uses the SHA256 hash algorithm as its "mining" method. SHA256 generates a 256-bit long hash output that acts as a document fingerprint. For a block to be accepted, it must have a SHA256 with a certain number of leading zeros, like this one, that was generated for block 732770:

00000000000000000000000f545cccf4f00a970c3339e007d0a3b7799956f07b52

Part of the block header data sent into the SHA256 function is a nonce, which is a number that is incremented until the right number of leading zeros is obtained — in other words, until the hash output is lower than a specific target number. Because miners have no ability to manipulate the output of the hash function, they must continuously increment a nonce and repeatedly input it into the hash function, until the resulting hash satisfies bitcoin's protocol criteria for the number of leading zeros. The number of leading zeros, with a higher number of zeros indicating a higher difficulty level and requiring more extensive SHA256 computations, determines the mining difficulty level.

A single SHA256 is not costly, therefore it is trivial for other miners to verify the validity of a proposed winning block. However, generating many SHA256. as fast as possible so to be the first miner, is the real challenge. For example, the hash shown above has a nonce set at 1,487,622,917, suggesting that many hash calculations by its miner (or aggregate of miners if coming from a mining pool) according to the nonce. This difficulty level is set to make sure that, on average, a 10-minute interval occurs between each bitcoin block. But the more miners that participate in the network, the more hash power becomes involved, and the more rapidly solutions are found; hence the network automatically adjusts to increase the difficulty by lowering this target number (more leading zeros) so as to maintain an average of 10 minutes between blocks.

Therefore, because the bitcoin protocol adjusts difficulty based on the amount of mining being done and because bitcoin has a fixed supply, the relationship between miners and supply differs from typical commodities, such as gold. For gold, the more miners active, the more gold will be extracted from the ground, and, therefore, the higher the yearly supply mined. And that's what differentiates bitcoin. If more miners join the network, and the total hashing power increases by say 10%, the discovery of a new block on average will take less than 10 minutes. To compensate for the decrease in time between blocks, every two weeks (actually every 2016 blocks), the network analyzes the average interval and adjusts the difficulty level accordingly. Not only will the difficulty be adjusted, but it also means that any blocks submitted by miners running a different version of the protocol will be rejected. Rather, miners must adhere to the adjusted difficulty level as set by the protocol. Similarly, if a large number of miners go offline as when China banned bitcoin mining in early 2021, the protocol notices that the average interval between blocks has increased, and the network will correspondingly adjust the difficulty level down to make it easier for the miners that remain on the network. This dynamic system results in making bitcoin's rate of new supply immune to the market's economic data. Or, said another way, the demand for new bitcoin has no effect upon the supply.

Mining bitcoin is highly competitive. Figure 14 depicts a scenario where two miners "win the lottery" at about the same time. If the miner who mined Block 1 is in one region of the world, other miners in that same region are likely to get that block first rather than the other block, and they will start work on mining Block 2. Other miners will get the alternative block 1, or Block 1 and start working on the other chain. This is called a temporary fork that will be resolved once a miner working on either of the two chains discovers the next Block 2. In the figure, another block is added to the top branch and therefore becomes the longest chain, and all miners proceed to mine Block 3, disregarding block 1.' As shown, if your transaction was included by the miner of Block 1 but not by the miner of Block 1, which later became part of the longest chain (hence officially recognized), it would have been wrong to assume the transaction was finally in the blockchain.

With one important exception, once Block 2 is broadcast, transactions included in Block 1 but not in Block 1 return to the mining mempool, where pending transactions are stored. But, if the sender of a transaction made another transaction to another bitcoin address (double spending) and that second transaction was included in the official Block 1, then the transaction sitting in Block 1 will not be included in the mempool as these BTC have already been spent (via Block 1). This highlights the importance of verifying the number of subsequent blocks that have been appended to your transaction's block, as it serves as additional confirmation. The more blocks, the better.

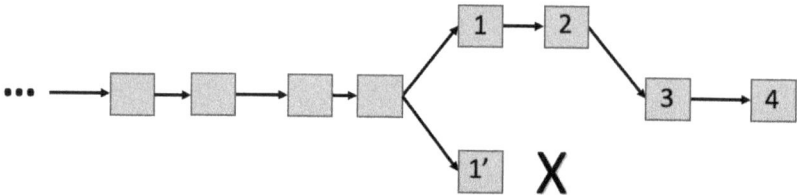

Figure 14: Bitcoin's Proof of Work temporary forks.

These essential elements form bitcoin's Proof of Work. Of course, there are other subtleties to account for but this covers the fundamentals. Although to the average person on the street bitcoin might appear complicated, once you understand PoW, you realize it is really not too complex. In fact, compared to Proof of Stake, Proof of Work is quite simple, as you will find out later.

ABOUT BITCOIN'S BLOCK SIZE HISTORY

As mentioned in Chapter 2, Bitcoin Cash was created as a fork of bitcoin, but with a larger block size. Not everyone agreed with changing the block size, so two groups of different miners ran the two different versions of the bitcoin software, which resulted in two live blockchains and their respective networks - bitcoin and Bitcoin Cash. As justification for creating the fork, the Bitcoin Cash folks insisted that Satoshi's white paper abstract defines bitcoin as a form of electronic cash:

"A purely peer-to-peer version of electronic cash would allow online payments to be sent directly from one party to another without going through a financial institution."

And to them, this required the capacity to send more transactions than the existing technological limit of about seven transactions per second, rather than on limiting the block size to only 1 megabyte. The goal of keeping the block size lower, however, is that the lighter technical requirements provide a lower barrier to entry for new miners, resulting in more node[36] operators joining the network worldwide, thus increasing its decentralization and — importantly — its ability to withstand attack.

As for the original block size limit, it is an interesting story in itself. Initially, bitcoin's block size was limited by the number of database locks required to process it, which effectively was around 500-750 Kbytes. This restriction was either forgotten, or not realized by all, except perhaps Satoshi Nakamoto himself. What's fascinating is that in 2010, Satoshi released a new software version of bitcoin in which he quietly added an explicit block size limit of 1 megabyte. But, because the database lock restriction setting was even lower than the block size limit, the database lock restriction was rendered irrelevant. It wasn't until March 2013, over two years after Satoshi's disappearance, that the discovery of the database lock limit was made, almost unintentionally, with the release of bitcoin software version 0.8.0. This version eliminated the undocumented database lock limit restriction, enabling miners to produce blocks larger than 750 kilobytes. At that time, however, about 60% of the miners were still running version 0.7.0, which rejected these large blocks as they were considered invalid by their software. This created a hard fork; it was then agreed

---

[36]Bitcoin node only runs the bitcoin software without doing any bitcoin mining. They are part of the network and participate in the relay of valid blocks and the rejection of invalid blocks.

that all miners would downgrade to version 0.7.0 until a resolution was applied.

Since this database lock limit was an undocumented block size limit found in every prior version, bitcoin developers decided to officially remove it and proceed with a hard fork that would allow for larger blocks up to 1 megabytes. They scheduled the official hard fork for May 15, 2013, when all miners were required to apply a patch that would remove the limitation. This hard fork was not the last, but it was the last that was non-controversial.

The most contentious issue regarding bitcoin has been settling the maximum block size dispute. With this code, Satoshi Nakamoto "clandestinely" added an explicit block size limit in 2010, just a few months before he disappeared from the bitcoin space:

```
static const unsigned int MAX_BLOCK_SIZE = 1000000;
```

The issue of the block size continued to resurface, and in 2014, Mike Hearn, a bitcoin developer, saw the need to increase this limit. He proposed a hard fork that would introduce Bitcoin XT with an 8 megabyte limit, but it was never adopted. The debate intensified and culminated in a conference held in Montreal in 2015 that aimed to address this issue of bitcoin's block size. At its core, the philosophical debate was about the impact of full blocks. Should bitcoin's block be large enough that they are never full, allowing for enough transactions to be included without any wait time, or should they always be full to avoid transaction fees spiraling down to near zero?

You might wonder why transaction fees would spiral down to zero if blocks were never full. To small blockers, as those in support of small blocks came to be called, full blocks would always be inevitable. They posited that if blocks are not full, the extra space would ultimately be used to store any kind of information submitted by users. And since miners would make more from fees by adding as many transactions as they can, they will include as many as possible, even if the fees are small. In a cascade effect, users making bitcoin transactions would know they can offer as small transaction fees as possible, because miners will still include their transaction anyways, even if only included at the very end.

Right now, bitcoin miners generate the bulk of their revenue from block rewards (6.25 btc per block at this writing), but eventually rewards will be much smaller; around the year 2140, they will diminish to zero. Conversely, large blockers found this concern irrelevant and had no need to solve a problem that may or may not be present in 100 years or more. Another concern small blockers foresaw was serious stress on the network if blocks size were to increase. By necessity, disk space requirements must increase, too, making it more difficult for small node operators to enter the competition. Relatedly, small blockers also expressed reservations about the networking issues stemming from broadcasting larger blocks within the network.

But then came the development of Segwit, short for "segregated witness," a soft fork of bitcoin. This reorganization of the bitcoin transaction format resolved the problematic transaction malleability issue, as well as essentially increasing the number of transactions that can be contained in a bitcoin block. If all users were using Segwit transactions, it would essentially be as if the bitcoin block size more than doubled, going from 1 to 2 megabytes. Nevertheless, this was not sufficient for large blockers, so it led to the split we discussed earlier. Bitcoin Cash became popular enough for cryptocurrency exchanges to add it to their trading offerings. Ironically, later Bitcoin Cash experienced its own hard fork that created Bitcoin SV (for Satoshi Vision) with an even larger block size. Again, for an in depth historical perspective on the politics behind this debate, I recommend *The Blocksize War*, an excellent book by Jonathan Bier. Today, with the market mostly losing interest in both Bitcoin Cash and Bitcoin SV, many exchanges are delisting them both.[37] Another challenge Bitcoin Cash and Bitcoin SV are experiencing is that their large blocks are too demanding for their networks, causing frequent "block reorgs" (temporary hard forks).

---

[37] https://www.coindesk.com/tech/2021/02/19/okcoin-delists-bitcoin-cash-bitcoin-sv-to-avoid-misleading-new-bitcoin-clients/

With the emergence of the lightning network, the need for regular users to operate a bitcoin node (a non-mining operation) has grown increasingly important. We will explore how the lightning network operates in a later chapter, but part of the requirement is to open channels. Nothing prevents anyone from using any or all publicly available nodes, but many hard-core users prefer to run their own node to remove any dependencies on others and provide for greater privacy. With Lightning, small block size requiring much smaller disk storage for node operators becomes a more relevant feature so that anyone can run their own nodes.

MINING POOL

Big picture: The mining of bitcoin blocks is analogous to a lottery: miners combine their hash power and share their revenue to get a higher chance to win blocks so that they can receive a more streamlined revenue. By joining together with other miners in mining blocks, winning a block occurs more often, thus providing a more reliable and constant stream of income. True, the rewards are smaller as they must be shared, but payouts are more predictable and more frequent. The first mining pool was created in November 2010. The idea caught on, and today there are at least 15 well-known mining pools, each of various sizes, including BTC.com, AntPool, and F2pool.

Within mining pools, every miner can have a node, but just a single node is required to connect to the bitcoin network. This node maintains a copy of the current blockchain and collects any new transactions sent by users to include in its mempool. When a new block is to be mined, this node will assemble a set of transactions from the mempool into a block and then send, to all miners, a copy of the block along with a range of nonce it should focus on. So, miner A might be assigned nonce from 0 to 9,999 while miner B will be assigned 0,000 to 19,999 and so on. Periodically, each miner sends back a status report and asks for a new range of nonce to work on as it goes through its assigned nonce. When a miner discovers a nonce that produces the correct hash (correct number of leading zeros or rather, lower than a certain number), it sends it to the pool node which immediately broadcasts the block to the bitcoin network. Later, the mining rewards are distributed according to how much hash was done by each. If miner A, for example, went through 10 sets of 10,000 hash, while miner B went through only two, then miner A will receive five times more of the share of the rewards than miner B.

For this discussion a mining node is defined as a node broadcasting new mining blocks by its miners. By comparison, a non-mining node, one that anyone can run, is simply connected to the network, keeping its own copy of bitcoin's blockchain. This node's purpose is to validate blocks and transactions as they are broadcast to the network, without producing its own blocks as no mining is undertaken. As mentioned earlier, in the case of the mining pool, a single mining node is technically required. Such nodes determine which transactions from the mempool will be included in the next block, while a non-mining node can only validate the blocks and the transactions they contain. It's an important distinction, and we will see why later.

DECENTRALIZATION ASPECT OF PROOF OF WORK

PoW allows miners to quickly and easily begin mining. All that is required is to turn on a bitcoin mining node and it will immediately begin competing with other miners for the right to mine on the very next bitcoin block. In comparison, as will be explored in the next chapter, PoS requires a miner/staker to first run for several days as a mining/staking node before it is permitted to mine blocks. As for other consensus mechanisms, such as those used by XRP or bitcoin Liquid, one's reputation needs to be established and become known for other nodes to include you. The key, here, is two-fold. First, the greater the number of nodes in a network, particularly mining nodes, the better. If a cartel or government attempts to force miners to only accept certain transactions, thus censoring others, the more nodes that exist and the more they are distributed worldwide the more difficult it is to force them into compliance. Second, the more dynamic this network can be, with new nodes being rapidly included in the network, the more resilient. As word spreads that attackers, cartels, or governments intend to force node operators or miners to break bitcoin's fungibility by blacklisting addresses, new miners in other geographic locations will be incentivized to operate a node, circumventing these attacks. When compared to other consensus methods, PoW is the most open and easy for anyone to join. Granted, if you have little hash power, your impact will be minimal, but still present. But even a simple mining node further decentralizes the network by forwarding valid bitcoin blocks and transactions.

> Bitcoin is a permissionless network, meaning that anyone can join the network instantly. In addition, bitcoin blocks are small, making it feasible for small computers to participate as bitcoin nodes. Finally, both bitcoin nodes and miners validate blocks according to the bitcoin protocol, and with over 15,000 existing bitcoin nodes, this makes bitcoin the most decentralized cryptocurrency.

In the case of bitcoin, even bitcoin's ownership has been formally decentralized with its founder, Satoshi Nakamoto, vanishing in December 2010. All he left us with, other than the original code and the white paper, is his discussion in forum posts over a span of two years from 2008 to 2010. You can read more about this in *The Book Of Satoshi*, published in the Spring of 2014.

Mining pools are an integral part of PoW. One argument advanced by anti-bitcoin folks is about how few mining pools exist and how much more centralized this *could* become. After all, mining pool operators select the transactions that will be included in the blocks. Bitcoin miners joining any of these pools are all mining for the same exact block. In short, a bitcoin mining pool is like a giant miner that subdivides the mining task to multiple individual miners. The mining pool operator collects the revenue from transaction fees and the block rewards and distributes the revenue equally among all the nodes, based on how much hashing each has contributed, regardless of which node discovered the correct nonce.

On the surface, it may appear that mining pools contribute negatively to the decentralized nature of bitcoin, and this concern has been raised by anti-bitcoin folks as a counter argument in the decentralization debate. But, critical to this analysis is if and how mining pools could be leveraged to attack bitcoin. By attack, I mean any disruption to proper bitcoin operations such as always mining empty blocks, applying a blacklist on transactions or any other kind of misbehavior.

To put these concerns into perspective, it's important to understand the very nature of mining pools. In 2015, a particular mining pool approached 51% of the total hashing power; when this was reported in blogs, social media, and articles, many miners immediately began voluntarily exiting that pool and joining others, dropping that mining pool's share of hashing power. The fact that it is so easy for miners to rapidly leave and join mining pools, and the fact that the mining pools themselves do not require much infrastructure to create, the power effectively lies in the hands of the miners, whom history shows have chosen based solely on principal and maintaining bitcoin ethos.

So if mining pools readily redistribute themselves, then perhaps distribution of hash power among individual miners is of concern. If the hashing power is concentrated, it becomes easier for a malicious entity to target or take over the few large miners and attack the bitcoin network. It is worth noting that although mining pools are public and advertise themselves, the identity and information of individual miners are not publicly available, but they can still be traced. According to a study from the National Bureau of Economic Research (NBER) released in 2021,[38] the top 50% of miners hold almost all the mining capacity, while the top 10% have 90%, and just 0.1% of miners, which is about 60 miners, have 50% of the mining capacity. The study concluded that just over 60 miners have more than 50% of the hashing power. Note that the study defined a bitcoin miner as

---

[38] https://www.nber.org/papers/w29396

an organization or corporation or even an individual that controls a bitcoin node (and likely a large number of ASIC hardware devices that calculate the hash).

Essentially, if these 60 miners were all under European Union's jurisdiction, or if there was enough hash power in these countries to get to 51% of the hash power, these miners could exclude transactions outside government-approved, whitelisted bitcoin addresses or even worse, all empty blocks making bitcoin practically useless. We covered this subject in Chapter 2, but it is important to revisit it here. To better understand this problem, the next figure illustrates a situation where a ban on a blacklisted address was activated by top miners:

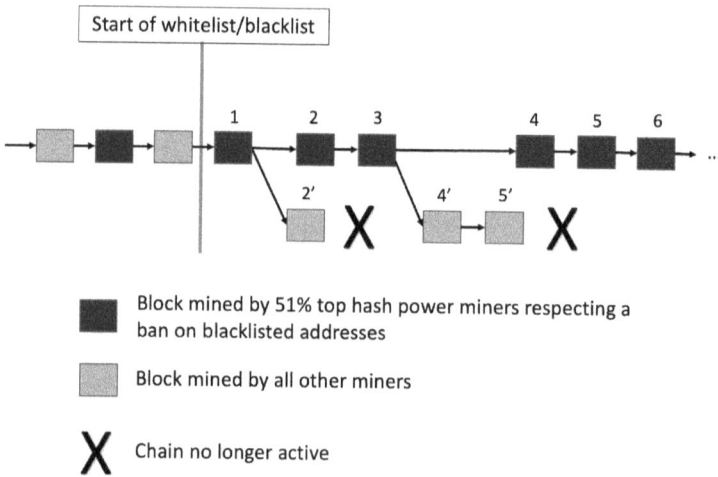

Figure 15: Top 51% hash power miner respecting whitelist and blacklist.

The darker blocks have been mined by this "cartel" of miners, while the lighter ones have been mined by all the other miners. Before the start of this whitelist, all miners created blocks in some random distribution, loosely tied to their proportion of the hash power. Once the whitelist/blacklist was activated, the 51% top miners run a modified software that filters bitcoin addresses, determining which transactions to accept in a block. These miners only create blocks respecting this whitelist and reject blocks not respecting it. In the figure, Block 2 is mined by the cartel and Block 2 , containing non-approved transactions, is mined by the other miners. In this scenario, the 51% top miners, with the help of a modified bitcoin software, pretend this block never occurred and continue mining. When a blacklisting miner working on that branch (or fork) finds a block with only approved transactions, it is added by the others – See, Block 2. And because the top 51% of miners applying this blacklist have more hash power, they are more likely to discover Block 3, the next block. At this point, the other miners will accept this as the longest official chain, and the chain with Block 2 vanishes, along with the blacklisted transactions that are perpetually pushed back into pending transaction mempool.

Blacklisted transactions are again included in a new block, this time Block 4. And now it gets promising as Block 5 has been added to the chain, which may or may not contain other blacklisted transactions. But because the mining cartel won't accept Block 4 since it contains a blacklisted transaction, these blacklisting miners are still mining for the block after Block 3. Once they find new Blocks 4, 5, and 6, which of course makes their chain longer, the other chain vanishes again. So, in this case, bitcoin's decentralized nature suffers and why decentralization is a spectrum. The fact that there are some points of weakness prove this — without even mentioning the havoc that a worldwide concerted government could implement. Having said that, I give this a very low chance of occuring, and even if it did, bitcoin developers would be working on an updated version to counteract this attempted hostile takeover. Solutions might include adding the choice of which transaction to be included as part of the bitcoin protocol, where then all the thousands of bitcoin nodes would act as policeman against such behavior. Interestingly, Stratum V2,[39] an updated mining pool protocol, is designed to provide more control to miners joining pools and increase decentralization. As for a hostile action by our hypothetical global government, this too is unlikely to happen considering the great number of cryptocurrency users at large. As stated earlier, one

---

[39] See https://bitcoinist.com/stratum-v2-bitcoin-mining-software-gets-facelift/ and https://braiins.com/stratum-v2

thing the banking cartel fears about bitcoin is the education it brings to the masses, and how this education skews the future towards favorable politics for bitcoin.

Let's now delve into what a decentralized cryptocurrency means. This is best illustrated by using its the opposite: a centralized currency where a single government or organization (or a very few) can control one or more of the currency's attributes:

1. The total supply of the currency;

2. The creation, deletion and management of accounts that can hold that currency; or

3. The prioritization of currency transfer from one account to another, or the decision of which transfers to allow or to be blocked;

Clearly, central bank digital currencies (CBDC) are fully centralized as they satisfy all three prongs.

For bitcoin, however, it is different. Currently, there are more than 15,000 bitcoin nodes distributed worldwide. This number combines mining and non-mining nodes, and they all validate the blocks, ensuring that the supply corresponds to the directives of the bitcoin protocol and its software.

Regarding the first prong - the total supply - bitcoin is highly decentralized, meaning that any block violating the supply side of the protocol would be rejected. Prong two and three are somewhat linked. Anyone can anonymously download a free bitcoin "wallet" (signing device) app, but if they're prohibited from receiving bitcoins to it, then it's just an empty, useless account. This is why the last two attributes are somewhat tied together. Taken individually, each miner has the power to mine empty blocks, but they cannot prevent other miners from mining non-empty blocks and vice versa. If a hostile group exerted control of the top miners, however, it would have complete authority to determine which (or whose) transactions are included.

That's a play on the 51% attack. Together, these top miners would theoretically use a modified bitcoin software that does not accept any blocks containing blacklisted bitcoin addresses. They would essentially generate a soft fork of bitcoin where they are the more restrictive chain. Since they have the hash power needed to dominate the network, whenever a block with a blacklisted transaction is mined by any of the other smaller miners, the cartel of miners would disregard it as if the block were invalid and continue mining, leading to a fork. And, since they dominate in hash power, their chain would eventually become the longest chain. Because the miner cartel has a greater hashing power, its blockchain will eventually become the longest, and the other 49% miners will adopt it because they are still running the traditional bitcoin software that would not reject the top miner's block as it does not violate any of their rules.

One of the arguments against Proof of Stake repeated by bitcoin maximalists is how the rich will get richer, and how this type of consensus will concentrate power to just a few. Currently, the non-mining bitcoin nodes are responsible to validate whether correct blocks are being passed, but they have no power to determine which transactions miners should include in the next blocks. But of course, it would not be long before this type of transaction filtering by a cartel of miners is detected, outraging the bitcoin community and inspiring developers to release critical updates to resolve the vulnerability. Bitcoin's software development might be extremely conservative but there are still major improvements that have been made.

If the situation surfaced where only empty blocks were generated, I can quickly imagine a bitcoin software update that will reject empty blocks when the mempool is not empty. Non-mining bitcoin nodes could participate in this block monitoring if they too maintained a mempool. However, the attackers (top 60 miners) could get around this by sending each other their own transactions. Also, this would not prevent the blacklisted addresses concern.

An enhanced approach would involve updating the current bitcoin protocol to integrate a pre-consensus mechanism that determines which transactions from the mempool should be included in the upcoming blocks. This could entail, for example, if a transaction with a very high transaction fee has been languishing in the mempool for more than three blocks, nodes would then reject any new blocks that fail to include it. Obviously there are complications to work out, considering that currently a mempool is different from one miner to another, hence this concept is pure speculation on my part. The benefit is that the protocol ensures transactions with above average transaction fees are accepted. Rather than a fixed number of blocks, perhaps the threshold should be a factor of the transaction fee multiplied by the number of blocks mined during the time it has been in the mempool. To avoid the inclusion of spam transactions, the calculation of this factor might include a log function to drastically lower the possibility of tons of near zero fee transactions to be processed. I am thinking out loud but the point I want to convey is I'm convinced a solution would be found if it comes to this.

But I doubt it would get to this point, just as I doubt a worldwide ban of bitcoin mining could ever happen, at least for the foreseeable future. As I mentioned earlier, what the central bankers are most afraid of is the education that bitcoin brings to the public more than bitcoin itself. With a more educated population, such flagrant behavior would be rejected by the majority. Only if they could create a major panic such as an imminent world war or staged alien attack where "war measures" needed to be implemented, could they perhaps influence enough of the majority to accept their heightened control. History shows that fear itself has been used often by governments to influence, or outright control, their population's behaviors.

When I was young in the 1980s, I remember a story my mother told me after coming back from a trip to visit the USSR with her friend. While there, they had a guide in charge of monitoring their movement, since foreigners' interaction with the locals had to be supervised. While at a restaurant, a group of Russians at the other table looked over at my mother and her friend saying "Peace! Peace!" while raising their two fingers as the peace sign. In short, the USSR subtly controlled its population by feeding a fear that the West could be attacking them at any time. The United States has played this card as well — after September 11, 2001. Regardless of whether such means were justified, the point is governments understand mass psychology, and they know that fear tends to keep people from thinking clearly, if they can think at all.

The crucial idea is to have a thoughtful approach or multiple approaches to ensure that bitcoin's strength, its decentralization, can be further decentralized if the situation demands. This implies that having a potential solution on standby, known and ready for activation, could serve as a sufficient deterrent for governments or cartels, dissuading them from attempting an attack and obviating the need to implement the protective strategy.

PROOF OF WORK BY OTHER COINS

An important aspect of bitcoin's Proof of Work is obviously the hash power. Although some object to bitcoin's use of energy, this also means it is extremely difficult to execute a 51% attack against the bitcoin network. And, any other cryptocurrency using PoW immediately faces a potential 51% attack from bitcoin miners, particularly those using SHA256 as bitcoin does; this strength is one of the main reasons why bitcoin maximalists call all other coins shitcoins.

Maximalists first establish PoW as the most solid consensus method and because energy and power will be directed at the most important cryptocurrency, bitcoin, all other PoW cryptocurrencies are significantly more vulnerable to attacks. Consider Bitcoin Cash (BCH), which uses SHA256 as it is a fork of bitcoin. In April 2023, BCH has 0.5% of the market capitalization of bitcoin, or rather, its price is more than 100 times smaller than that of bitcoin. The total hash rate by all miners of BCH sums to 1.57 EH/sec (1.57x1018 Hash/sec) while bitcoin's total hash rate is 223 EH/sec or 142 times more. Meanwhile, the hash power of U.S.-based Marathon Digital, one of the largest miners in the world, is about 13 EH/sec. So, one mining company has more hash power than BCH by a factor of seven, which means that this single mining company could overtake the BCH network by switching its software to mine Bitcoin Cash. Core Scientific, another major miner, has over 8 EH/sec of hash rate; it too could perform a 51% attack on BCH quite easily, as it has more than four times the hash power.

Before continuing, let's enhance our explanation of what comprises a 51% attack. One example has been explored earlier - where a cartel of miners (assumed to be under concerted instruction from a bitcoin-hostile government or organization) is using a whitelist of addresses which they deem allowed to transact. Ethereum, in fact, is in the midst of experiencing something along those lines with ETH stakers becoming compliant with the Office of Foreign Assets Control (OFAC). Another is what is called "selfish mining" which was detailed in a November 2013 paper by Eyal and Sirer:[40]

> The key idea behind this strategy, called Selfish Mining, is for a pool to keep its discovered blocks private, thereby intentionally forking the chain. The honest nodes continue to mine on the public chain, while the pool mines on its own private branch. If the pool discovers more blocks, it develops a longer lead on the public chain, and continues to keep these new blocks private. When the public branch approaches the pool's private branch in length, the selfish miners reveal blocks from their private chain to the public.

Their paper proposes a successful attack can be launched is something notably less than 51%, perhaps as little as 33%. The general idea is that once this small group of miners (selfish miners) are the first to discover a block, they begin the attack by not releasing or holding the block. In this way, they would already have a head start on mining the next block while all the other miners are still mining for the current block, the one already solved by the selfish miners. Selfish mining however is specific only to an

---

[40]https://arxiv.org/abs/1311.0243

economic attack against other miners, would not last very long and would only be at most annoying to regular bitcoin users for dealing with these temporary forks. Further investigation into the various types of attacks relies on a specific and highly complex area of mathematics called game theory. One of the authors of the Selfish Miner paper later concluded:

> **When two pools can attack each other, they face a version of the Prisoner's Dilemma. If one pool chooses to attack, the victim's revenue is reduced, and it can retaliate by attacking and increase its revenue. However, when both attack, at Nash equilibrium both earn less than they would have if neither attacked. {…}**
>
> **The fact that block withholding is not common may be explained by modeling the attack decisions as an iterative prisoner's dilemma.**[41]

After more than a decade of mining pool operations, no such attack has been reported for bitcoin, at least nothing significant. This suggests that our conclusion is valid, as big miners have found no gain to exploit by deploying their intense capital and infrastructure to disrupt the network. In addition, bitcoin rewards are frozen in the blockchain until 100 additional blocks have been mined before the miners can collect them. Thus, any kind of disruption from an attack on the network would negatively affect the bitcoin price, which would reduce the attacker's ultimate payoff. In short, sometimes, academic papers do not account for all economic incentives in play.

Another avenue for the "51% attack" could be to perform a double-spend attack by altering the transactions recorded in the blockchain. This tactic works particularly well with a cryptocurrency of little value to the attackers. This happened twice to Bitcoin Gold (BTG), where a malicious actor or actors stole nearly $18 million worth of BTG from exchanges. Figure 16 walks us through their scheme.

---

[41] https://www.sciencedirect.com/science/article/pii/S2405959522000443

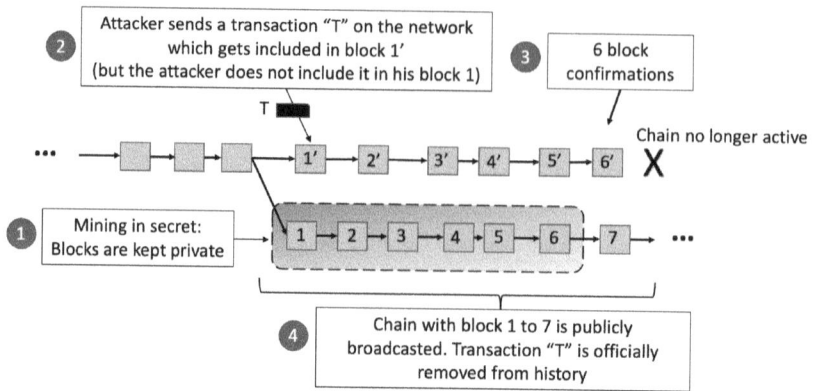

Figure 16: Block Withholding or selfish mining attack.

The double spend strategy is similar to selfish mining, where the attacker strategically gains extra mining as certain blocks and transactions are circumvented. In both scenarios, blocks are mined in secret, but the double spend attack starts with the malicious actor secretly mining while sending BTG coins to an exchange (Textbox 2). Most exchanges require six blocks before a transaction is considered confirmed. During this window, the malicious actor continues mining in secret for several blocks. Once confirmed by the exchange, the BTG is traded for BTC, which is immediately withdrawn. And once the exchange has sent the BTC, the malicious actor releases its version of the blockchain, which erases this BTG transaction from history, allowing it to spend them again.

According to that study from NBER, it would take about 60 of the top miners (corporate/individual) acting in concert to perform a 51% attack on the bitcoin network, yet it would take just a fraction of the hash power of the largest bitcoin miner to attack BCH.

The vulnerability is not as acute for cryptocurrencies that do not share the same hash algorithm as bitcoin. For example, Litecoin uses Scrypt rather than SHA256, and, therefore, the specialized ASIC hardware equipment meant to generate SHA256 are not as effective in mounting an attack against Litecoin by bitcoin miners. The source of energy by these mega miners, however, could still be diverted to specialized hardware to mine on other blockchains, so the danger still exists. Additionally, cryptocurrencies with small market caps sharing the same hash algorithm are at greater risk than those with a larger market cap. Typically, a correlation can be spotted between hash power and market cap. For instance, if the price of BCH doubled tomorrow, the price of the currency per total hash power would suddenly climb, making it more financially viable for miners to redirect their machines towards mining it. As a sidenote, there are websites that aggregate the list of cryptocurrencies per current hash power and will sort those with the best return; small miners might see it more viable to mine those more profitable. However, considering that the price of altcoins is more volatile, by the time one can switch, mine, and collect the block rewards, the price could have changed unfavorably.

WASTED ENERGY AND CO2 EMISSION

A current argument raised against PoW is the network's energy consumption, which detractors believe increases costs and reduces the energy available to you and your neighbors. In any heavily government-regulated society, particularly where subsidized electric energy is involved, miners are incentivized to take advantage of the lower energy price. But in many areas of the world, electric energy is cheap enough to be used as the main source of heating during the winter. In Quebec for example, the government-owned Hydro-Quebec generates electricity from major dams in the northern part of the province. A friend who lives in Quebec profitably mines bitcoin during the winter months. By locating his mining rig in the basement, he is able to warm the whole house while earning bitcoin in exchange. Since he would have spent money on electricity to warm the house anyway, the cost in electricity was the same with the added benefit of obtaining bitcoin. I can see companies creating mining rigs with the explicit goal of warming houses or water heaters where the complexities are taken care of for the buyer. Such products were mentioned in Chapter 2.

And, of course, the nations of El Salvador have made bitcoin legal tender. Interestingly, the Central African Republic followed in the footsteps of El Salvador by making it legal tender too in June 2022 but reverted back on this decision in early 2023. El Salvador was already using the U.S. dollar, and although the Central African Republic has its own currency, it is pegged to the euro. So, neither have a local fluctuating currency. Not only has El Salvador adopted bitcoin as currency, it also mines bitcoin using geothermal energy generated from its inactive volcanoes. Inactive, volcanic geothermal energy becomes available when engineers dig towards the magma chamber, the large pool of liquid rock where the molten rock and water meet. There, the extreme heat and pressure push steam up to the turbine, which generates electricity.

Similarly, Private firms[42] harness Iceland's abundant geothermal energy and tap into dedicated geothermal power stations to mine bitcoin without negatively affecting energy price and availability for local residents. In colder climates, like Iceland and Siberia, operators can simply open the doors to cool the computer room rather than spend additional electricity for air conditioning.

In short, apart from the production of mining hardware, mining with geothermal energy destroys both the waste of energy and the CO2 emission arguments, particularly when performed in remote areas. Another beneficial-use technology application is capturing vented methane emissions. Methane venting, or gas flaring, is a direct emission of methane into the atmosphere as a byproduct of crude oil extraction. Oil extraction is typically sited in remote areas where no marketable use for methane is available. Already some major oil companies, such as Exxon, operate bitcoin mining rigs, using the methane to generate the electricity needed for mining.[43] Although located in more populated areas compared to oil extraction sites, mining at landfills offers an important function by collecting methane, a gas targeted for reduction by U.S. EPA, from gas flares and

---

[42] https://www.wired.com/story/iceland-bitcoin-mining-gallery/
[43] https://www.cnbc.com/2022/03/26/exxon-mining-bitcoin-with-crusoe-energy-in-north-dakota-bakken-region.html

utilizing it in mining bitcoin, often generating sufficient energy to sustain mining and waste operations.

Bitcoin mining in remote places is growing. Several hydroelectric plants are being repurposed for bitcoin mining worldwide. One such instance is the town of Ocean Falls located in British Columbia, Canada. In the 1950s, the town had a thriving population of 5,000, and a paper mill was powered by a nearby hydroelectric power plant. By 1990, the population had dwindled to less than 100, and the paper industry had vanished. In the meantime, the hydroelectric plant continued to operate, producing surplus energy to power the remaining residents in the nearby town. But local demand only accounted for one-third of the plant's total energy output. More recently, a bitcoin mining company has taken advantage of this excess energy by establishing mining operations in Ocean Falls, reviving the town's economy.

The reclamation of coal refuse in Pennsylvania, along with numerous other stories, share a common characteristic - they involve ghost towns with idle or deserted power plants located in remote areas, making it economically unfeasible to transport the electricity generated to other regions. To claim this stranded electricity for bitcoin mining, a mining rig operation only requires a reliable supply of electricity, an internet connection, and a small workforce to operate the facility, rendering such locations ideal for mining operations.

OTHER ARGUMENTS

Some bitcoin maximalists also count the hard work behind PoW as another positive. They believe hard work should be rewarded so that no one gets money for free (as opposed to the Cantillon effect, whereby those closest to the source of money creation benefit first), and the opportunity to mine bitcoin is available to anyone, not just the connected or the government.

Returning to the argument against gold bugs who contend that money should derive its value from a commodity that serves a practical purpose, think gold for jewelry, we have addressed how the market disregards this notion because the value of an asset stems from the interest people have in it. The key factor, here, is sustained confidence in the currency's stability and its future demand. In my view, PoW's significance lies in its permissionless nature, which enables anyone to immediately participate in mining and validation. Gold only requires effort to extract it from the ground, it does not necessitate any work to sustain its value. Even if all gold mining were to cease tomorrow, the gold in your possession would retain its value or potentially increase in value. In contrast, bitcoin and any other altcoin would be rendered unusable if all miners ceased operations.

This brings us to another argument made by gold bugs, who claim that owning physical gold (or silver) entails zero dependencies on any network, third parties, or the electric grid. Proponents often highlight how much better gold and silver would fare in the event of a nuclear attack, for instance. Given the abundance of new investors with limited knowledge of bitcoin's underlying principles, along with the fact that bitcoin was not in existence during World War I and II, this argument is compelling. They often cite the fact that bitcoin's network function relies on the operation of miners and nodes, whereas gold coins held in hand require no such system.

Should a major event cause only 10% of the existing miners and nodes to remain operational, bitcoin would still be functional. During the first few weeks after the event, block times would be significantly extended until the network adjusts the difficulty level, which occurs every 2016 blocks. Under normal conditions, this process takes approximately two weeks with an average of 10 minutes per block. But if 90% of the hash power were to disappear, the network may experience up to two hours between each block during this adjustment period. Nevertheless, the market will eventually recognize that bitcoin is still operational and available for use by those with internet access. Indeed, some bitcoin coders have even managed to transmit a Lightning payment using radio waves, while other solutions such as using CB ham radio, mesh networks also exist.[44] In contrast, I am uncertain about how the banking sector would fare in similar

---

[44]https://www.coindesk.com/markets/2019/03/04/bitcoin-coders-send-international-lightning-payment-over-ham-radio/

circumstances, but it would not be pretty, and even worse in affected regions. To date, bitcoin's price action since 2009 has been highly correlated to the stock market. This has been another argument advanced by bitcoin's critics. What they forget is bitcoin unifies two dimensions:

1. It possess attributes similar to gold allowing it to become the preferred store of value; and

2. Its digital nature offers an alternative to existing payment systems rooted in government fiat currency

Some have pointed to the fact bitcoin tracts the stock market more than gold. However, bitcoin's value began at 0 in 2009 and therefore could only be destined to rise as more people discovered it. During its first few years of existence, only those active in the cryptography space knew about it. It wasn't until 2012 that I became aware of it. Intrigued, I began studying and understanding it, as most of us do. Indeed, the rise in bitcoin's price tracks with the recovery of the stock market and economy after the crash of 2008. Further, whenever the stock market hit a pause, it was often due to bureaucrats at the Federal Reserve changing their policy, which affected the money supply and, in turn, the price of bitcoin.

But bitcoin's gold-like store of value will be tested when and if the stock market experiences a significant decrease in value compared to gold and other commodities. It is important to note that the stock market may remain unchanged in nominal terms (priced in dollars), but with high inflation, this essentially means that the stock market is losing value along with the dollar, albeit not as rapidly. But, if bitcoin increases in price, along with commodities, gold, and silver, this indicates that bitcoin has transitioned from a risk-on asset correlated to the stock market, to a risk-off asset. A risk-off asset is an investment that is perceived as relatively low risk and tends to hold its value or even increase in value during times of economic uncertainty or market turmoil. Such assets are typically seen as safe havens by investors seeking to protect their wealth during times of instability. Only time will tell when bitcoin has achieved this lauded status.

5

PROOF OF STAKE

A philosophical battle is being waged between those who favor PoS and those who prefer PoW and bitcoin. On the one hand, Proof of Stake promoters contend that Proof of Work wastes energy, a topic covered in chapter 4. On the other hand, bitcoiners say Proof of Stake is prone to centralization and so recreates the current power system in which the rich become richer without effort, accruing more power and rights. They also point out that Proof of Stake involves no work, and so nothing is really accomplished with this method. To be able to properly evaluate the arguments of each side philosophically and technically, we first need to understand how both methods work. As we covered Proof of Work in the prior chapter, we will now present a Proof of Stake implementation.

Proof of Stake is undeniably more complex than PoW and entails more overhead with respect to data usage. At its core, PoS is a permissionless network that requires participating nodes to put their holdings in the currency at stake in order to be granted the right to mine blocks. While PoW uses a hash value with specific properties (leading zeros) to determine which miner has the right to create the next block, PoS requires complex coordination between all nodes. Those nodes intent on mining (or staking) coordinate with one another to establish mining rights prior to creating a set of future blocks, which are sometimes called cycles (or epochs). Currencies have employed several different implementations of Proof of Stake, many of which vary greatly. Peercoin (PPC), a first PoS coin launched in 2012 and which today ranks about 854 in market capitalization, employs a combination of PoW and PoS. It was followed by NXT in 2013, and, eventually, more prominent ones such as Cardano (ADA), which was launched in 2017, adopted Ouroboros,[45] which employs cryptography, combinatorics, and mathematical game theory. A currency called Bitcoin PoS that is not a fork of bitcoin adopted some elements of bitcoin's implementation.[46] Bitcoin maximalists are justified in pointing out the lack of decentralization in some of these implementations. In fact, at some point, more than 70% of Ethereum's nodes are compliant with the Office of Foreign Asset Control's (OFAC) standard[47] since its migration to PoS.[48] Most articles critical of Proof of Stake are directed against weaker implementations, and their authors tend to generalize, treating all PoS implementations as having the same flaws.

Proof of Stake has recently received more press, particularly since Ethereum converted from Proof of Work to Proof of Stake. The goal of this chapter is to measure Proof of Work against, hopefully, one of the currently best implementations of Proof of Stake. Proof of Stake is more complex than Proof of Work, regardless of the cryptocurrency employing it. Although this chapter might scare those uninitiated in technical matters,

---

[45] https://dl.acm.org/doi/10.1145/3243734.3243848

[46] See https://bitcoinpos.net

[47] Meaning they are censorship compliant, that is, they will block transactions if required by the authorities.

[48] https://cointelegraph.com/news/51-of-ethereum-blocks-are-now-compliant-with-ofac-standards-raising-censorship-concerns

we will explore Proof of Stake piece-by-piece using the implementation of Tezos (XTZ). A quick, important note, as stated in chapter 3, Tezos uses governance to update its protocol, making what would be considered an update leading to a hard fork in bitcoin just a soft fork in Tezos. Because of this, several important changes have occurred seamlessly. Bakers, the Tezos designation for miners/validators, vote for a proposal; if passed, the software is upgraded to include the new code; and, according to the protocol, the upgrade then occurs automatically at a given block number. I believe Tezos is unique in this regard; to my knowledge, no other cryptocurrency projects have this feature.

Before investing in Tezos (XTZ is the symbol), however, you should know that, as of this writing, its price in BTC is approximately 450 satoshis. At its ICO in 2017, it was sold at a price of 2000 satoshis (5000 XTZ per bitcoin) or the equivalent of about 40 cents per XTZ at the time. Although this represented a gain in US dollars, it was a loss when measured in bitcoins. But, like many other altcoins, at some point, XTZ was traded at 4,000 satoshis, meaning any trader who sold at the time would have doubled their bitcoin holding. I do not know the future of Tezos, I do know it is based on some very good concepts, but market adoption is another thing. Tezos became an important playground for NFT, but the competition is increasing with so many blockchain supporting smart contracts and with Ethereum maintaining its dominance.

Interestingly, because of this governance, Tezos made a radical change in its consensus, moving from Nakamoto-style to Byzantine-style consensus, which is another argument in favor of using Tezos for this study as we will cover both of these consensuses in this chapter. You might wonder why I am using Tezos rather than Ethereum. At the start of this writing, Ethereum PoS was not yet officially operational, and, since I prefer Tezos PoS because of its delegation (another topic we will cover), I focus on Tezos while contrasting it with Ethereum. Tezos perhaps had a controversial beginning, and its funding might be seen as questionable by many, but its PoS implementation is significantly better than most, in my opinion.

Developers offer different reasons as to why Proof of Stake was created, but one of the major arguments is to provide an alternative to the heavy energy usage associated with Proof of Work. Another is simply to explore other forms of consensus. That there are multiple type of consensus that has been developed is just the situation we'd expect in any free-market environment where scientific discoveries are uninhibited by regulations or government constraints. An argument has been advanced that since stakers can make income from transaction fees without having to spend heavily on energy, PoS is a passive income generator. Rather than invest in stacks of $ASIC^{49}$ computer hardware suited for hash discovery that depreciated, stakers instead invest in the currency they intend to stake. Unlike bitcoin mining, which is heavily reliant on the cost of energy, PoS-associated daily expenses are limited to the operating costs of running a server and maintaining an internet connection. This reduces the risk of stakers going bankrupt, except in cases where the value of the cryptocurrency drops to zero. For instance, in December 2022, Core Scientific, a bitcoin mining company, declared bankruptcy due to the sharp decline in bitcoin's value while energy cost increased.[50]

HOW IT WORKS

Among the variety of different implementations of Proof of Stake, Tezos uses a delegated Proof of Stake protocol. We will cover the Nakamoto-style consensus with which Tezos started and which resembles bitcoin's consensus, where the longest chain prevails. We then discuss the Byzantine Fault-tolerance consensus, which Tezos now uses and which Ethereum has also adopted. The Byzantine Fault-tolerance consensus has a rapid finality, but, as we shall see later, this comes at a cost. By rapid finality, we mean a transaction has been accepted and is now part of the blockchain, with absolute certainty. This contrasts with Nakamoto-style

---

[49] Application-specific integrated circuit.
[50] https://www.bloomberg.com/news/articles/2022-12-21/core-scientific-files-for-bankruptcy-as-crypto-winter-lingers

consensus, which lacks complete certainty but rather an increasingly higher probability a transaction is official, as more blocks are produced.

Many PoS criticisms that I have seen in blog posts and articles are often directed at PoSs without delegation, and hence many of their points are not applicable here. Note that Ethereum does not use delegation in its Proof of Stake. Delegated Proof of Stake means that any owners of cryptocurrency can delegate their staking rights to a miner who, comically, was termed a baker in Tezos by its French founder Arthur Breitman. These owners still control their private keys, and only they have the right to spend their coins and can do so at any time. So, as there is so much control by the owners, the term liquid Proof of Stake has sometimes also been used to describe this PoS implementation.

As discussed in Proof of Work, establishing which miner has the right to mine the next block is determined by a race to find a hash output to the respective block that has the correct number of leading zeros. There is thus randomness involved; in some way, it is like a lottery ticket where the more computing power a miner uses, the greater the chances he wins the lottery.

PoS also has a randomness component; all bakers coordinate to create a seed to feed a pseudo-random generator to establish baking rights for future upcoming blocks. A pseudo-random generator is an algorithm that generates a series of seemingly random numbers, which are not truly random, however, as they are completely determined by an initial number called a seed that is input. From the same seed will come the same sequence of numbers. This is the principle by which hardware wallets in bitcoin generate private keys starting from the seed constructed out of a set of mnemonic words. One could use SHA256, for example, to hash a seed phrase. In this case, the hash appears as a random output of 64 numbers between 0 and 15. The two important qualities of the hash are that the outcome is unknown to all parties before the seed is selected and that, from the established seed number, the same exact result is obtained. We will see later how this is employed in establishing "baking" rights.

Most blockchain implementations, including bitcoin, measure time in blocks rather than days, hours, or minutes. This makes sense since the blockchain is a series of blocks constantly being added to one after the other, with varying time intervals between each block. In contrast, Proof of Stake operates on a fixed schedule block-adding. For Tezos, a block is added every 30-seconds. To establish baking rights, Tezos groups blocks into cycles, (Ethereum calls them "epochs") each containing 8192 blocks, and baking rights are established for an entire cycle.

Baking rights for all blocks of a given cycle are assigned using the pseudo-random generator, and so, each cycle is associated with a seed. As you can imagine, the process by which a seed is generated must avoid any kind of exploitable weakness, and therefore providing a fair advantage to all parties is crucial. The following figure illustrates the seed generation process for cycle 467.

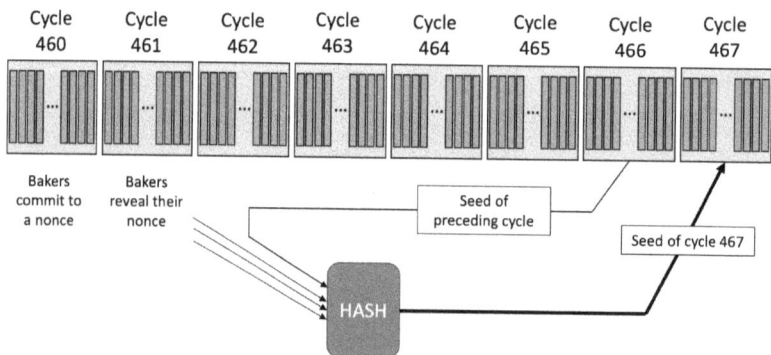

Figure 17: Proof of Stake seed generation in Tezos.

In Figure 17, the vertical dark rectangles represent a block containing transactions as well as overhead information shared by bakers. The process to generate the seed for cycle 467 starts seven cycles earlier, at cycle 460. The overall protocol uses "commit and reveal," in which, during cycle 460, bakers randomly generate a nonce (a large number) to which they commit by creating a special kind of transaction that records the hash of their nonce in the blockchain along with the bakers identities. Any bakers who fail to commit are excluded from the baking (or mining) of the blocks comprising cycle 467, and so committing constitutes a hard requirement. During the following cycle, i.e., cycle 461, bakers reveal that cycle's nonce, and other bakers then verify that the hash of this nonce matches that to which a baker committed in the prior cycle. At the end of cycle 461, all nonces have been revealed and, along with the seed of the prior cycle (which, in this example, is that of cycle 466) are input into a hash algorithm (typically SHA256), resulting in the seed for cycle 467, which is publicly available to all. Obviously, not all bakers will be happy about the result. The lucky ones will be awarded more blocks, but, on average, the process should be fair over many cycles. However, because they committed a hash of their nonce, bakers cannot change their minds and supply another nonce that would lead to a seed more favorable to themselves. Their only option would be to withhold their nonces and see the difference, but by then it would be too late, as some bakers will have published their nonces in the very last block of the cycle.

In the example given above, at the beginning of cycle 462, everyone has access to the cycle seed which derives, through an official algorithm that is part of the Tezos protocol, all assignments of block rewards and endorsements. Based on the seed fed into the sequence generator (i.e., the pseudo-random number generator), for each block, the algorithm allocates priorities to each baker. For example, the first block of cycle 467 might have priority 0 be assigned to baker Donots4Us while priority 1 is assigned to baker C, and so on. When it is time for that block to be created, because Donots4us has the highest priority (0), it is given the first opportunity to bake the block. If after 30 seconds, the expected time between processing of each block, the baker with priority 0 has not broadcasted his block, the network awards the baker with priority 1 the opportunity to bake that block and so on. Then, the process then moves to the next block in the cycle. Note that all bakers know ahead of time exactly when they will be baking (mining) a block. Since a cycle lasts on average 2.7 days, and the seed for a given cycle that allocates baking rights is known five cycles before the start of that cycle, bakers know 14 days in advance which block they will bake. This important difference with Proof of Work has advantages and disadvantages as we will see later in this chapter.

As part of the process of block creation, other bakers are scheduled to check the validity of and provide an endorsement for a block. Just as there are rewards for baking a block, bakers also receive rewards, albeit smaller, for validating blocks after having been scheduled to do so. Tezos started with 64 endorsements per block but later increased this, first to 256 endorsements, and even more in the latest update. Several bakers will endorse blocks created, provided they see them as valid.

So far, we have seen how baking (mining) rights are assigned, but other elements that constitute parts of this particular Proof of Stake implementation are worthy of discussion. Earlier, I mentioned that the Tezos implementation of Proof of Stake is sometimes called liquid Proof of Stake because owners of the currency can hold their coins in cold storage, remaining in full control and yet delegating their staking rights to a baker of their choice. As part of the staking process, the network must establish how much staking is done by each of the bakers. While baking rights are randomly assigned based on the cycle seed generated, they are directly proportional to how much each baker is staking. In Tezos, in addition to the baker's own coins, a baker also acquires the staking rights of the coins that other owners have delegated to him. To establish how much staking is associated with each baker, the protocol randomly takes a "stake snapshot" during the cycle to determine the distribution. In Figure 17, the stake snapshot is taken in cycle 461 so as to establish the baking rights of cycle 467, meaning that there is a lag of five cycles before staking leads to baking rights. In return for their delegation, bakers typically return a portion of the rewards to their delegators directly proportional to the amount delegators staked minus a 2%-20% fee set by the baker.

In contrast to the liquidity those delegating enjoy, bakers must tie up their coins in a bond. If a baker has 100,000 tez (the name of the Tezos currency) in its Tezos address and an additional 500,000 tez have been delegated to this baker by other currency owners, the total staking for this baker amounts to 600,000 tez. As part of the protocol, the baker is required to put 10% of that amount in a bond, meaning 60,000 tez will be locked up, leaving only 40,000 tez available to this baker. The purpose of the bond is to penalize any bakers that broadcast invalid blocks or broadcast two different versions of the same block. This is another important distinction with Proof of Work, where invalid blocks are simply discarded without any penalties to the miner who produced them.

With Proof of Work, two miners may, sometimes at approximately the same time, discover a solution for the next block, but these solutions will obviously have differing content as they are submitted by different miners. When this happens, the first block received by other miners is accepted, but, since not all miners will receive the same first block, the chain splits but only temporarily. With Proof of Stake, the same circumstance may happen, but, because of the priorities associated with mining a given block, the behavior differs. Figure 18 below illustrates this process. The last block created was block 49446, and the next expected block 49447, after an expected elapsed time of 30 seconds. That's the amount of time bakers with the highest priority (i.e., 0) have to create and release versions of the block. In this instance, if baker 54 does not broadcast block 49447 within thirty seconds, baker 21, which has priority 1, will broadcast his version of block 49447. In the example shown, this occurred for block 49442.

What could have occurred is that baker 54 timely sent his version of block 49447, but congestion on the network prevented it from being communicated in time. For a blockchain to be decentralized, its consensus must also be decentralized. Therefore, when two versions of a block are baked - baker 21 created block 49447 and baker 54 created another version of the same block that was received later - a resolution must be reached. A share of the nodes will believe block 49447 was created by baker 21, while another believes it was created by baker 54. When this happens, we say that the blockchain is forked or is in a forked state. However, in any good implementation, such as in bitcoin, this fork eventually collapses, and a consensus is resolved to a single branch, which is then said to have

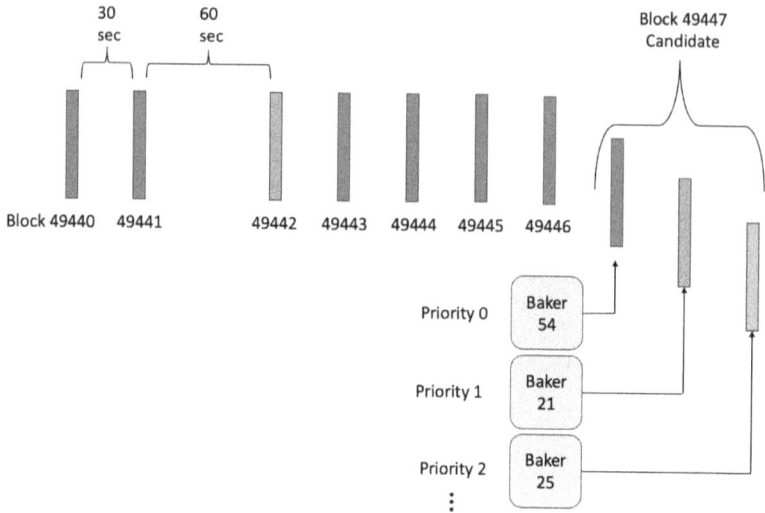

Figure 18: Proof of Stake seed generation in Tezos.

reached finality. Determining if a particular transaction is fully confirmed is highly probabilistic in bitcoin, and, in fact, Satoshi addresses this in his white paper.

The important question then arises as to how many blocks must be added to the blockchain of such a Proof of Stake network to solidly confirm that a transaction is secure, often referenced as the number of blocks needed for confirmation. With PoW, it's a matter of probability, and typically six blocks is required by exchanges to feel confident enough, with some accepting only three. With bitcoin, consensus coalesces around the longest chain, as discussed in the previous chapter.

There are multiple ways a Proof of Stake implementation can deal with forks. Since in Proof of Stake the time scheduling of block creation is deterministic and priorities are assigned to block producers (i.e., miners), a fork can be resolved by using a combination of priority and endorsement.

Say, for example, that baker 54 wants to hold its block with the goal of creating an alternative chain for financial gain. In this case, baker 54 would make a payment transaction to some third party that would be included in block 49447 as proposed by baker 21. Then, later, baker 54 would send his version of block 49447, which does not include this payment transaction. To allow for this possible circumstance, exchanges wait until a certain number of confirmations (i.e., creation of a certain number of additional blocks) have occurred before confirming transactions. This number of confirmations varies greatly across cryptocurrencies.

Let's see how many more blocks must be created and added to the blockchain on top of block 49447 created by baker 21 before the absence of a fork can be assumed with high certainty. If the next two blocks after 49447 are created by the baker having priority 0, then this chain is gaining traction toward assured confirmation, or as it's known in bitcoin, the "longest chain." But, for the acknowledged fork to gain traction, the alternative blockchain containing block 49447 created by baker 54 must have many more blocks added by priority 0 miners. Moreover, the number of endorsements counts as weights. Therefore, the more bakers who endorse the chain containing the block 49447 created by baker 21, the more difficult or at some point impossible it would be for baker 54's block to be accepted instead. Like bitcoin, probabilistic finality is still achievable, albeit differing somewhat from that in bitcoin since the total number of participants is known. If the network detects that a large majority accept a given branch/fork, this will eventually be accepted as the official branch, and the one with a much smaller portion of stakers will be rejected.

In an earlier version of Tezos, only 32 endorsements were required per block. With over 200 bakers, this meant only a fraction of them were acknowledging a given block through endorsement. Later, Tezos increased this to 256 endorsements, enabling the network to obtain consensus with respect to a branch based on the number of endorsements much more rapidly.

Now let's check what would happen with a 51% attack such as we covered earlier with bitcoin and apply this to PoS coins using the Nakamoto-style algorithm. Again, assume a group of stakers located in Canada, the USA, and European countries are forced to respect a whitelist/blacklist of tez addresses (tez is the currency in Tezos). In Figure 19 below, a baker, not part of the cartel group, holds the top priority to create the second block following the start of the whitelist. However, because that block contains a blacklisted transaction, the cartel bakers refuse to accept it and ignore it, waiting the extra 30 seconds to let another baker with priority 1 bake that second block. In this hypothetical scenario, a second non-cartel baker has priority 1 which respects priority 0 block and as such, does not create a block. So, the cartel must wait for another interval to have a chance for the baker with priority 2 to come in. Priority 2 in this case is owned by a cartel baker and creates the block, officially splitting the chain into two forks.

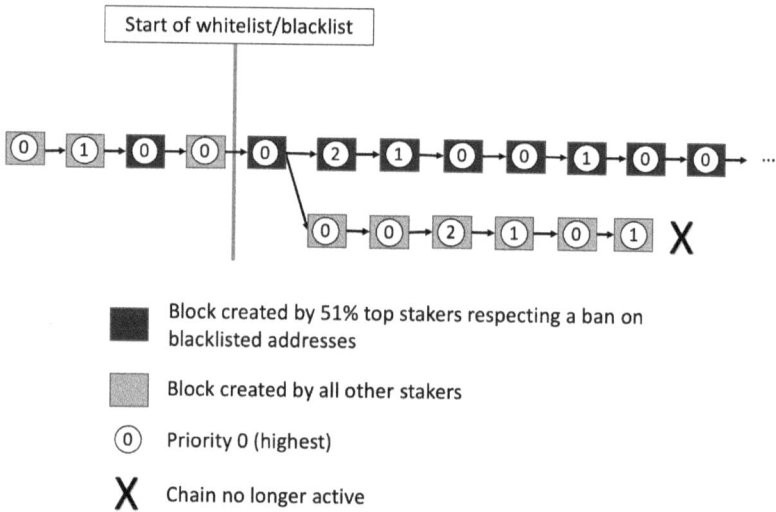

Figure 19: PoS with 51% staking attack.

Note, however, that, since Tezos employs a delegated Proof of Stake protocol, other stakers that were staking the cartel bakers are more likely to change their delegations to a baker outside of that group. This is analogous to the bitcoin mining pool, where individual miners change their pool selection to one outside the cartel. This does not eliminate the possibility that an individual baker (or bakers), on its own, possesses enough tez to mount a 51% stake attack, like the 60 top bitcoin miners discussed previously. Currently, based on information provided by the blockchain and

Baker's name	Type	Total staking (tz)	Percentage overall	Cumulative percentage
Coinbase Baker	Exchange	92,466,302	13.34%	13.34%
Kraken Baker	Exchange	46,294,436	6.68%	20.02%
Everstake	Baker	46,293,833	6.68%	26.7%
PosDog	Baker	33,755,285	4.87%	31.57%
Stake.fish	Baker	28,079,866	4.05%	35.62%
P2P Validator	Baker	27,220,926	3.93%	39.55%
Tz1Nf6... (address)	Private baker?	19,821,496	2.86%	42.41%
PayTezos	Baker	16,218,950	2.34%	44.75%
Chorus One	Baker	15,029,055	2.17%	46.92%
Foundation Baker 5	Tezos Foundation	12,698,866	1.83%	48.75%
Foundation Baker 7	Tezos Foundation	11,705,267	1.69%	50.44%
Foundation Baker 3	Tezos Foundation	11,671,822	1.68%	52.12%

Table 4: Top bakers and their respective staking in Tezos.

available at a Tezos blockchain explorer such as tzkt.io, the top bakers in Tezos are as shown in Table 4 along with their staking balances as of May 2022.

As this table shows, Coinbase exchange held 13.34% of staking in Tezos with Kraken exchange in second place at 6.68%, making the two exchanges' combined holding 20.02%. Rather than the 60 miners needed in bitcoin, Tezos requires only 12 bakers to cumulate a 51% staking amount. In Proof of Stake, exchanges own coins for trading purposes, just as they do bitcoins. However, exchanges holding PoS coins can participate in blockchain consensus, but their bitcoin holdings do not give them any edge over the bitcoin network, they can only run a non-mining node.

Mining, as you will recall, is an entirely different business with its hash power and energy requirements, and therefore exchanges are not in the business of PoW mining. More often than not, in PoS, exchanges own many altcoins just as they do bitcoins, and so the situation from the get-go is not as good for PoS as with bitcoin because of the staking power exchanges have. I would suggest that the top two reasons why coin ownership is more concentrated for Tezos (and likely other PoS coins) than for bitcoin is not only the involvement of the exchanges but also the size of the market. More often than not, better distribution accompanies large capitalization, which gets us back to the network effect which bitcoin is enjoying the most.

However, as for miners in a bitcoin mining pool where it is easy to switch to another mining pool, owners of PoS coins on an exchange can also switch exchanges. If these exchanges were to comply with black-listing, investors would be highly incentivized to move their coins off the exchange. The same would apply for bakers. Since Tezos uses delegated Proof of Stake, wherein owners of coins securely hold their coins in their private wallets but delegate their staking rights to a baker, they can easily move to another baker at any time. Regarding exchanges, the same applies to bitcoin and any other cryptocurrencies; that is, if an exchange operating in a country obeyed a government censorship or blacklisting, bitcoin own-ers could remove their bitcoin from the exchanges, assuming they know ahead of time. For all cryptocurrencies, exchanges are easier targets for the government to impose their restrictions. Coming back to PoS, once coins are off an exchange, however, the coin holder can (re)delegate coins to a baker in any country.

Interestingly, in the end, however, a solution to a 51% blacklist attack on bitcoin as we referred to in chapter 4 could also apply to a PoS coin that uses Nakamoto-style consensus.

BYZANTINE FAULT TOLERANCE CONSENSUS

Tezos used to employ a Nakamoto-style algorithm, what is used by bit-coin, but later moved to what is called Byzantine Fault Tolerance (BFT)[51] type of consensus, which Ethereum's Proof of Stake implementation also employs. It is important to distinguish between the two styles. Nakamoto consensus has a probabilistic finality since it is based on the longest chain. Whether a consensus has been achieved never gets a 100% certainty, but this probability increases over time as additional blocks are added to the

---

[51]https://en.wikipedia.org/wiki/Byzantine_fault

existing chain. Cardano, another Proof of Stake coin, uses as its consensus Ouroboros,[52] which is also a Nakamoto style algorithm.

Because Proof of Stake incorporates deterministic scheduling of block creation and pre-allocated priority rights assigned to miners/validators/bakers, this allows for other types of consensus algorithms. Tezos "Ithaca2" upgrade to a BFT consensus algorithm was considered a significant update to the protocol. The BFT mechanism employed is called Tenderbake[53] and was derived from Tendermint first published in a 2018 paper.[54] Tenderbake settles firmly after only two blocks but makes an assumption about the network to be discussed below. By providing a deterministic finality, once a block has been validated, it will never be discarded thus contrasting with a Nakamoto-style of consensus, where the inclusion of a given block in the longest chain is never 100% certain.

The BFT style of consensus can achieve complete certainty as it has specific rules about who can approve a transaction and how many approvals are required before all participants agree that the transaction is 100% final. Obtaining consensus is essential. Consensus indicates that all parties agree on the makeup of the current blockchain; provides consistency and finality (i.e., eliminates the possibility of long-lasting forks); and allows the chain to continue growing, even if some nodes crash or act maliciously or some part of the network was disrupted by delays or partially partitioned.

With BFT active in Tezos, creation of the next block in Tezos is now done through rounds. When the network runs smoothly, only one round per block is needed. However, because of timing-related or other types of issues, one or more additional rounds might be needed. Each round has a specific duration and represents an attempt by bakers to agree on the makeup of the next block, and so, if one attempt fails (i.e., consensus cannot be reached), the network undergoes still another round[55] with each

---

[52]https://eprint.iacr.org/2018/378.pdf
[53]https://arxiv.org/abs/2001.11965
[54]https://arxiv.org/abs/1807.04938
[55]https://tezos.gitlab.io/active/consensus.html

round's duration increasing to account for delays or situations where network reliability has declined. A reminder that Ethereum's PoS also uses BFT style consensus but terminology and some minor details might be slightly different.

Let's return to block 49447 in Figure 18, where rounds are composed of three phases:

1. The block proposal phase. Here, the *proposer*, the validator with the first right to create a block, proposes a block containing transactions from his mempool, i.e., the list of pending transactions not yet included in a new block. This proposal is disseminated to all other nodes comprising the network. Barring network delays, this proposal should be received by all nodes. In this instance, baker 54 is the proposer.

2. The preendorsement phase. In this phase, validators send a preendorsement or supporting vote on the content of the candidate block, in essence: "I am validator 21 and I endorse the block content proposed by validator 54 for round 1."

3. The endorsement phase. Assuming validators have observed a quorum on the preendorsement, validators send a confirmation vote for the candidate block and for the preendorsement quorum. Put simply, this is equivalent to stating: "I am validator 21 and I affirm to having observed a quorum of preendorsements for the block content proposed by validator 54 at round 1." When network delays occur, all nodes might not receive the proposed block or some might receive it after a delay so significant that the preendorsement/endorsement messages failed to reach them before the current round's timeout.

A benefit of this mechanism is quick finality in determining the next block. Yet, the rapid finality produced by Tezos and other cryptocurrencies using this form of consensus comes at a cost. If a quorum is not reached because of network delays, another round is initiated. For a quorum, and hence consensus, to be reached regarding acceptance of a block, two-thirds of the nodes/bakers must endorse the block's proposal. This is an important point as it means that, if more than one-third of bakers/nodes are not participating because either they are down, have no network connectivity, or fail to respond due to some other cause, a quorum is never reached with respect to a given block, and the consensus mechanism continues, round after another round, seeking to reach quorum. Basically, the blockchain is dead, well let's just say not functioning while in this state. In addition, when we say one-third of bakers/nodes, it actually translates to the staking amount. If only five bakers hold one-third or more of total staking and are down, no new blocks can be created. When this happens, the blockchain would be inoperable until the developers created a fork that fixes the situation, or the nodes come back online. Here, the simplicity and conservative of bitcoin's approach demonstrates its values and its reputation as digital gold, evidencing the importance of having bitcoin as a core element of one's portfolio with other cryptocurrencies acting as a higher risk playground. At the risk of repeating myself, I view bitcoin as akin to gold in the 1800s, that is, as today's secure repository of value.

An important point is worth mentioning, however. The higher market cap a cryptocurrency has, the more users will be involved. Although ownership distribution will always somewhat be following the 80/20 Pareto principle,[56] the number of players part of the top-20 percent will increase with the importance of the cryptocurrency. Also, the Tezos developers are well aware of this issue and have formulated what would happen if one-third of the bakers were not available. The first step would be to determine if there were some means to bring one or more of these bakers back online. If all fails, a more drastic solution involving what is known as a "user-defined" software version would be implemented, where, for example, the one-third of bakers were removed from the list of bakers from whom the protocol expects to receive confirmation. Such "user-defined" updates are

---

[56]https://en.wikipedia.org/wiki/Pareto_principle

a hard fork because they would not be going through governance. So much for governance you might say, but like stated before, it is the price to pay to guarantee achievement of finality. However, in my personal opinion, this situation is definitely not something we should expect in a currency that intends to become a long-term storage medium for value. Attaining 100% finality comes with a heavy price with respect to system durability and stability without outside intervention by its developers to 'fix' it.

So far, the current version of Tezos's protocol at the time of this writing has been running since March 2022 without any such issue. It has fared better than Solana, another Proof of Stake cryptocurrency that has repeatedly experienced so many episodes of downtime that jokes about it have been flying on Twitter. However, a much more highly distributed ownership would be needed to reduce the risk of a network jam, which will likely come if Tezos market capitalization and adoption increases in importance. The concept is interesting, but, when seeking digital gold, bitcoin remains unchallenged. The question then arises: what would be the situation if Tezos, retaining the current set of features (or even others), were the number 2 cryptocurrency, similar in market capitalization to Ethereum? A much higher number of bakers would mean that, instead of just five bakers, it would be more like 60, for instance, who would hold one-third of the total amount staked. The ownership of mining or staking for cryptocurrencies like bitcoin or Tezos will likely be distributed according to the Pareto principle, meaning a small percentage of miners (or bakers) would hold a large proportion of the mining (or staking), but this would not necessarily increase the risk of network disruption. With bitcoin, the key metric to watch is the 51% of mining, whereas, with Tezos and Ethereum, 33% would be required to prevent immediate finality and temporarily stall the network until operator and developer could intervene. No specific intervention strategy has been outlined should this occur with Tezos or Ethereum, but because bitcoin uses the Nakamoto-style consensus (eg: the longest chain), the situation described is of no concern for it.

51% ATTACK WITH PROOF OF STAKE

The subject of transaction censorship that we covered for PoW is still applicable for PoS, but in this case, it is a 51% staking attack, but that only applies to PoS that uses the Nakamoto-style consensus. In this case, where the longest chain prevails, a group of stakers holding 51% of staking could mount the same kind of attack. This attack might come in the form of double spending as elaborated earlier, or it could be an application of censorship on certain transactions. With the Byzantine fault tolerance algorithm, however, it would require 67% of staking, and, in regards to its governance, an attack on Tezos would require 81% of staking to pass an amendment unfavorable to the remainder of the users. In all cases, those acting maliciously so as to negatively impact the protocol would cause the value of the coin to plummet and, correspondingly, the attackers' own holdings. In addition, for Byzantine-Fault-Tolerance, there is the 34% attack to worry about where the network is non-operational.

To recap:

- The Nakamoto-style consensus is subject to the 51% attack (staking or mining)

- The Byzantine-Fault-Tolerance consensus is subject to the 68% attack for transaction censorship, and the 34% network attack (or issues if by accident) if the quorum is not achieved.

ETHEREUM'S PROOF OF STAKE

Let's go over Ethereum's current implementation. As of this writing (end of 2022), Ethereum has recently switched to PoS but it differs somewhat from what we have described so far. Ethereum's PoS also uses the Byzantine Fault Tolerance to achieve consensus. But strangely, staked ETH are locked and cannot be withdrawn until the Shanghai upgrade scheduled to be implemented in 2023. Bitcoin maximalists are having a blast pointing out that the definition of the word shanghai is "to put by trickery into an undesirable position."[57] Personally, I do not understand why they have locked staking and intend to modify the system in the future. They have had more than two years to work this out, but I have been told that the reason for the delay is to reduce the complexity of the initial implementation. To an outsider, the uneasy feeling is akin to coins locked in Alcatraz with a release date set in a future upgrade. It means anyone who staked ETH must continue doing so until the update is released. Perhaps by the time you read this, the issue will have been resolved. However, this temporary lock has created a peculiar ecosystem where alternative reactions and solutions might appear. For example, some ETH holders are not interested in running and maintaining a node but would be happy to have others perform this service for them. With Tezos, this can conveniently be done by delegating staking rights for coins in cold storage to a node operator (baker). But, with Ethereum, only actively staked ETH are participating; hence the operator of a staking node might sell its staking rights to another but would still need to operate the nodes that are attached to the ETH's private keys, a different undertaking with a different risk analysis. With delegation, the only risk is that the baker doesn't pay back the portion of the rewards promised based on the staking contribution. Here, however, if the node operator screws up, gets hacked, or loses the ETH by any means, the owner loses both the rewards and the staked ETH. This Ethereum change to PoS is very recent, and so we will have to see how things progress in the future.

So, in short, an ETH owner can either run a validator node themselves and stake the minimum 32 ETH; pay a node operator to run it for them; pool their ETH with others and give it to a node operator; or, lastly, deposit it in an exchange like Coinbase that will stake the coins for the owner and credit part of the rewards. Except for the first scenario, the user relinquishes control of his coins. Staked ETH addresses are called Beacon Chain addresses whereas existing ETH addresses are simply called normal ETH addresses. Although staked ETH are frozen until that future upgrade,

---

[57] https://www.merriam-webster.com/dictionary/shanghai

rewards from transaction "fee tips" that validators received are credited to a normal ETH address, meaning that the revenue derived from staking is not frozen.

Additionally, given that withdrawal of staking is not currently possible, validator balance transfers are also not implemented, meaning staked ETH cannot be transferred or sold to others except by giving one's private keys, which obviously is not an option. Unless the payment itself was locked in an escrow account, who would want to buy your staked ETH when you could keep a copy of the private keys? I sent a series of questions to Preston Van Loon, one of the lead developers of Ethereum. He kindly replied on December 6, 2022, and allowed me to reprint his responses:

Q.1) Apparently it seems withdrawal of staked ETH is not yet possible. Why was it done this way? Is there a link to ETH official website about this or only via a message sent?

> **This is correct. Withdrawals are currently not possible in Ethereum Proof of Stake. However, it is expected to be part of the next network upgrade. Withdrawals have not been implemented in the original launch in an effort to reduce complexity of the initial Beacon Chain. I'm not aware that this is mentioned on ethereum.org.**

Q.2) Is it possible for a staker to move staked coins to another address. In other words, if my ETHs in my ETH address are staking and I want to sell my staked coins to somebody else, is that possible? Without them having to take over my existing ETH address by me giving them a copy of the private keys, which they know I will still have a copy.

> **At this time, validator balance transfers and withdrawals are not implemented so you would not be able to securely transfer ownership of staked funds. There is one caveat that any transaction fee tips that a validator receives as part of a block proposal are sent a normal Ethereum address rather than a Beacon**

Chain address. These fee tips are immediately liquid and may be transferred as freely as any other Ethereum account.

Q.3) Is the only way to participate in ETH staking rewards by having the ETH in a staked address? (Is there a possibility of delegating your ETH to a staker—similar to what is done in Tezos?

Correct. Only the validators are eligible to receive staking rewards and Ethereum does not allow for delegation in Proof of Stake. At this time, there are no plans to implement stake delegation for Ethereum's Proof of Stake. However, there are several staking pools with various levels of trust assumptions and decentralization. With that said, the Ethereum protocol discourages staking pools by increasing slashing penalties to validators that violate the protocol en masse.

Q.4) The rewards for a staker are the transaction fees and the creation of new ETH per block, correct? Is any of that shared with the other validators or does all of it go to the proposer?

The rewards for a block proposal include a protocol reward for successfully creating a block as well as any transaction fee tips. The protocol reward goes towards the validators' balance on the Beacon Chain while the transaction fee tips go towards the validators' specified Ethereum account. The rewards for creating the block are not shared with any validator other than the one that created the block. However, all of the validators in the Ethereum Proof of Stake network earn rewards for voting on blocks and having their votes included in a block.

Q.5) What is the inflation rate of ETH? Is it still a fixed amount of ETH per block?

The inflation rate of ETH varies since EIP-1559 which enabled the majority part of transaction fees to be burned. When transaction fees are high as a result of network demand then it is possible that the amount of ETH burned per block exceeds the amount of ETH created as a reward. The exact amount of ETH that is created per block depends on the number of validator votes that the proposer included into that block. At the moment, the network is floating around 0.05% issuance per year.

Q.6) Since its migration to PoS, Ethereum apparently has more than 70% of nodes compliant with the Office of Foreign Asset Control (OFAC) standard (meaning censorship). Why do you think that is?

Since the Merge, many Ethereum validators have chosen to outsource transaction ordering of new blocks to "MEV" services where Searchers provide advantageous and profitable transaction ordering to validators and those validators receive a premium bid. These MEV services have elected to cautiously refuse to build transaction ordering with any transactions that interact with any OFAC sanctioned Ethereum addresses. This action may not be necessary for US based parties, but the lack of clarity and guidance from OFAC may have led these groups to conclude that the risk of sanctions violations is not worth the reward. It is important to note that no one is openly refusing to cast votes on blocks or children of blocks that contain interactions with OFAC sanctioned addresses and as long as some portion of the network is not censoring block production then those subjected transactions will eventually be included on chain within a reasonable timeframe. More on MEV here: https://ethereum.org/nl/developers/docs/mev/

Q.7) What happens if only 60% of stakers are available/online or desire to vote on the checkpoint block?

In the event that less than two thirds of the Ethereum network are not participating in consensus, then the blockchain will not reach a finalized state until the two thirds quorum is restored. A finalized state is important for Proof of Stake as it means that an attacker or any other party cannot build blocks upon an older checkpoint state without being subjected to heavy slashing penalties and ejection from the validator set. During a time of non-finality, the penalty for being offline increases exponentially over time. Eventually, the weight of the votes from the offline segment of Ethereum has been diminished so much that it now accounts for less than one third of the validating votes and the blockchain can therefore reach two thirds quorum again to finalize.

Q.8) What does the reference in the Ethereum docs that states "unless there is a consensus failure in which an attacker burns 33% of the total staked ether" mean? What is the attacker doing to have a consensus failure, not voting? A consensus failure happens when there are not enough stakers voting to have higher than 66%.

This phrase is referring to a common attack in block production where an attacker can choose to build on an older block and secure enough votes (or build a longer chain in the case of PoW) such that everyone is convinced that the attacker's block is the canonical block. They may want to do this to "undo" a recent transaction for any number of reasons. One of the key benefits to Ethereum's Proof of Stake is that blockchain finality exists such that a block producer cannot build upon any block older than the most recent finalized checkpoint without receiving heavy slashing penalties. There is one caveat here that an attack could successfully reorganize the Ethereum blockchain in Proof of Stake, but they would have to perform slashable actions that would result in a permanent loss of 33%

stake of the entire total staked Ether. That is to say, they would need to first secure more than 33% of all of the ether at stake valued which is about $6B and they would probably need more than 50% of the total stake to be successful in practice.

You can read more on these known attacks and how the value of Ethereum makes it difficult for an attack to be successful here:

https://ethereum.org/en/developers/docs/consensus-mechanisms/pos/attack-and-defense/#attackers-with-33-stake

As we can see, the Byzantine-Fault Tolerant protocol boasts the fantastic benefit of achieving finality very rapidly, something a smart contract blockchain like Ethereum relies on given that major financial transactions, including trades, occur on its blockchain. Byzantine-Fault Tolerant, however, comes at the cost of a major disruption should the number of nodes participating drop below the number needed for a quorum. In other words, it works well if the network runs normally. Granted, this is what we typically observe, and the higher the number of participants, the more resilient the network should be, but it is nonetheless a potential point of disruption that people should be aware of. A system having the benefit of rapid finality without this encumbrance would be even better.

The inflation rate numbers are particular; if this continues, Ethereum's supply is virtually fixed. Ethereum experienced quite a drastic change that took several years to complete, but it is finally done. Time will tell whether it was worth it, but, if necessary, Ethereum developers are not afraid to make dramatic changes while bitcoin developers are well known for moving conservatively. In addition, the Ethereum foundation projects an important, authoritative voice supporting these major changes. The Ethereum foundation was created prior to Ethereum's launch and was behind the ICO. Since it was a PoW coin at the time, funding wasn't necessary other than to pay for its development. As you might remember, bitcoin was launched without any fanfare other than the publication of the white paper and, two months later, the source code, by an author whose identity still remains unknown.[58]

ECONOMIC ASPECT OF PROOF OF STAKE

Distribution of staking in PoS is interesting.   When new PoS blockchains are started, very few nodes are operating, leaving these few with the bulk of the rewards. For example, assume that the new coins given as rewards (just as new BTC are awarded miners per block) leads to an inflation rate of 5%. If only 20% of coins are staked initially, the stakers receive a 25% return, whereas if every coin is staked, the return is the same as the inflation rate—5%, thus mimicking a classic stock split.

Another distinction between PoS and PoW regards operation requirements. A bitcoin miner is invested heavily in ASIC hardware and wants to make use of it as much as possible but can deal with being offline for a few minutes. A staker, on the other hand, should be online during the window of time its node is scheduled to mine (or propose to mine) a block; otherwise, the staker loses the reward, which then goes to the backup staker that took his place. In addition, the operator of a staking node must be wary of hacking threats. If a hacker took over a node and caused it to misbehave, the network would penalize it by destroying the node's coins held in bonds. Recall that to be able to stake, PoS typically requires a node to tie up a portion of all staked coins in bonds. Any double mining of blocks, for example, would be seen as an attack on the network, and the responsible node would be financially penalized. Depending on the protocol implementation, another threat might be a hacker withdrawing the coins stored in a staked address that are not held in bonds if the staking node holds the private key. PoW miners do not worry about these issues, as private keys

---

[58]To read more about Ethereum's PoS, you can check out these sources: https://www.blocknative.com/blog/an-ethereum-stakers-guide-to-slashing-other-penalties https://ethereum.org/en/developers/docs/consensus-mechanisms/pos/

can be safely stored offline. The bitcoin mining software only needs to know what bitcoin address is to be credited block rewards.

PROS AND CONS OF PROOF OF STAKE

With the overview of Proof of Stake, we can now consider its pros and cons and how it compares with Proof of Work, in particular bitcoin. Two of the main recurring negative points often advanced by those opposed to Proof of Stake are its complexity and the overhead in bandwidth and space it entails. Critics say greater complexity increases the likelihood a flaw will be discovered and capitalized on by an attacker. It is true that PoS is more complex and so to satisfy skeptics, a cryptocurrency would need to run, issue free, for a longer period than bitcoin did to demonstrate its stability. Even with bitcoin's lightweight level of PoW complexity, similar concerns were voiced during bitcoin's beginning. This was so new that many could not avoid asking what would happen if some sort of a flaw was later discovered. Since bitcoin has been running for more than 14 years now, this concern has scaled down appreciably in importance, if it even exists at all.

Another criticism is that staking nodes perform no real work, and therefore no value is created. Let's break this argument down into two parts. First, running a staking node involves risk. PoS has a punitive component, and so hacking or administrative mistakes are a source of financial risk. Because the PoS network destroys coins placed in bonds by a staker whose node broadcasts invalid blocks or two different versions of the same block, a hacker who caused the staking node misbehave can cause the staker to lose his stake. Additionally, depending on the implementation of PoS, the private keys linked to staking node addresses are not in cold storage and could be accessed by a hacker. A bitcoin miner, however, can hold private keys securely in a hardware wallet, and the mining node knows only the bitcoin address to which to credit the rewards. Additionally, because when a staking node is to create a block is determined ahead of time, were the node to be down at that time, it would lose the associated rewards it was scheduled to earn. Consequently, that the node has a reliable internet connection secured from hacking is of paramount importance.

But the number one criticism of Proof of Stake advanced by Proof of Work folks is its resemblance to central banking, where the rich get richer and control more.This comparison is, in my opinion, flawed, as a central bank's currency is run on two major philosophical principles: proof-of-guns-and-jails and proof-of-debt. In all countries, those failing to pay taxes in a particular country's currency end up in jail. Also, since these currencies are born out of debt, particularly in the commercial banking sector, people are forced to use that currency to pay back their debt.

This suggests another tool used by central bankers: they use debt level to influence the country's economic activity and so create a recession/depression to slow down inflation and benefit their insider friends, who hunt bargains among the bankruptcies induced by the recession or depression. Proof of Stake entails none of these elements. When critics say the rich have a larger controlling stake in a PoS system, in what way is that different from a rich bitcoin miner? Both must submit to the protocol or, in PoS, possibly be penalized by part or all of their stake. As mentioned earlier, some coins such as Tezos use delegated Proof of Stake under which everyone benefits from coin inflation, which is more like a stock split in which a company multiplies the number of shares outstanding by a factor greater than one. For a factor of two, for instance, each person owning a share then owns two shares. Based on the stock split analogy, I do not see this comparison as valid. However, for those Proof of Stake blockchains where only a few major actors benefit from staking rewards (the process of new-coin creation), this criticism would be valid.

One of the most ridiculous arguments I often see is that it costs validators nothing to maintain a PoS blockchain compared to bitcoin, where miners must expend a lot of energy and purchase highly specialized hardware. Proponents of this argument contend that the marginal cost of a database is zero, even if it is cryptographically signed, i.e., requires a digital signature. Since validators stake their coins which are then managed by a consensus that requires very little energy to maintain, they contend that the PoS currency is worth nothing, that there is nothing at stake, and that the currency is doomed to fail. Hilariously, this argument is also used by gold bugs, i.e., those who favor investing in gold, who claim that bitcoin is worth nothing and is just "digital air" or some other two-word descriptor.

Why in human social interactions and regarding market-driven forces do we see opinions similar to those found in religious debates? Again, as the Austrian School of Economics holds that it is the market that decides the value of anything. Not you, nor I, nor anyone can claim that updating an entry in a simple SQL database costs zero, and the same holds for PoS. And, if the market says a given PoS coin is worth $100 or 0.001 BTC, then that's what it is worth, at least at that time—and the coin's worth perhaps has more to do with the network effect than the consensus. Their counter-argument to this might be that, in the long run, since no energy is expended, it will go to zero. But, again, in valuing bitcoin, the market is more likely to care about the network effect than about the energy bitcoin miners expend. However, it is true that there is self-reinforcement—the more energy expended in maintaining the network, the more secure it is against a 51% attack, thereby making the currency more attractive. It might if some governments introduced carbon legislation, but that would be a case of outside forces affecting localized miners, just as fiat currency has value driven by proof-of-guns. But that's beside the point.

Another argument involves the unlimited future supply of hash-mining hardware that can be created for bitcoin mining while the supply of coins that can be acquired for staking under PoS is finite. This is a stronger argument, at least on the surface. The same principles apply to both PoS and PoW. In PoS, we first need to define the type of threat that a group or organization obtaining the largest stake in a Proof of Stake coin—or, equivalently, the largest hash power in a Proof of Work network—can pose. A specific case, perhaps more specific to Tezos with its form of governance than to other PoS systems, is the major stakers' regrouping and voting for a protocol amendment (which requires support from those holding 80%

of the staking) that would give them an advantage over the others, alter the blockchain, allow for censorship, or any combination thereof. We will cover this later.

However, such inequality will always exist, and hence wealth within any currency will always be widely distributed. After all, the Pareto principle applies. I believe the middle class is stronger in a free market environment. We can therefore assume that the same inequality will be apparent in distribution of mining equipment as it is in coin ownership. Certainly, the supply of hardware can be replenished indefinitely whereas the supply of coins is limited, but just as they could be acquired constantly by those with most of the capital as well. It's also important to bring up the environment in which this important group who has a large stake holding must deal with. Are merchants required to accept a currency defined by a legal tender law or is the public able to decide which currency they want to use? If a currency is not imposed by the government and currency chosen by the free market dominates, large stakeholders would have an interest in not acknowledging the rise of another currency out of a fork in an existing currency. Imagine a fork where the blockchain content is altered slightly so that large stakeholders who perform censorship have their ownership revoked. This constitutes somewhat of a revolt, but it is done peacefully by a simple hard fork wherein the prior currency becomes less and less relevant and the new one more accepted and dominant. Altering the blockchain is certainly not recommended, as it violates an important principle of blockchains, i.e., that their content should be permanent. Of course, such a move would be disruptive, but it would be a solution if a group leveraged its members' resources in a nefarious way. As for bitcoin miners performing censorship, we elaborated in Chapter 4 how bitcoin's developers, nodes, and honest miners could apply a mechanism to exclude such bad miners from acting, perhaps under the aegis of a set of governments. However, in such a situation—which we haven't seen—experts might develop new methods that we, and even themselves, haven't yet thought up.

One solution could be that a new supply of ASIC hash hardware comes online, beyond government reach, which could be used to displace bad-acting miners by censoring their actions, thus leading to a hash race. True, if pro-censorship governments were to help finance these miners, the race might be a difficult one, but other solutions are possible, some that might surface only if/when such a problem arises.

Although we are far from this point, the question remains, how will the ecosystem react in 2140 when the last bitcoin is mined? The exact plays and counterplays that will then occur can be extrapolated or imagined, but none are certain. Will the importance of Layer 2 be so great as to make mining less attractive as only transaction fees will generate revenue? How high will those transaction fees have to be to keep mining sufficiently financially viable to justify the hashing power that we have today? I am not worried about this, particularly because this will happen so gradually that the market, and hence the coding experts, will have adequate time to adjust.

To evaluate this threat, we need to estimate the overall conditions that will prevail at that time so as to define the world PoS and PoW may then face. Importantly, as was discussed in a previous chapter, we are entering an era of complex mathematics and science. In particular, game theory, the discipline of mathematics that models the strategic interactions of two or more rational players in a non-cooperative game, is increasingly relevant. Game theory entered the public spotlight with the 2001 movie A Beautiful Mind starring Russell Crowe playing mathematician John Nash.[59] Nash, was a recipient of the Nobel Prize in Economic Sciences for discovery of the Nash equilibrium,[60] which states that, when each player in a game of strategy knows the equilibrium strategy of the other player(s), none will gain by changing strategy. Stated differently, if Player 1 using Strategy A is obtaining the best result possible against Player 2, who is using Strategy B, and, if Player 2 using Strategy B obtains the best possible result against Player 1's use of Strategy A, then Player 2 has nothing to gain by

---

[59]https://en.wikipedia.org/wiki/John_Forbes_Nash_Jr
[60]https://en.wikipedia.org/wiki/Nash_equilibrium

changing strategy since Strategy B gives the best result. Moreover, Player 2 will assume Player 1 thinks the same and so will keep using Strategy A. Depending on the game, if both players were to change strategy simultaneously, they could reach another Nash equilibrium using different strategies from before. However, neither gains advantage by changing strategy once a Nash equilibrium is reached.

Game theory can be applied to trading as well. People read the chart of an asset, say bitcoin's pricing against the US dollar, and, during a downtrend, bullish traders attempt to determine the price when the bottom occurs so that they can buy. All traders in the market try to second guess each others' strategies, and the price eventually bottoms out at a certain level. Of course, such traders want to buy at the lowest price possible, but they are competing against each other to buy at this lower price. Hence, second guessing occurs with every trader trying to discern the strategies of the other traders in trying to find the bottom. Whereas the little fish in the market are scared as they watch the price go down and sell, the heavy investors strategize their buying. This might partially explain why Fibonacci numbers and trendlines are very often, but not always respected.

Returning to Nash, I wonder what he would have to say about bitcoin, Proof of Work and Proof of Stake in his prime years. Just as gold bugs or other anti-bitcoin folks are not accounting for game theory when pointing out bitcoin's flaws and mulling over how a government or third party might either destroy or render the cryptocurrency useless, game theory applies to Proof of Stake. When individuals like you or me try to speculate how the players involved would act and counteract each other's moves, we assume that we are able to consider all the possibilities and strategies that all players could devise. That's actually quite a challenge, in fact, nearly impossible, in my opinion. But we can still speculate, as there is room for this. Using our now-known game theory skills, let's return to the list of potential threats that could arise when a group or organization attempts to take control of a cryptocurrency:

1. Make the coin/blockchain unusable. (Empty blocks, or stuck, or constantly re-write transaction history)

2. Apply a blacklist/whitelist to transactions and/or operations

3. Increase the supply or change the balances of existing accounts by altering the blockchain

Other threats by large stakeholders might be possible, but any that deviates from the ordinary is noticed by all the other users could justify creation of a fork. Here's where game theory comes into play. It is humanly impossible to anticipate all the possible angles, and I will readily admit that I cannot imagine many, but I do recognize that game theory is at play. Even if a government were involved and forced a currency manipulation, that would not differ from the current situation with bitcoin and other cryptocurrencies emerging as competition to state-imposed currencies.

Because PoW requires this constant race—whereas PoS does not—the latter can achieve rapid consensus due to its deterministic approach. In PoS, all nodes know which miner is expected to mine the next block, and so it's just a matter of letting enough time pass to allow the network nodes to share the latest block among themselves, resulting in faster confirmation. In PoS, miners or bakers MUST be up and running at the time at which they have the right to bake a block or otherwise they lose it. This contrasts with PoW, where miners can come and go immediately, and there is only a 10-minute window between the start of their mining activity and when they might gain the reward. With PoS, miners, validators, or bakers (depending on the terminology used by the given cryptocurrency's blockchain) must wait several days between the time they start participating and the time they are rewarded by creating, endorsing, or validating a block.

As discussed previously, fewer than 60 miners have more than 51% of the hash power in bitcoin and could, if all were taken over by a set of governments or attackers, be able to filter out certain transactions following an approved whitelist. Miners outside of this group not wanting to apply such filters would be forced to modify their software to handle a fork or other provision to avoid the filtering. In PoS, however, the simplest solution I personally can conceive of is to eliminate this condition for the developers to alter the blockchain by removing the nefarious large stakers. The amount of data overhead used in PoS is much larger than in PoW. To handle all the arbitration and establish who has the rights to add a block, and all these endorsements require this to be recorded as part of the block along with the regular transactions performed. The PoS bandwidth requirement is higher as well. Even though a massive amount of data is accumulated in the entire blockchain, nodes and validators/miners can operate with just the blocks generated over the past three weeks. Some coins have the option for a node to store the blockchain information in a way that only records the balance of each address on the blockchain as well as all the smart contracts and their respective data. Along with the latest blocks that dictate the baking rights for the upcoming blocks, this information is distributed across the entire set of nodes. It is convenient for these blockchain playgrounds, but this brings back how much safer and more secure bitcoin looks by all nodes having the ability to easily store the entire blockchain. Ethereum's entire blockchain is over 1 terabyte, and that's after slashing prior redundant transactions, a contrast with bitcoin nodes, which retain everything. Obviously, these attributes also make PoS more fragile. For instance, what if an pivotal event fragments the network or the internet for several days or even weeks. A pivotal event could include a solar flare (geomatic storm) like the Carrington Event[61] or one even stronger that disrupts the grid over a good portion of the globe. Depending on the scope, both PoW and PoS networks would be affected. The problem, at least for bitcoin, centers on those isolated with a smaller chain. Perhaps two weeks later, when the internet is restored worldwide, those running bitcoin's longest chain (having the most hash power) will have had the benefit of using it for the past two weeks, while those on the smaller chain will not have any of the transactions performed during that time. But, at least, in this disruptive situation, some bitcoin users would still be benefiting from it, and no coins would be

---

[61] https://en.wikipedia.org/wiki/Carrington_Event

lost by the bitcoin users due to the situation. For most PoS implementations, the situation would be similar. I say for most because Tezos's latest implementation requires a quorum. So, either the blockchain will have stopped operating until the developers adjust the calculation of a quorum, or it will wait until the network is restored globally.

I sometimes run over a Mad Max scenario or similar circumstance in my mind, where the internet is suddenly unavailable on an entire continent. The effects would be devastating and widespread. Banks and other internet-dependent systems would not be any more operational than bitcoin, but bitcoin could actually have an advantage. Bitcoin mining, which would still be continuing elsewhere in the world, would simply adjust; after 2016 blocks, the difficulty level of solving bitcoin blocks would decrease to bring the average solution time between blocks back down to 10 minutes. Ironically, a Mad Max scenario is what gold bugs often refer to as justification for not owning bitcoin and owning only gold or silver. The catastrophic events that occurred in our planet's past leaves little doubt that another such major event will one day occur. If one believes it will arrive within the next year or decade, then it would make sense to invest only in gold, buy an underground shelter (something like the Blast from the Past movie), although this will only pay off if the disastrous event actually occurs. On the other hand, if you believe we have at least another few centuries, then owning bitcoin makes a great deal of sense. Sure, there could be wars or other smaller scale events, but that's a lot of if's. If you are a bitcoin maximalist who believes bitcoin would be more resilient than any other coin during disruptive events and assigns a reasonable probability to the actual occurrence of such an event, then you should also own some physical gold and silver coin, as they are even more resilient. Returning to the argument that PoS allows the rich to get richer, which, as you will remember, doesn't apply to delegated Proof of Stake, which allows anyone to participate in staking and receive the associated rewards. In Tezos, because about 75% of all coins are staked, three-fourths of all owners receive extra coins from the additional supply created for baking rewards. The strategy here is to encourage coin owners to participate in staking. With their delegation, they can choose their baker, typically supporting those with similar views on voting, and, as such, this delegated Proof of Stake counteracts the typical criticism associated with PoS regarding distribution of new coins and their corresponding power. Since rewards are distributed equally based on the amount staked (minus some fees delegators charge bakers), it does not differ from a stock split. Consequently, from a market capitalization perspective, it is as if no rewards were created. However, it does give more power to exchanges, something users of these coins should understand.[62]

DECENTRALIZATION ASPECT OF PROOF OF STAKE

As mentioned earlier, I believe decentralization is not an absolute, meaning that the system is either completely decentralized or completely centralized. Rather, decentralization is a continuum or shade of gray in that it is extremely difficult to obtain a system that is completely decentralized with no failure or attack dependencies. I believe bitcoin is the top dog in terms of decentralization and, as such, the most secure. Imagine the 1800s when gold was the world's reserve currency, when people stored their wealth in gold and speculated in anything else. Land held second place as a means to store value, but, depending on war, floods, or governments (like Russia's tumultuous evolution into the USSR), people still speculated, geopolitically speaking, how things would go. But how does PoS measure up regarding decentralization? Obviously, it all depends on the type of PoS implementations, so let's stick to the type we discussed earlier. As mentioned previously, a major difference between PoW and PoS involves the process by which consensus is established. One involves a constant minute-by-minute hashing battle to win the next block, while

---

[62]If you are interested in reading more about Proof of Work and Proof of Stake, download the report written by the Kraken Exchange: https://blog.kraken.com/post/14885/pow-vs-pos-securing-the-chain/

the other requires a long process where the right to mine future blocks increases with the amount staked. Let's go over the key points.

Among the factors raised by Proof of Stake proponents is that an attacker would need to invest in the coin it wants to manipulate or destroy. In contrast, a Proof of Work miner can attack a rival coin it does not like by mounting a 51% attack where double spending occurs. This is the famous attack we talked about in the Proof of Work chapter: A miner holds his version of the block and releases it later, thereby creating a fork where they might have spent on both, i.e., double spent coins. Although exchanges have wised up to this possibility and now wait longer for confirmation on coins with low hash power, this nonetheless proves the point. Given that users must wait longer to receive confirmation, these coins are not very practical.

At its core, Proof of Stake proponents have a point about economic interest preserving value. The question is, under what conditions would a dominant holder of a coin alter its blockchain's operations in his favor? Any activities on the blockchain would be publicly visible to all. If people start to see preferential treatment in, for example, the order of transactions included in the blockchain that always favor one group over another, such activities might be detected. Transaction ordering might be more relevant and valuable when smart contracts involving financial operations are involved, like a trade for example. Imagine a miner/baker who knows in advance—not the case with Proof of Work—that it will be mining block number #30,020,404 in a minute. The miner would run special code on his mining node to select a transaction he is about to make over others occurring at the same time in a time-sensitive trade, in short, front running trades. With an anonymous address, this would be difficult to detect, however, and, if repeated often, others who have been cheated might eventually start to look at the statistics. With PoW, miners have no idea when they will be able to win a block, and so, in that sense, PoW is clearly better.

Government action is another threat that decentralization guards against. We could go over a myriad of scenarios, but it boils down to a few major cases. Could a government invest in a PoS significantly enough to control, filter, or censure transactions? Yes, but, just as with a rich investor, a fork could be applied. Let the government re-invest again and again in something that the public will eventually reject and choose another one. Of course, a government could make that currency legal tender and regulate its use, which, again, is not terribly different from our current situation. Just as we have the fiat euro, pound, and dollar along with bitcoin and other cryptocurrencies, we would have a forced PoS-government-coin along with others. Since the Pareto principle would apply to all, we would typically have something close to 20% of miners owning 80% of the hash power, or the coins. Overall, 80% of the wealth will be owned by roughly 20% of the population. Even though anyone can invest in new hardware to increase hash power while a fixed amount of coin exists for the staking, the principle still fits these players. Ironically, because Proof of Stake forces players to own a stake, to invest in the coin, it is more secure than all other PoW coins except of course for bitcoin, which is king with its Proof of Work hash power. It seems to me that any new coins (although I don't see the point for more) should choose PoS as its consensus method; otherwise, its security can be compromised with PoW due to bitcoin's tremendous hashing power. Granted, the hash algorithm is often different, but many algorithms are shared by more than one coin.

Another important point regarding Proof of Stake involves its environment. We are so accustomed to the "legal tender" laws imposed on us that Proof of Stake critics often neglect to analyze the free market angle. In a free market environment, given that all source code is open source, if large stakers in Proof of Stake started to do nefarious things that were somehow permitted by the cryptocurrency blockchain's protocol (censoring transactions, for example, may not deviate from the protocol), other users could decide to fork the blockchain and remove the miscreants' ownership. Think of what happened with the Ethereum and Ethereum Classic hard fork and imagine this done to penalize a large staker, who may have perhaps abused his power using his governance in Tezos. With the free market competition principle also applied to money, game theory comes into play.

In a free market environment, large holders of Proof of Stake will lose their investment if they mismanage their staking rights. I have watched many Proof of Stake critics create a philosophical cathedral in which they analyze the entire altcoin ecosystem, except the impacts of a free market on a currency. If another form of metal had been discovered in the 1600s that was better gold—more portable, for instance—but just as rare and capable of serving as either a small or large payment, it would have displaced gold as a currency. In a free market environment, large holders of Proof of Stake lose their investment if they mismanage their staking rights. But in the end, I still believe that the market will eventually lead to a more dominant bitcoin with perhaps a few other cryptocurrency playgrounds. Bitcoin's network effect and rapid, ongoing development, combined with PoW's flexibility for participants makes it the strongest decentralized contender. As discussed earlier, among PoW systems, other cryptocurrencies cannot compete against bitcoin as to CPU power and energy. Others should stick to PoS or other consensus types, even ones that have not yet been invented should leave PoW to bitcoin.

A SIDECHAIN OF BITCOIN RUNNING ON PROOF OF STAKE

The lightning network and other developments such as CoinPool demonstrate that side chains on bitcoin can offer additional benefits. Such a chain could allow for various implementations, experimentations, or any operations currently performed on other blockchains such as smart contracts on Ethereum. Such a sidechain exists today. It is called the Liquid Network; we will cover it in a later chapter.

But, as already discussed, such side chains should not be running on Proof of Work unless bitcoin miners were combining the work of both chains, and a hard fork in the current implementation of bitcoin would most likely be required to support this. An alternative is to run on Proof of Stake where, obviously, no new coins are created. Miners/Stakers on that sidechain would be rewarded only from transaction fees, just as will be the case with bitcoin in the year 2140 and beyond.

For example, were the Tezos implementation copied, modified such that no new coins were created, and the currency changed to satoshis with different labeling so as to indicate it had been transferred onto that side chain. The hardest part here is finding a mechanism to transfer the ownership from bitcoin's main blockchain to the sidechain. Once transferred, the users on the sidechain must be assured the corresponding bitcoins on the main blockchain are frozen, that is, non-spendable until they have been transferred back to the main blockchain. Ideally, this mechanism doesn't require trusting a third party like so many of those "wrapped bitcoin" uses on Ethereum or other blockchains. Since we want to avoid hard forks on bitcoin, a solution might involve using lightning network or a CoinPool-like method combined with the traditional functions of miners/stakers.

Miners/stakers on that sidechain would be responsible, as a group, for locking and releasing these coins using CoinPool or something equivalent, while adding incentives (fees) to perform the transfer and penalization (loss of bond) in response to bad actions. Just as with Proof of Stake, miners/stakers on the sidechain would need to place satoshis in a bond to have the right to create new blocks on that sidechain. Any misbehavior would be penalized, whereas collecting fees from the sidechain transactions would increase their revenue.

Sidechains are not a new idea. One such solution was proposed in BIP-300 and BIP-301 (BIP stands for Bitcoin Improvement Proposal) called Drivechain.[63] However, due to concerns about the increase in miners' power, its implantation lacked support by many. A PoS sidechain using a CoinPool or lightning network method for transfers, would mitigate these concerns, as stakers would be involved in the sidechain, not miners. Granted, nothing would prevent a miner from becoming a sidechain-staker as well, but the distribution of players would be different.

---

[63] https://www.drivechain.info/

The Liquid network, covered in more detail later, is a sidechain of bit-coin that uses LBTC as a currency pegged to BTC. Ideally, a sidechain would use something like Zero-Knowledge Proof (ZK-Stark)[64] as a means of freezing the bitcoins on the bitcoin's blockchain while they are repre-sented in the sidechain. Unfortunately, we will need to be patient as this integration will require additional soft forks to the bitcoin protocol before it could be used.

---

[64]https://eprint.iacr.org/2018/046

6

BITCOIN'S LIGHTNING NETWORK, COINPOOL AND BEYOND

Bitcoin's development is conservative, with a strong preference for soft fork changes, which are less disruptive and do not require immediate updates by all parties. A hard fork, on the other hand, is rare and requires all parties to update immediately, or else the chain will split due to incompatibility. For instance, Bitcoin Cash (BCH) was created through a hard fork when developers introduced software changes - increasing the maximum size of a block by a factor of 4 to facilitate more transactions - incompatible with the prior version. Nonetheless, this does not imply that bitcoin development is stagnant. As we discussed in a previous chapter, the introduction of segregated witness (segwit) paved the way for the deployment of the lightning network without necessitating alterations to the bitcoin protocol or software. Integrating segwit required only a soft fork. Other notable changes, such as Taproot, have already been implemented or are in the works, offering innovative, new functionalities, while implementing backward compatible changes and avoiding contentious hard forks. Most bitcoin critics ignore these developments. This chapter will delve into recent and expected major changes slated for the future.

BITCOIN SCRIPT

Before exploring new functionalities such as the lightning network, it is worthwhile to understand bitcoin Script,[65] which has been around since bitcoin's inception. Bitcoin uses a scripting language that is executed as part of the outpoint in a transaction. Interestingly, bitcoin Script is not a complex language, as it does not contain loops, recursion, or "gotos." Because of this, it is said that it is not Turing complete as it cannot express complexity and has a very defined and predictable path of execution. Nevertheless, it provides the fundamental building blocks for implementing the lightning network, as we shall see. Bitcoin Script is stack based using reverse polish notation, similar in a way to how Hewlett Packard calculators operate. For example, to add 3 and 4, you would type 3 then press enter to move it up the stack, and then type 4 and then press the add button which takes the last 2 on the stack and adds them together. Although simplified compared to major language, it does have several commands allowing for interesting operations such as:

- Flow control based such as OP_IF statement;

- Logical operation such as OP_AND or OP_OR;

- Arithmetic such as OP_ADD, OP_SUB, OP_MUL, or OP_NUMEQUAL;

---

[65]https://en.bitcoin.it/wiki/Script

- Cryptographic operation like OP_CHECKSIG and many others; and

- Lock time where it returns true or false based on time value, typically defined as the current bitcoin block number.

Combined, these operations allow for powerful directives that can be called "smart contract," although they are rudimentary compared to what Ethereum can achieve. But they do offer the added benefit of most likely being bug free. Not all of these operations have been around since bitcoin's release but have been added as the need presented itself.

Before discussing the specific operations bitcoin Script can perform, let us first review the details of how and when they are executed. In a bitcoin transaction, the rules for spending the bitcoins in the future are written in bitcoin Script and included in the Outputs section. The figure below illustrates how transactions form a chain, even though they are rarely in consecutive blocks and certainly never in the same block. They do, however, show the movement of bitcoins as they are divided into smaller amounts or combined back together, constantly moving as they are "spent." Frequently, multiple inputs and outputs, meaning more than one transaction, can be part of the input to a new transaction.

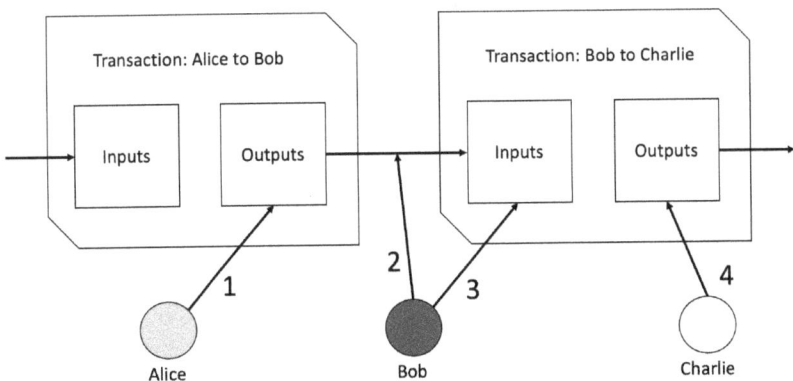

Figure 20: Bitcoin transaction chain.

In Figure 20, when Alice sends bitcoins to Bob, she sets rules on how these bitcoins can be unlocked and be part of a future transaction (See "1" in the figure). Those rules are written using bitcoin Script and included as part of the Outputs section of a bitcoin transaction. Alice's transaction includes a script ("1") that specifies how Bob can unlock and spend the bitcoins she sent him. Bob must have control over the bitcoins to send them to Charlie or anyone else. Later, Bob creates a new transaction to pay Charlie, which includes the same script from Alice's transaction ("2") in the Inputs section to prove he has the authority to spend those bitcoins, and a new script in the Outputs section ("3") that specifies how Charlie can spend them in the future. This creates a transaction chain that continues as Charlie may send those bitcoins, along with the corresponding scripts ("3" and "4"), to other bitcoin addresses. In a transaction, the sum of all bitcoins in the input must match the sum in the output. Even in the case of the mining rewards, the input is what is called the coinbase.

A single bitcoin transaction can have multiple inputs, which is useful when the sum of the bitcoins in one address is insufficient to cover the sum of the outputs. In a typical transaction, bitcoin is sent and associated with a specific bitcoin address. The original bitcoin address (non-segwit) started with a 1 and is generated by first running SHA256 on the public key, and then hashing the result again using a different hash algorithm, RIPEMD160. These addresses specified in the transaction's output script as follows:

```
OP_DUP
OP_HASH160
b6a6395fd3d6ddf3515b57a57c047faf34260a54
OP_EQUALVERIFY
OP_CHECKSIG
```

Here's an overview of the stack concept as applied to this process. The OP_HASH160 first performs both the SHA256 and RIPEMD160, one after the other. Since a bitcoin address involves a public key undergoing

SHA256 and then RIPEMD160 hashing, the reverse must be done to validate it. When Bob creates a transaction to pay Charlie, he includes a digital signature with the public key of his bitcoin address in the inputs section. Miners validate the transaction if Bob has the authority to spend these bitcoins by executing the script in the Output section of Alice's transaction. The OP_HASH160 is used to verify that the public key matches the bitcoin address in Alice's output, and OP_EQUALVERIFY confirms that the digital signature corresponds to the private key owned by Bob. Basically, if a bitcoin address has never been used before, it has two layers of security. Satoshi Nakamoto probably chose this method for two reasons. First, it shrinks the bitcoin address to 160 bits (RIPEMD160 hash) making it a bit more compact. Second, it adds an extra layer of security in case a flaw or exploitable weakness is discovered in secp256k1, the variant of elliptic curve cryptography used for the private key in bitcoin. An attacker is powerless, unless they have the public key, and for this, they will also need to break both SHA256 and RIPEMD160. Once a transaction occurs, the public key is exposed, but if Bob only sends a portion of the bitcoins from his address, his wallet automatically generates another output to spend the balance (the change) to another new address he also controls. But sometimes people publish a bitcoin address for donations, for example, and then receive other transactions after an earlier transaction was done with it, making the public key public. Although the exposure is not catastrophic since there are no known flaws with secp256k1, it is not ideal for privacy of bitcoin held for long term storage.

Timelock

Returning to the various operations available in bitcoin Script, one example with interesting possibilities is the OP_CHECKSEQUENCEVERIFY,[66] which puts a time restriction on a transaction in relative value. For example, if the operation stated: These bitcoins cannot be spent until at least 100 blocks since the transaction was included in the bitcoin network. If

---

[66]https://github.com/bitcoin/bips/blob/master/bip-0112.mediawiki

Alice had included this timelock in her transaction to Bob, Bob would have to wait for 100 bitcoin blocks to be added to the blockchain before he could create a new transaction using these bitcoins.

It can be used in multiple ways. For example, this is the script for a two-of-three multisig escrow account that times out 30 days after it has been funded:

```
IF
     2 <Alice's pubkey> <Bob's pubkey> <Escrow's pubkey>
     3 CHECKMULTISIG
ELSE
     "30d" CHECKSEQUENCEVERIFY DROP
     <Alice's pubkey> CHECKSIG
ENDIF
```

Including this script in the output section of a transaction allows the funds to be spent with the signatures of any two of Alice, Bob, or "Escrow" at any given time. After 30 days, however, Alice's signature alone would suffice. It's worth noting that the use of OP_NOT enables us to reverse the restriction where Alice alone could spend the funds, but only during the first 30 days. Additionally, a single transaction may contain multiple inputs and outputs.

Hashlock

Coming back to hash operations such as OP_SHA256, they could also be used to create a Hashlock, which can either be the only restriction on a transaction or combined with OP_CHECKSIG that requires a digital signature. An interesting feature of a hashlock is that the same *secret text* used to generate the hash can be employed to lock multiple transactions, and once the secret is revealed, all of these transactions can be unlocked. This method, however, is not very secure because the secret key is revealed to everyone when one transaction is broadcasted on the network, allowing an attacker to replicate the transaction with a higher transaction fee to encourage a miner to include it. Thus, it is better to combine it with a digital signature.

Hash Time Locked Contracts (HTLC)

But as we will see, a hashlock combined with a timelock can create a powerful tool called Hashed Time Locked Contracts (HTLC). In short, a hashed timelock contract is used to reduce counterparty risk by creating a time-based escrow that requires a cryptographic passphrase (the secret text that was hashed that will unlock the hashlock portion of the contract) to unlock a transaction output. The lightning network is among the most well-known use cases of HTLC.

LIGHTNING NETWORK

How often have I seen a post on twitter where someone compared a coin with thousands of transactions per second to bitcoin's 7 transactions per second without mentioning the lightning network?[67] Too many to count! On chain transactions implies major issues. Either the blockchain supports a lot of them at the cost of being less decentralized, or it limits them to ensure stronger decentralization. But, imagine a scenario where the primary use of the blockchain is to secure an agreement between two parties wishing to exchange bitcoin transactions at any rate they choose. Such an agreement would guarantee the security of any payment, similar to sending a transaction on the bitcoin blockchain. This is precisely what the lightning network enables - a layer two payment system that operates on top of bitcoin's layer-one blockchain.

A viable payment suited for everyday use, the kind that you might already be using with a credit card, must have these three attributes:

---

[67] https://lightning.network/lightning-network-paper.pdf

1. Certainty/Finality (although even a credit card does not always provide this for merchant because of chargebacks);

2. Rapid confirmation (merchants don't want to wait an hour to sell a cup of coffee); and

3. High throughput to serve everyone.

The first attribute, certainty/finality, is highly regarded. When paying with a bank check, trust is necessary that the check won't bounce or the bank account is not empty or closed. In some transactions, however, this level of trust cannot be guaranteed. Therefore, having a certified payment method that is also quick and can handle high traffic is crucial. The lightning network fulfills all these requirements, but it still has some drawbacks. Fortunately, CoinPool aims to address most of these drawbacks, as we will discuss later in this chapter.

The second attribute, scalability, is a concern that dates back to bitcoin's early days, first documented in James A. Donald's first reply to Satoshi Nakamoto's announcement of bitcoin's whitepaper publication. Hal Finney also raised this issue in a private email exchange with Satoshi:[68]

The intriguing part is where Finney refers to other transactions utilizing an alternate payment system, possibly built on the foundation of bitcoin. Despite no technology resembling the lightning network at that time, Finney envisioned a comparable parallel network established on bitcoin.

Things would have been very much difficult for bitcoin in the last few years if the lightning network (LN) had not existed. Bitcoin's dominance would have been seriously more challenged, if it weren't for LN. Scaling without LN would have been arduous, and the only alternatives would have involved custodians, which could lead to a loss of trust and market manipulation and cause significant losses for the majority of participants.

---

[68]https://www.coindesk.com/markets/2020/11/26/previously-unpublished-emails-of-satoshi-nakamoto-present-a-new-puzzle/

```
From hal@finney.org  Wed Nov 19 07:20:46 2008
Return-Path: <hal@finney.org>
X-Original-To: hal@finney.org
Delivered-To: hal@finney.org
Received: by finney.org (Postfix, from userid 500)
        id A78D414F6E2; Wed, 19 Nov 2008 07:20:46 -0800 (PST)
To: hal@finney.org, satoshi@vistomail.com
Subject: Re: Bitcoin source files attached
Cc: bear@sonic.net, jamesd@echeque.com
Message-Id: <20081119152046.A78D414F6E2@finney.org>
Date: Wed, 19 Nov 2008 07:20:46 -0800 (PST)
From: hal@finney.org ("Hal Finney")
X-Bogosity: Ham, tests=bogofilter, spamicity=0.000000, version=1.0.3
Status: RO

Ah, I see, thanks for the corrections.

Some of the discussion and concern over performance may relate to the
eventual size of the P2P node network. How large do you envision it
becoming? Tens of nodes? Thousands?  Millions?

And for clients, do you think this could scale to be usable for close
to 100% of world financial transactions? Or would you see it as mostly
being used for some "core" subset of transactions that have special
requirements, with other transactions using a different payment system
that perhaps is based on Bitcoin?

Hal
```

Figure 21: Finney email to Satoshi.

The lightning network uses a combination of elements, including multi signatures, to allow two individuals, who may not trust each other, to transact bitcoins as safely over a lightning channel as they do on-chain, only exponentially faster. Before we go over LN, let's start with a crude implementation of such a layer 2. Initially, the parties send BTC to a two-of-two multi-signature bitcoin address. For instance, if Alice and Bob planned to conduct several transactions, they would create a special channel. If Bob were a merchant who would only receive funds from Alice, it would make sense for Alice to fund the multi-signature address. If Bob were also paying Alice, however, they could agree to a funding ratio, such as two BTC by Alice and one BTC by Bob. To accomplish this, they would create a multi-signature address where Alice owns one private key, and Bob owns the other, and then send their funds to the address. They would keep track of their balance using a spreadsheet, metaphorically speaking, adjusting it accordingly each time Alice makes a payment to Bob or Bob pays Alice. When they eventually decide to withdraw funds, the transaction would look something like this. First Bob and Alice create two transactions: one where 0.4 BTC goes to Alice's bitcoin address and one where 1.6 BTC goes to Bob's bitcoin address. But what would be the point of this? Using this multi-signature approach requires trust between the parties involved. If Alice's balance is zero BTC, while Bob's balance is three BTC, a bad-intentioned Alice might refuse to sign the transaction, leaving Bob's funds stuck in a multi-signature address requiring two signatures, because he controls only half of it.

Using a multisig alone is pointless, additional functionality is required. What's needed is a mechanism where both Bob and Alice can withdraw their balance from that multisig address whenever they desire. Let's get one step further and imagine both Bob and Alice could construct a transaction that allows them to withdraw their respective balances, without publishing it to the blockchain until they are ready. This commitment is only finalized and the channel is closed when the final transaction is broadcast to the bitcoin network for inclusion in the blockchain. The next figure, Figure 22, shows such a transaction. Since the two-of-two multisig address requires both signatures, and they would withdraw both their initial balances, they would have agreed to prepare this initial commitment transaction at the time they first constructed the two-of-two multisig address and built the transaction to fund it. Note that the Commitment 1 transaction is prepared and signed by both Bob and Alice before they fund the initial transaction with their respective BTCs. This way, if Bob disappears right after the funding, Alice would still be able to get her funds back.

Recall that, the lightning network allows two parties who do not trust each other to use a payment system. If one person dies or refuses to close the channel, the other can broadcast the commitment to officially close the channel. So far, this system looks great. But there is a problem when the balance is updated and a new commitment is created. Say, Alice pays Bob 0.2 BTC, a new commitment is created between them, and just like before, it is held in their respective lightning network wallet rather than broadcast to the bitcoin network. According to this new balance, this means Alice

Commitment 1
(Held by both parties until one decides to close)

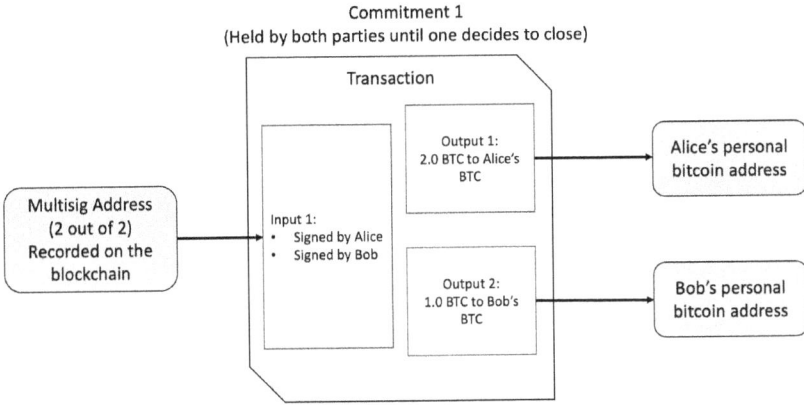

Figure 22: Opening a "Channel".

now has 1.8 BTC and Bob has 2.2 BTC. The concern is that Alice could cheat Bob out of 0.2 BTC by broadcasting the first commitment where she had 2 BTC instead of the latest one where she only has 1.8 BTC. What would prevent an unsavory Alice from broadcasting the first commitment? Figure 23 illustrates the situation.

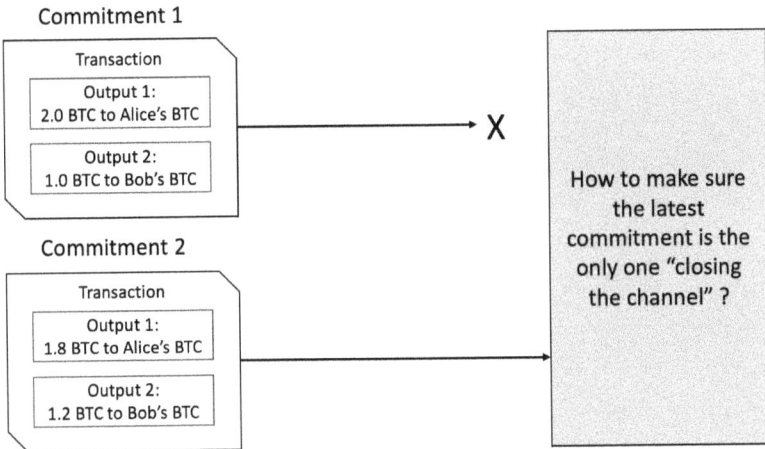

Figure 23: New commitments.

The solution lies in the complexity of the lightning network. Let's take this in steps. What we need is a way to invalidate prior commitments, and by using Hashlock, we can solve the problem. Imagine if Commitment 1 had been created through a transaction that included an extra condition in Output 1 requiring the transfer of the 2.0 BTC that was initially credited to Alice.

```
Output 1:
if hash(A) == hash (hence unlocked):
send the 2.0 BTC to Bob's personal address
else if signed by Alice:
send the 2.0 BTC to Alice's personal address
```

If this condition were part of Commitment 1 and Alice were to broadcast this older commitment, Bob could use the secret text A (which we will cover later) to unlock the "if statement" and prevent Alice from not only stealing his 0.2 BTC but penalize her by taking her entire balance. Essentially, if Bob unlocks the hashlock, 2.0 BTC will be sent to Bob's BTC address, otherwise, if Alice unlocks it with her private key, the 2.0 BTC in Output 1 goes to her address.

Many have been conditioned to think the amount in an Output portion of the script is "owned" by a bitcoin address, but that's only a valid analogy when the script condition to spend the output only requires a signature with the corresponding private key associated with a bitcoin address. When the script involves a set of "if" and "else statements," along with other more complex bitcoin operations, it then all depends on which conditions will be satisfied to discover to which bitcoin address the balance would eventually be sent.

In the midst of a lightning transaction where Commitment 2 is created, Alice would reveal to Bob the secret text (A) that she generated when she created the hash for the Hashlock of Commitment 1. The purpose of revealing the secret (text) A for the Hashlock is to invalidate the prior commitment. This secret text is an arbitrary text to satisfy the if statement with the hash() used to protect Bob. This output script aims to prevent a scenario where Alice broadcasts the older Commitment 1, which is unfavorable to Bob. If this were to happen, Bob would take advantage of his knowledge of the secret text "A" to unlock the hashlock. After updating the ledger to Commitment 2, then after Alice wrongly broadcast Commitment 1 and it has been added to the blockchain, Bob can immediately broadcast a new transaction that based on it where he satisfy the if hash of Commitment 1 where it reveals the hashlock that satisfies the "if" portion of the script. This way, Bob can seize Alice's entire current balance – the 1.8 BTC, plus her previous payment of 0.2 BTC, leaving Bob access to the entire contents of the original multisig address. So, the "invalidation" of a prior commitment is accomplished by this threat of penalty for broadcasting it. Note also that there is a corresponding hashlock with a secret text B that Bob would also reveal to Alice to penalize him if he were to send a prior commitment.

This scenario sets up a race that is won or lost over the blockchain. When Alice, who wants to cheat Bob out of the 0.2 BTC, broadcasts the older commitment transaction and it's added to the blockchain, Alice would then broadcast a subsequent transaction where she signs the "else" portion of the script in Output 1 to obtain the 2.0 BTC to her address. Bob must act quickly and send his version of this transaction where he provides the secret "A" in hope that miners will pick his transaction rather than hers. Obviously, this is not a sound or practical solution. What's needed is a time constraint on Alice to ensure that Bob has enough time to act before Alice attempts to cheat. This can be done by introducing the a TimeLock operation in the output script, like this:

```
Output 1:
if hash(A) == hash (hence unlocked):
send the 2.0 BTC to Bob's personal address
else signed by Alice and after 24 hours:
send the 2.0 BTC to Alice's personal address
```

```
Output 2:
if hash(B) == hash (hence unlocked):
send the 1.0 BTC to Alice's personal address
else signed by Alice and after 24 hours:
send the 1.0 BTC to Bob's personal address
```

Problems solved! Well, nearly. After broadcasting and integrating the older commitment into the blockchain, Alice would have to wait for 24 hours before she can withdraw from it. This waiting period gives Bob, who holds the secret for the older commitment, sufficient time to unlock the first part of the script and claim the funds. Now you might wonder, what would prevent Bob from broadcasting himself this transaction instead of hoping Alice tries to steal from him? Indeed, this is a new problem, which shows we are not fully there yet. Figure 24 recaps the conditions:

Figure 24 walks us through a possible outcome after the Commitment 2 has been made between Alice and Bob. The first transaction contains 3.0 BTC that can only be unlocked with a two-of-two multisig. Either of the two commitments can be transmitted as the next transaction since both Alice and Bob have signed these two commitments. What's important to understand is a commitment transaction that closes the channel may require another one shortly after, as it serves the purpose of closing the channel and establishing rules for withdrawing the bitcoins. In the upper portion of the figure, it shows what would happen if Alice were to broadcast Commitment 1 to the bitcoin network, trying to steal from Bob. If that were to

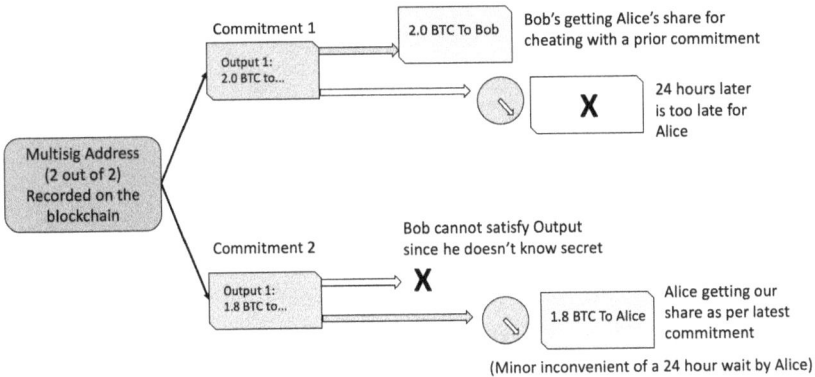

Figure 24: Timelock added.

happen, Bob has 24 hours (or whatever time set in the contract) to penalize Alice by broadcasting his variant of the following transaction, which will withdraw those bitcoins locked under the rules set in the output part of the Commitment 1 transaction. Because Alice must wait several hours or days under those rules, Bob has ample time to penalize her, if necessary, thus eliminating the race.

If, on the other hand, Alice were to broadcast the Commitment 2 (which is the current), Bob could not penalize her as he only has the secret text to Commitment 1's Hashlock. Alice has not revealed the secret text of Commitment 2 to Bob, but if there were a third commitment, she would have shared it with him. But in this case where the two are at Commitment 2, Alice just waits out the timelock period knowing Bob cannot penalize her. Once the timelock has expired, she can create a subsequent transaction to move her current balance of 1.8 BTC to any new BTC address of her choice.

But there is still one last point to address. You might wonder, although it is not in Alice's favor to broadcast the older Commitment 1, why wouldn't Bob broadcast it and use the secret key to the Hashlock to his advantage. The reason is simple, Bob doesn't have access to that version of Commitment 1. Both Alice and Bob have their own version of each commitment as shown here:

```
Alice's version of commitment 1            Bob's version of commitment 1
Signed by Bob (Alice will need to sign)    Signed by Alice (Bob will need to sign)
Output 1:                                  Output 1:
if hash(A) == hash (hence unlocked):       send the 2.0 BTC to Alice's address
send the 2.0 BTC to Bob's address
else signed by Alice and after 24 hours:   Output 2:
send the 2.0 BTC to Alice's address        if hash(B) == hash (hence unlocked):
                                           send the 1.0 BTC to Alice's address
Output 2:                                  else signed by Bob and after 24 hours:
send 1.0 BTC to Bob's address                send the 1.0 BTC to Bob's address
```

Although Bob signed Alice's version of the commitment, he does not have the actual copy of it, what he signed was a draft version. The same applies to Alice. And with this, we have a complete solution. As long as Alice closes the channel with the latest commitment, she can be confident that Bob cannot penalize her and take her balance. She also knows Bob will not broadcast an older commitment of hers, as he has a different version and his balance is higher in the latest commitment, he would have nothing to gain by wrongly sending an older commitment. But if he did, Alice would be able to penalize him and take his old 1.0 BTC balance while she would get her entire initial balance.

Now it seems like it would be tiresome for Bob to constantly monitor the blockchain to ensure that in case Alice does not broadcast the older commitment with a higher balance for herself. Lightning Nodes and specialized nodes called "watchtowers" can be charged in looking for these conditions. Should Bob's node goes down, he can safely rely on one or more watchtowers that he has tasked with this job. Although this may seem complicated for non-technical folks, a growing service industry will facilitate this mechanism so that you, Alice, Bob, and anyone else not a fan of maintaining computer software can benefit from the lightning network without the major complications. Even better, such services will allow you to easily maintain your own lightning channels.

Currently, the lightning network is easily accessible to anyone with a smartphone via a variety of bitcoin wallets that support it. Some wallet providers act as custodians of your bitcoins, while others do not. For instance, with the Phoenix wallet (https://phoenix.acinq.co) or the Muun

Wallet (https://muun.com), users are custodians of their private keys, but they still rely on the channel, which they control, to be maintained by these services. This allows non-technical people to securely hold their bitcoin without any of the headaches and complexities associated with maintaining a bitcoin client and other software updates, as well as network maintenance. And as is the trend in bitcoin development, I expect more improvements as new bitcoin opcodes are introduced to facilitate the use of layer 2.

Chaining payment

One thing we have not yet discussed is payments through intermediaries - how Alice can pay Charlie through Bob, given that she does not have a direct channel with Charlie while Bob does. The malleability of the lightning network lies in its ability to facilitate such transactions, which would otherwise be inconvenient and costly if limited to one-to-one channels. By chaining multiple individuals, with the same level of security through decentralized smart contracts, the lightning network establishes a secure layer 2 network, running bitcoin's blockchain, thus enabling anyone to make payments to anyone else.

This principle requires a tiny twist on the type of contracts we previously discussed. In the earlier agreement, two outputs were committed, with one using a hashlock to penalize anyone who would broadcast an older commitment. In a multi-party contract, three outputs will be used in the commitment, with the third using this Hash Timelock contract (HTLC) not for penalizing, but to facilitate this transfer through the chain via multiple parties. Fundamentally, the purpose of the HTLC is to provide proof that the payment was made. So, let's walk through how Alice can pay 0.2 BTC to Charlie. but what Alice wants to make sure is that Bob will pay Charlie rather than keeping it to himself. To begin, Charlie must create a secret text (C) for the third output, which will be passed through a hash function to produce an hash output shared with both Alice and Bob. It's the hash of the secret text that is shared, not the secret text (C). Alice will then create a new commitment with Bob containing a third (temporary) Output where Alice will pay Bob 0.2 BTC if Bob can prove he has paid 0.2 BTC to Charlie. This commitment will reference the hash output that Charlie shared to create a hashlock. Similarly, Bob will create a new commitment with Charlie, allowing Charlie withdraw funds from the commitment by revealing the secret text. Here is the output in this commitment that would be used:

```
Alice commitment to Bob              Bob's commitment to Charlie
Output 3:                            Output 3:
if hash(C) == hash (hence unlocked): if hash(C) == hash (hence unlocked):
send the 0.2 BTC to Bob's address    send the 0.2 BTC to Charlie's address
else signed by Alice and after 24 hours: else signed by Bob and after 24 hours:
send the 0.2 BTC to Alice's address  send the 0.2 BTC to Bob's address
```

We say Output 3 here because Alice and Bob still have Output 1 and 2 as we have shown before. For simplicity, let's assume all parties have 1.0 BTC in their respective channel, meaning Bob has 1.0 BTC in the channel he has with Alice and 1.0 BTC in the channel with Charlie. Equivalently, Alice has 1.0 BTC in her channel with Bob and Charlie also has 1.0 BTC with his channel with Bob. Bob therefore has a total of 2.0 BTC when summing up both channels.

Alice's new balance with this commitment to pay Charlie via Bob would be 0.8 BTC, while Bob's will be at 1.2 BTC with Alice and 0.8 BTC with Charlie, hence his balance overall will remain at 2.0 BTC. Note that in addition to that 0.2 BTC, Alice might have to provide a little extra BTC to pay transaction fees to Bob for his trouble (temporarily locking funds, transfers). Now looking at this commitment, Alice is protected if Bob suddenly disappears, as the timelock allows Alice to recover her fund and try another intermediary to pay Charlie. Additionally, Bob will only be able to get paid from Alice if he knows the secret text (C). Once all commitments are signed and shared between parties, including Alice's commitment to Bob which then allowed Bob to make a commitment to Charlie, the secret text can be exchanged. Since Charlie is assured that he can receive the 0.2

BTC from Bob from Output 3 by using the secret text C that he himself generated, two outcomes are possible.

In the first option, Charlie can broadcast this commitment on the blockchain where the secret text is revealed, demonstrating his intent to close the channel with Bob. Then Bob knows about the secret and can close the channel he has with Alice. Another scenario is where Charlie wants to maintain the channel with Bob (the typical case) in which case Charlie reveals the secret text to Bob so that Bob can either close the channel with Alice or create a new commitment with Alice. In this new commitment, Bob and Charlie (as well as Bob and Alice), only 2 Outputs will be involved while they revoke this prior commitment with 3 Outputs in the same method as we mentioned earlier. That's why I said earlier (temporary) as the need for 3 Outputs adds complexity that is only required temporarily until all the commitments have been set up and the secret text (C) is shared.

So Alice and Bob could create a new commitment, which would exclude Output 3 and consist of only two outputs, with adjusted balances:

Alice: 0.8 BTC

Bob: 1.2 BTC

Equivalently, in the channel between Bob and Charlie, Bob's balance would be at 0.8 BTC while Charlie's balance would increment by 0.2 BTC to 1.2 BTC.

For those readers interest in greater detail regarding balance management and payment routing, I recommend expanding your knowledge base by reading books such as *Mastering the lightning network*,[69] by Andreas M. Antonopoulos. Many criticize the lightning network for being too complicated compared to their favorite altcoin that processes tens of thousands of transactions per second on the blockchain itself. The focus, however, should be on making transactions user-friendly with the proper infrastructure, which is continually responding to market demands. The end user

---

[69]https://github.com/lnbook/lnbook

buying a coffee doesn't care how the lightning network works, just like grandma doesn't care how pistons and electric motors interact and move while she drives her Prius.

One of the primary concerns with LN is its liquidity. For example, if Alice wanted to pay Bob 3.0 BTC, she would have to make the transaction on-chain, as she doesn't have enough in her own balance in their LN channel. This issue also extends to intermediaries. If Bob and Charlie only had 0.1 BTC in their channel, Bob wouldn't be able to pay Charlie 0.2 BTC on behalf of Alice. This is an important limitation to consider, but remember, whenever a problem is identified, engineers and developers work toward finding solutions. Work is already being done to reward people who lend their bitcoin in these channels to add liquidity in return for a yield via a liquidity market.[70]

It is also important to consider how the lightning network might open the door to custodian services. Currently, many bitcoin lightning wallets available as mobile apps act as custodians for their users. This is similar to having a bank or exchange with third-party risk. While running one's own node is the most secure option, it may not be practical for everyone, especially our Prius-driving grandma. In the near term, however, we will likely see the development of infrastructure-as-a-service and new security measures designed to protect wallet users from the risks associated with third-party custodians.

The main take-away, here, is how the lightning network employs bitcoin's basic script functionality to enhance bitcoin's scalability in a way nearly inconceivable in the early years. Further, integrating zero-knowledge proof technology with the lightning network's current framework has the potential to overcome obstacles in self-custodial lightning wallet applications. Adaptations of this magnitude demonstrate that regardless of the current hurdle, developers and entrepreneurs will forge a solution that amazes us all. Of course, time will tell whether these innovative, solution-driven projects will solve emerging bitcoin needs,

[70]https://www.coindesk.com/tech/2020/11/19/lightning-networks-new-liquidity-marketplace-attracts-a-surprising-mix-of-individuals-enterprises/

but remember, few imagined a successful layer 2 integration at bitcoin's inception.

A final point worth noting, the lightning network generates a new stream of income from routing fees. In our example, for his trouble, Bob can charge Alice a fee. And, if there were multiple intermediaries between Alice and Charlie, they too could charge a fee. Although these fees are very small, the sheer volume of transactions can add up. Remember, unlike bitcoin, the lightning network has no restrictions on the number of transactions per second; it is only limited by your connection speed and your computer's power. Also note, even as little as one satoshi can be transferable on LN, enabling a new economy based on micro-payments.

TAPROOT

Much like segwit, Taproot is an example of a bitcoin improvement that appears insignificant, but actually opens the door for more significant and beneficial features in the future. Segwit paved the way for the lightning network. Similarly, Taproot[71] enables the combination of multiple signatures into one, thereby reducing transaction size. Since November 2021, Taproot has been integrated and running as part of bitcoin. Without taproot, bitcoin's protocol necessitates the verification of digital signatures, individually, against their public key. For example, a multisig three of N requires the verification of three digital signatures with their respective public keys to prove they satisfy the original multisig. With Taproot, it is possible to aggregate and verify multiple and complex signatures, such as multisig, as if they were a single signature. To accomplish this, Taproot moved away from the Elliptic Curve Digital Signature Algorithm (ECDSA) and instead employs Schnorr signatures joining two core technologies together, Merklized Abstract Syntax Trees (MAST) and Schnorr signatures.

---

[71] https://cointelegraph.com/bitcoin-for-beginners/a-beginners-guide-to-the-bitcoin-taproot-upgrade

By allowing multiple signatures to be combined as a single one, Schnorr facilitates the inclusion of more transactions in a block. This process also enhances privacy by not disclosing the number of signatures or whether an address is a multisig or regular address. Schnorr avoids using bitcoin script. Unlike bitcoin script, which involves combining individual signatures, Schnorr signatures are linear, making it possible to combine them naturally. In fact, the sum of two or more Schnorr signatures results in another valid Schnorr signature, which is not the case with ECDSA signatures. To be more explicit, the Taproot upgrade was actually composed of three interconnected Bitcoin Improvement Proposal (BIP):

- BIP 340[72] introduces Schnorr signature;

- BIP 341[73] details Taproot, which adds support for Schnorr signature; and

- BIP 342[74] covers the validation of Taproot scripts.

You might wonder why Satoshi Nakamoto used ECDSA, instead of Schnorr signatures. The timing might have a lot to it considering Schnorr signatures were patent-protected until February 2008, almost a year before the release of bitcoin's software. Perhaps Satoshi avoided Schnorr signatures, unsure of his own project's timing. We will never know. But the current developers are not locked up on what Satoshi used, which is excellent. Too many, particularly fans of Bitcoin Cash, consider bitcoin's white paper, his blog posts, and the original bitcoin release as sacred communications. Although I titled my first book, *The Book of Satoshi*, it was merely a reference to the analogy with a savior who liberated us from the evil of central banking.

Taproot's significance lies in its ability to enable the construction of other layer 2 mechanisms, like CoinPool, which are expanding and im-

---

[72] https://github.com/bitcoin/bips/blob/master/bip-0340.mediawiki
[73] https://github.com/bitcoin/bips/blob/master/bip-0341.mediawiki
[74] https://github.com/bitcoin/bips/blob/master/bip-0342.mediawiki

proving on the lightning network. Even with the conservative nature of bitcoin development, the engineers have made remarkable progress improving the network, particularly on layer 2. Development on layer 2 can be faster and more experimental without facing the same issues or challenges that would arise on bitcoin's base layer. Perhaps most importantly, missteps on layer 2 will not impact bitcoin's core security and functionality. Proposed with BIP 114[75] and BIP117,[76] Merklized Abstract Syntax Trees (MAST) improves privacy and reduces data storage. :

MAST combines multiple information in a tree of hash, where only the relevant portion must be revealed without revealing the rest of the information. This means, a single hash can represent a vast amount of information from multiple combined data sets. In the case of taproot, the data set would enable the execution of a transaction. The diagram below illustrates this concept.

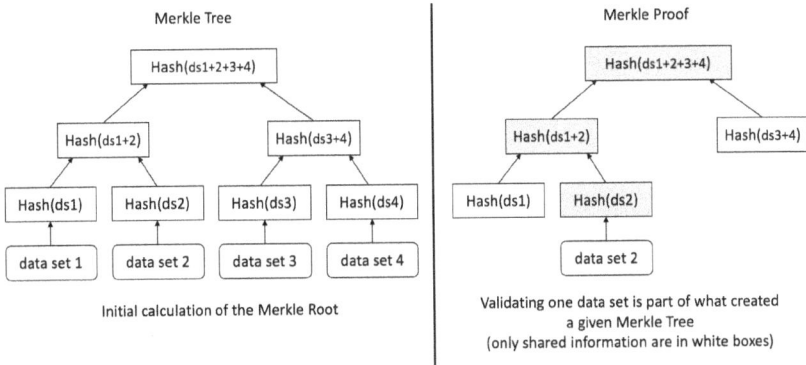

Figure 25: Merkle Tree.

The left side depicts the process for generating a Merkle tree from four different datasets. The top value (Hash(ds1+2+3+4) is what gets to be published. The right side shows the minimum amount of information required to be shared to prove that a particular dataset (data set 2, in this example) is

[75] https://en.bitcoin.it/wiki/BIP_0114
[76] https://en.bitcoin.it/wiki/BIP_0117

part of the Merkle root, while only the hash of the other data set is shared, hence all the other data set remains private information.

Bitcoin uses Merkle trees to reduce the amount of information stored for transactions, specifically for unspent transaction outputs (UTXOs). This does not, however, have any impact on the secrecy since these UTXOs are already visible on the blockchain. Taproot's implementation of MAST is different. MAST is used to organize possible conditions for advanced transaction types or conditional payments in a Merkle tree, allowing the spender to only reveal the specific condition without exposing any others. This saves space and time, while maintaining privacy. By combining Merkle trees and Schnorr signatures, bitcoin can support more complex conditions without increasing bitcoin's block size.

TARO

The introduction of Taproot in 2021 enabled the development of Taro,[77] which can be used to issue assets on the bitcoin blockchain that can be transferred over the lightning network. As we saw earlier, the lightning network allows for instant, high volume transactions, with low transaction fees. By assets, we mean the creation of tokens or NFTs, similar to what Ethereum allows with its smart contract. Critics of bitcoin maximalists might note: "So it's not only Ethereum that will allow shitcoins to be created on its network, but bitcoin will too." It is a bit ironic, indeed, that bitcoin's Layer 2 now allows for tokens, when bitcoin maximalists are so critical of them. These tokens may eventually include "stable coins," meaning coins tied to government fiat currencies. Well, labeling them as stable is a bit of a stretch when the inflation rate might reach 20% or more per year. But, despite high inflation, demand for a US dollar-based stable coin on the lightning network exists in communities worldwide.[78] This preference for a stable coin tied to the U.S. dollar is likely to continue for as long as the dollar remains relevant and the

---

[77] https://lightning.engineering/posts/2022-4-5-taro-launch/
[78] https://bitcoinmagazine.com/technical/community-banks-improve-bitcoin-adoption

dominant global currency. It is worth pondering whether stable coin development on bitcoin would have ever occurred had Etherum and other altcoins never pushed its adoption. To me, the bitcoin community's response highlights that competition of ideas accelerates discoveries. For certain, the absence of regulations in the wild, wild west of cryptocurrency facilitated rapid development and exchange of ideas.

Refocusing on Taro. Taro, an open-source protocol developed by Lightning Labs, is an acronym that stands for Taproot Asset Representation Overlay. With Taro, users can create one or more assets by initiating a single Taproot transaction on the bitcoin blockchain. Indirectly, it will allow bitcoin miners to continue receiving fees as a source of revenue beyond the year 2140. But because of the nature of Taproot, Taro transactions look like any other regular transactions on the blockchain.

You might recall that when using smart contracts on Ethereum or other similar blockchains to create new tokens, a significant amount of storage is required to track associated metadata, such as the number of tokens in circulation, ownership, and ownership transfers. Bitcoin's blockchain is immutable, and only stores Merkle tree roots, not Taro transfers. Instead, participants in Taro transfers are responsible for covering the expenses related to verifying and storing string Taro witness data, which occurs off-chain.

Suffice it to say, the introduction of tokens on bitcoin's decentralized financial ecosystem will be fascinating. Not only does it underscore how bitcoin continues to evolve, but also may push other, less relevant cryptocurrencies to extinction. Time will tell how much of Ethereum's established network effect, particularly in the areas of NFTs and tokens, will be affected by Taro. But, given bitcoin's strong security features, significant market cap, and continued development, it is possible that this new technology could lead to substantial expansion, provided the necessary infrastructure is put in place. Although decentralized trading platforms, like Uniswap, are not yet in the picture, Taro's use of the lightning network gives rapid finality without any quorum issues.

Are you intrigued by Taro? Visit:

https://docs.lightning.engineering/the-lightning-network/taro

COINPOOL

Numerous criticisms have been levied against the lightning network since its inception, particularly regarding its scalability and the difficulty in opening channels with multiple parties and locking funds in each of them. CoinPool offers a promising solution to these issues. Proposed in February 2022, CoinPool allows multiple parties to share a bitcoin unspent transaction output (UTXO), the output section of a transaction. Unlike the lightning network, which only permits two parties to transact and requires an on-chain bitcoin transaction whenever one party wants to withdraw from the channel, any user on CoinPool can withdraw their funds at any time without permission from other users. In addition, CoinPool accounts can interface with the lightning network, thus expanding the existing lightning network infrastructure and enhancing its functionality.

The introduction of CoinPool[79] allows multiple users to have partial ownership over a single UTXO, boosting bitcoin's scalability. This capability allows for instantaneous layer-2 off-chain transfers of partial ownership, which in turn allows for faster and more efficient transactions without requiring any on-chain transactions when updates occur in the CoinPool ownership distribution. Unlike the lightning network, where only two parties are involved, and any changes in the parties requires closing the existing channel and creating a new one, CoinPool can accommodate multiple parties, and no on-chain transactions are necessary when one or more members of the pool decide to leave and wants to transfers their ownership of bitcoin in the CoinPool to a new member.

Successful implementation of CoinPool depends on the introduction of a new bitcoin soft fork, similar to what occurred with SegWit and Taproot. Like the lightning network, which required bitcoin support for SegWit be-

---

[79]https://lists.linuxfoundation.org/pipermail/bitcoin-dev/2022-February/019968.html

fore it could be utilized, CoinPool will necessitate bitcoin's integration of three modifications: SIGHASH_GROUP, SIGHASH_ANYPREVOUT, and OP_MERKLESUB. This process, however, could take some time, as bitcoin's conservative development requires debates, discussions, proposals, reviews, and testing before any updates are implemented. But because major benefits were accrued with Taproot and SegWit, if developers do not see any issues, these new opcodes will likely be introduced.

It is premature to delve into the technical aspect of CoinPool as we did with LN, as changes will likely be made throughout the process, assuming it is adopted at all. As proposed, implementation of CoinPool is not scalable beyond a pool of more than 20 participants, though developers are working to increase this number. If you are interested in learning more about CoinPool, read the latest white paper.[80]

I find it amazing that the mechanics behind CoinPool, along with the introduction of new opcodes to support it, have the potential to pave the way for a sidechain. Currently, the bitcoin Liquid network operates with some form of Proof of Authority to represent tokens on the side chain that are tied to frozen bitcoin on bitcoin's blockchain. We will cover this in greater detail in the next chapter, but CoinPool's techniques could potentially be leveraged to facilitate movement between sidechains and bitcoin blockchain without relying on any third party.

DRIVECHAIN

Another recently released project is Drivechain. This project allows any other blockchain to function as a bitcoin sidechain. Chaindrive developers describe it as the "altcoin killer." This innovative project obviates the need for altcoins to pave the way in experimental consensus mechanisms and other technological breakthroughs. At this point, however, Drivechain's future is very uncertain. Current discussions reveal that additional opcodes are required for its support, and it seems unlikely that

---

[80]https://coinpool.dev/v0.1.pdf

such opcodes will be accepted and integrated. Despite this impediment, if a platform such as CoinPool becomes available, it could facilitate compatibility with Drivechain. Even if the project never comes to fruition, it stands as an example of progress in the bitcoin ecosystem.[81]

TAKE AWAY

Bitcoin's layer 2 is here to stay and will only improve with time. CoinPool is just one example of proposed improvements or alternatives to the lightning network. Many other white papers proposing new methods and techniques, nearly all requiring soft fork for bitcoin wait in the wings for their opportunity to improve the functionality.

It's simply a matter of time before we see sidechains, running new blockchains using Proof of Stake or other consensus mechanisms, underpinned by bitcoin's stalwart currency protocol. As the lightning network continues to mature and CoinPool is eventually integrated, the enhancements to layer 2 will make it increasingly challenging for bitcoin critics to highlight its sluggishness and transaction limitations. Further, transactional privacy concerns, attributed to the blockchain recording every activity, will decrease significantly. And, as time progresses, additional infrastructure, companies, and services will emerge around these features, making them more user-friendly. The halcyon days of a new altcoin being launched every month, will soon be over. As the entire crypto space continues to evolve and the infrastructure surrounding bitcoin becomes more vital, the relevance of altcoins will diminish. Some altcoins may still emerge in the future, but I am convinced that the majority of activities will consolidate around offering sophisticated, new services that leverage bitcoin as the currency of choice. A few blockchains may continue to operate alongside bitcoin, with their respective currencies, but their significance will likely decline over the long term. In a free market environment, people will gravitate towards a major currency for practicality purposes, and

---

[81] If you are interested in reading more about Drivechain, check out the project's website at https://www.drivechain.info

if smart contracts and other capabilities provided by altcoins are available using a sidechain or blockchain that uses bitcoin as the currency, these alternative cryptocurrencies will gradually disappear. Apart from speculators and short-term traders, there is little incentive to store your wealth in an alternative blockchain with its own currency, unless you truly believe it could rise in value against bitcoin, or at least maintain its value against it.

The key takeaway from this chapter is how significant enhancements to fundamental operations can be achieved using the basic operations accessible in bitcoin's contract. As noted earlier, during the early years of bitcoin, innovations like the lightning network were merely far-fetched ideas. The reoccuring lesson is to recognize that countless astonishing improvements are just around the corner. In my opinion, existing problems and critics' complaints about bitcoin will vanish one by one.

7

PROOF OF AUTHORITY: XRP, BITCOIN LIQUID

There has always been this great philosophical battle between those in favor of Proof of Stake and those in favor of Proof of Work, the consensus mechanism of bitcoin. On one hand, Proof of Stake promoters claim that Proof of Work wastes energy (a topic covered in a preceding chapter). On the other hand, we have PoW adherents who believe that PoS is, among other things, complex and probably prone to numerous problems not yet observed. But in addition to all this, we have those in favor of Byzantine-Fault Tolerant (BFT) type of consensus that can reach firm confirmation rapidly, although many bitcoiners believe it is at the cost of decentralization. But those two groups generally agree on one thing: Proof of Authority (PoA) is very weak when it comes to decentralization, if it even has any.

In this chapter, we will go over the two main PoA blockchain networks. First, XRP, a cryptocurrency created in 2012, which has maintained its status in the top 10 in market capitalization and importance since then. We covered some background history on XRP in Chapter 2. The other is the Liquid Network, which is a sidechain of bitcoin, meaning it uses a currency (L-BTC) that is pegged to bitcoin and can be exchanged for it one to one.

CONSENSUS ACHIEVED IN OTHER WAYS

Conceptually, proof-of-authority is a network of nodes where a few nodes are granted the right to become the validators of transactions, their ordering, and acceptance. Having these relatively fixed settings determining which nodes have authority removes any burden from the protocol to establish which nodes have the rights to create blocks (or whatever concept they use to prevent double spending) and to maintain a ledger keeping the balance of who owns how many units. The immediate benefit of removing this burden allows for an amazing scalability of transaction throughput. With dedicated hardware interacting through high internet bandwidth, the sky's the limit in terms of transactions per second. Given this remarkable advantage, you might wonder why it isn't PoA the most popular consensus method, and what could possibly be the controversy? We will discuss this controversy, but first let's delve into the details of XRP and then the Liquid Network. Other cryptocurrency networks also use proof-of-authority, alternatively called "permissioned" as opposed to bitcoin's permissionless network. Hedera Hashgraph is one example, although it is currently looking at moving to Proof of Stake[82].

---

[82]https://hedera.com/hh-decentralization-of-consensus.pdf

XRP

Rather than bitcoin nodes and bitcoin miners, where anyone can automatically participate by simply joining the network at any time, XRP validators must be included in the Unique Node List (UNL) of other XRP validators to participate in the network.[83] Compared to the number of bitcoin nodes and miners, XRP has far fewer validators. A small computer with little bandwidth can run a bitcoin node and can participate in the validation of blocks and transactions by either forwarding them to other nodes or rejecting them. Although any XRP validators can create their own list of other validators, most simply copy the list that the Ripple Labs company uses and provides. In addition, Ripple Labs owns a patent and the proprietary software called RippleNet that gives XRP its utility, which is used to facilitate international transfer payment by banks. Ripple Labs, therefore, will always remain the dominant voice regarding the validators and the direction of the XRP protocol since it controls an important economic incentive via this patent and its software. Even if a good portion of XRP holders were dissatisfied with some behavior from Ripple, forking the network will not give them any edge. This new forked blockchain would not acquire the utility embedded with RippleNet, the existing XRP network dictated by Ripple, which maintains the core value through its patent. In other words, its value is certainly not sufficiently decentralized.

The documentation on xrpl.org,[84] identifies XRP's consensus as the XRP Ledger Consensus Protocol, boasting claims that rival bitcoin and other PoW and PoS networks. Claims include that everyone who uses the XRP ledger can agree on the latest state regarding transaction ordering, and that all valid transactions are processed without having need of a central operator or having the risk of a single point of failure. Ironically, this same consensus would be used by the 12 banks of the Federal Reserve to run a "Fed coin," and we will see why.

---

[83]https://xrpl.org/run-rippled-as-a-validator.html
[84]https://xrpl.org/intro-to-consensus.html

At its foundation, all node operators on XRP's network must create a Unique Node List (UNL), where they identify other nodes they trust, and will, therefore, connect to. You might wonder, how do those node operators figure out which nodes to put in their respective UNL? This is where the distinction with bitcoin begins.

With bitcoin, all miners run the same software which will almost randomly connect with any other nodes on the network. Bitcoin clients use various methods to discover and connect to other clients. When a bitcoin client starts, it uses the list it built during the last time it was running. When a node launches the bitcoin software for the first time, it will query a DNS seed. Several domain names are maintained to resolve a list of IP addresses of well-known and established running nodes. A last fallback is a list of IP addresses encoded in the software that are set at the time to point at stable nodes. One method previously used but has since been abandoned, was having bitcoin clients discover each other using IRC (Internet Relay Chat) servers in a similar way to BitTorrent tracker. Once connected to the network, the client receives a list of other IP addresses and ports of other clients. Any bitcoin client can have an arbitrary number of other connections, which is configurable. In essence, who your client connects to is completely arbitrary, but the more connections made the better. Bitcoin node operators do not care to whom they connect, as long as these connections are as varied as possible. A node operator would not want to only connect to three other peers who actually might be bad actors, hence the need for numerous and various connections. This principle is at the core of decentralization — having no requirements about who can join, as long as they follow the protocol. On the other hand, a centralized system means a single point of attack by a government or a cartel, and for this, it need only be easily identifiable and fixed in location so as to allow for the inevitable "knock on the door."

Contrast this to XRP, where such a list of other nodes/validators is entirely configured. XRP's website notes:

The core principle behind XRP Ledger's consensus mechanism is that a little trust goes a long way. Each participant in the network chooses a set of validators, servers specifically configured to participate actively in consensus, run by different parties who are expected to behave honestly most of the time. ... As long as few than 20% of trusted validators are faulty, consensus can continue unimpeded; and confirming an invalid transaction would require over 80% of trusted validators to collude.

Depending on the network protocol, these validators work together, via round-robin or another method, to establish who is the next validator to coordinate the ordering of transactions. A block's status as being accepted is based on the validity of its content and whether the UNL-listed validator has signed it. Some might say it resembles a multicore processor database where each of the cores are located in different parts of the world rather than on the same CPU. With powerful computers and differing bandwidth, and an established pecking order for which node has the authority at any given time, it's no wonder that this network can generate multiple transactions per second.

This sounds so amazing... you would wonder why Satoshi didn't think of this! Jokes aside, let's go over more detail about the UNL and see how it differs from bitcoin. You will recall that, for bitcoin, the longest chain wins regardless of the identity of the node relaying the information or the node that created the block. And for blocks to be accepted, the nodes sending the blocks must validate and approve all transactions contained therein based on the information from the longest chain they are aware of. At its core, bitcoin's protocol is just as simple as XRP's. The main distinction between the two being the heavy consumption of hash power providing security to the bitcoin network while for XRP, security originates from trusting that 80% of the nodes you are connecting to are not colluding. Considering 80% is a large number, it actually does sound like a solid methodology indeed, yet also still diametrically opposed to the ingrained bitcoin ethos and practice which states, "Don't trust, verify." Bitcoin is designed to eliminate the need for any and all trust.

Conversely, the xrpl.org FAQ[85] explains that each server operator can choose their own UNL, but usually they are based on a default set provided by a trusted publisher. The main trusted publishers are the company Ripple Labs, the XRP Ledger Foundation, and recently Coil, (an online marketplace for creators and publishers to share and use content and, including NFTs running on XRP). But here is where things get amusing. With bitcoin, nodes themselves – which might not be mining – share the most recent block among themselves using a very defined methodology to establish consensus: the longest chain and, of course, all contain blocks with valid transactions in each block. The longest chain in PoW defines the absolute truth, no matter which miner created it or wherever it comes from in the worldwide network. This means that even in the advent of a bitcoin fork, a node connected with 200 other nodes will switch to the longest chain even if 198 of the other nodes stays on the shortest chain. As you remember, bitcoin forks happen sometimes when two miners find the next block at about the same time, but they will consolidate once one of the two chains gets an additional block, making it the longest.

If 40 of my friends and I decided to each start running an XRP node and connect with each other while only one of us has a connection to one of Ripple's nodes, our network will deviate from their network, creating and maintaining a fork of the blockchain since Ripple's node alone is just 2.5% of all validators in our network — well below the 20% threshold — allowing our network to stay active. In fact, this notion is well understood by XRP folks. Ripple's Consensus Protections[86] describes the overlap requirements for the selection of validators in the UNL:

For all participants in the XRP Ledger to agree on what they consider validated, they must start by choosing a set of trusted validators that are fairly similar to the sets chosen by every-

[85]https://xrpl.org/faq.html
[86]https://xrpl.org/consensus-protections.html

one else. In the worst case, less than about 90% overlap could cause some participants to diverge from each other. For that reason, Ripple publishes a signed list of recommended validators, including trustworthy and well-maintained servers run by the company, industry and community.

In other words, if you want to avoid any possibility of running a parallel network diverging from the current XRP consensus, you must have at least 90% of your UNL validators matching the list provided by Ripple. What's interesting is this 90% figure is well above the 80% of validators agreeing on the consensus, meaning Ripple has the power to make sure any kind of consensus remains in line with the company's expectations.

You remember my original point about how I perceive decentralization as a shade of gray; in this case, XRP sits acutely on the weaker side of this scale. Some would call it not decentralized at all considering the powerful position the company Ripple has, not to mention an enormous number of XRP held "in escrow" (approximately 50% of the supply). Ripple's CEO maintains that the XRP held by Ripple does not really matter because they are held in escrow. To be specific, the escrow[87] is on the blockchain using a timelock feature: Once the coins are unlocked, they most often return them back into the timelock. Regardless, Ripple remains in control of that XRP's future release.

Back to the validators, at the time of this writing, XRPscan[88] shows 135 validators, with at least four owned by Ripple Labs. Perhaps other organizations are running more than one node, as well. Applying the 80% quorum to validators means that so long as no more than 27 validators are acting maliciously or behaving inappropriately, the network will run fine. Of course, I am assuming the developers at Ripple will adjust the network state to remove from consideration any troublesome or nefarious nodes, considering that they dictate 90% of the UNL list content.

---

[87] https://ripple.com/insights/explanation-ripples-xrp-escrow/
[88] https://xrpscan.com/validators

Let's revisit the previous discussions about potential threats to consensus, such as network-based transaction censorship. The scenario we discussed involved all node operators being required to select 90% of their validators from a list provided by Ripple, the XRP foundation, and Coil. This exceeds the 80% quorum of validators required for consensus, leaving the remaining 10% of node operators powerless to prevent transaction censorship. Regardless of the cryptocurrency, transaction censorship could be the first form of attack that an opposing government would try to implement, as censorship does not require changing the existing blockchain, but rather just preventing certain new ones from being included. In such a case, perhaps the government decides to prohibit you from spending your cryptocurrency from your cold wallet because the government wants to penalize you for donating to a group that demonstrated their disagreement with said government — even if the demonstration was lawful and peaceful. Considering this UNL list is managed by Ripple, a company residing in the United States, it would be quite easy for the U.S. government, or perhaps some banking cartel, to force or bribe Ripple to only include nodes willing to participate in such censorship. And we haven't covered the case of forced transfer where your coins are moved to your respective government, but it would be just as easy.

We mentioned Ripple's patents earlier[89]... an important one is *U.S. Patent #10,902,416, "Network Computing System Implementing On-Demand Liquidity for Cross-Medium Transaction Services."*[90] This on-demand liquidity (which Ripple refers to as ODL), enables partnering banks and financial service providers to transfer funds cheaply and rapidly across the world. Part of the patent covers how the system can guarantee an exchange rate when different currencies are involved, but it can also transfer anything of value beyond just currencies. The prospect of enabling central banks to move away from the outdated SWIFT system excites many XRP holders. The company has expressed its readiness to collaborate with central banks in promoting the development of

---

[89] https://patents.justia.com/assignee/ripple-labs-inc
[90] https://patentimages.storage.googleapis.com/b4/77/51/2eea0acf0f4a68/US10902416.pdf

central bank digital currencies (CBDC). They believe their ODL system can efficiently facilitate payments across various currencies and are willing to work towards that goal. Although many see the convenience CBDCs could bring, the reality is they will drastically increase central banks' power to control or censor citizens' transactions. The bank and government could track everyday purchases, know which wallets hold how much currency at all times, and remove the basic privacy provided by cash payments, perhaps under the guise of attempting to curtail black market activity. CBDCs have been termed by many as "programmable currency," where your funds could be seized or frozen, say, if you contributed to the Canadian truckers' Freedom convoy or anything the government does not like. The draconian and already-in-use Chinese social credit scoring system, targeted now to curbing offenders' access to luxury goods or leaving the country, could easily be turned towards their centrally-controlled electronic finances. A system meant to enable these CBDCs is horrible, and bitcoin is the anti-CBDC. Bitcoin was made to frontrun and to compete against a government-issued digital currency panopticon, not to assist it.

We do not want to help and support the current central banking system. We should seek to eliminate and replace it with a fully decentralized currency that cannot be inflated, whose transactions cannot be censored, thus making the currency fully fungible. From an investment perspective, I understand that one might be interested in investing in XRP with an exit strategy of selling it at the next frenzy, possibly coming up from a deal with some central bank using it as a SWIFT replacement. What is strange to me is that some XRP holders are big fans of gold, yet they hate bitcoin.

To recap, Ripple:

- has authority over which nodes constitute 90% of the UNL list that XRP node operators must use, while only 80% of the nodes must agree;

- still owns approximately 50% of XRP in existence, owns many XRP related patents, including one related to ODL, providing significant economic advantage if the service becomes widely used by financial institutions and central banks.

So from a sound money perspective, and certainly from a "store of value meant to get rid of central banking" perspective, I would stay away from it. Anyone who invested some portion of their wealth in gold did so knowing that in 10 or 20 years, its atomic properties will be unchanged. The only things that could destabilize the price of gold are far out possibilities, such as a "Star Trek" replicator-style device, or cheap mining extraction from asteroids, the moon or Mars. Sure, any of these could happen, but is very unlikely that they do so within the next 20 years. With every year that passes, bitcoin rapidly gains the "store of value" status that gold held for thousands of years. In addition, within very recent years, bitcoin has gained more stability and over time, it will gain gold's perceived "intrinsic value" while keeping its core abilities. In fact, today bitcoin is only improving, thanks to new OPcodes, improvement proposals, and Layer 2 networks developing around it.

XRP, on the other hand, derives a large portion of its value from Ripple Labs, the company. Let's say Ripple dissolved and another organization would show up and start using and promoting XRP, then yes XRP would continue. But given that Ripple's ownership of XRP was obtained through pre-mining, it is more probable that other companies may choose to follow a similar business model by creating their own blockchain and engaging in pre-mining. Unless they were to obtain Ripple's XRP, it seems more likely that other companies would decide to pursue this approach while XRP the currency vanishes with Ripple.

In the end, from the perspective of providing security against attack or censorship from third party interference, whether governmental or cartel, XRP is not really decentralized. A reminder that decentralization should not be confused with high availability, which is a property that is sought after by organizations offering digital services through redundancy. If all of Ripple's nodes went down, the XRP network would still be running as long as 80% of all the other nodes are still running. But when it comes to influence on the direction of the network, anyone claiming XRP is decentralized is not being honest with themselves.

LIQUID BITCOIN NETWORK (L-BTC)

Liquid network is a bitcoin sidechain that also uses a form of proof-of-authority. According to the Liquid Network whitepaper, the currency used on bitcoin Liquid is a derivative of bitcoin called LBTC, which is pegged to bitcoin at a 1-to-1 ratio. This means that LBTC is a representation of bitcoin on the sidechain, as bitcoin Liquid operates as a side chain of the bitcoin blockchain. Specifically, the white paper states:

> As a sidechain, Liquid supports transfers of bitcoins into and out of the system by means of a cryptographic peg. Bitcoin pegged into Liquid is referred to as Liquid bitcoin or LBTC. The forward progress of the Liquid ledger and custody of the underlying bitcoin are controlled by a federation, and remain secure as long as over 2/3 of its members are honest.[91]

So just as Ethereum's latest move to PoS, the liquid network requires a 67% quorum. In fact, Liquid's white paper clarifies:

> If one-third or more of the functionaries are no longer operating, blocks will no longer be signed and the Liquid blockchain will be frozen until at least two-thirds of the functionaries come back online. Once a quorum of functionaries are communicating, block creation will resume.

As a federation, just like XRP, a select group runs the consensus on the latest state of the blockchain. And just like XRP, because it is a consortium of select nodes, this system avoids the typical PoS overhead or the energy and block delay issues associated with PoW. Of course, these

---

[91] https://blockstream.com/assets/downloads/pdf/liquid-whitepaper.pdf

benefits come at the cost of a no-longer-permissionless network, which is actually leaning quite a lot more towards becoming a centralized network. Sort of a distributed system operating a database, that's what PoA is in short. For this to work and be capable of high throughput, the number of those functionaries (Liquid Network) or nodes (XRP), cannot be in the thousands.

Liquid employs LBTC as its currency, which is tied to bitcoin by a federation that is the guardian of the original bitcoin (from the bitcoin blockchain) while creating an LBTC on the Liquid blockchain to represent it. The transfer of BTC to LBTC is known as peg-in. Conversely, if someone wishes to convert LBTC back to BTC, in a process called peg-out, they would initiate a specific transaction that designates a bitcoin address, and Liquid node operators, also known as watchmen, will unlock a portion of the original bitcoins and send them to that specified address.

Figure 26 illustrates this operation. The peg-in operations consist of two transactions that are illustrated in the figure by step 1 and 2. In step 1, a person transfers ownership of BTC to addr2 which is an address controlled by the Liquid federation. This in turn makes the liquid network operators create a brand new LBTC and transfer it to an LBTC address controlled by the original person who sent the BTC to addr2. Once on the liquid network, LBTC can be transferred to other users, in a similar way to any other blockchains. At some point, an owner might decide to move LBTC back to the bitcoin network, the peg-out. The peg-out also encompasses two transactions. In the first transaction, the user sends LBTC to an address managed by the federation on the Liquid Network, as demonstrated in step 3, which leads to the destruction of LBTC. This transaction also specifies a bitcoin address (addr3) to which the corresponding BTC, held in custody by the federation to represent the pegged LBTC, will be sent. Upon reception, the node operators responsible for the custody of the bitcoin create a bitcoin transaction sending the BTC to addr3.

The BTC that backs the LBTC on the Liquid Network are stored in an 11-of-15 multisig address, meaning 15 members of the Federation collaborated to create this multisig address with their own private keys, and

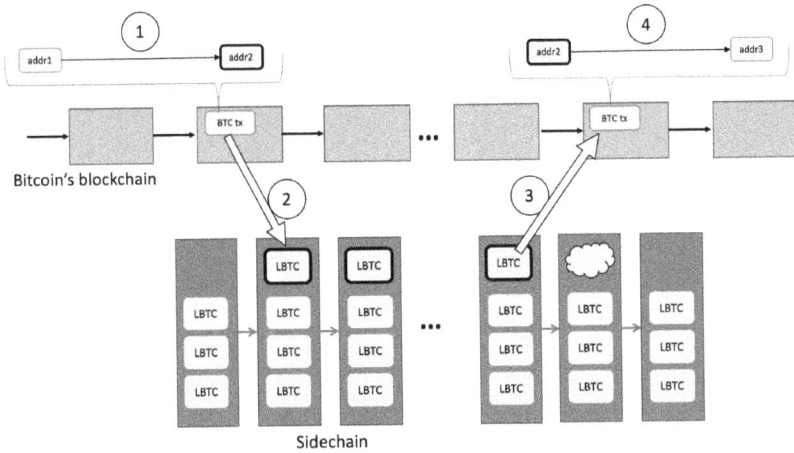

Figure 26: Sidechain with 1-to-1 peg.

11 of them are required to sign a peg-out. Any organization can apply to become members of this federation, but they must go through an approval process. It is not permissionless like bitcoin is, rather it is based on proof-of-authority (PoA). Note that you will rarely see, if ever, a blockchain utilizing PoA openly acknowledge its use.

> Regardless of how distributed the members/nodes are across the countries and continents, proof-of-authority consensus relies on a group of humans, an authoritative entity of sorts, to determine whether you may join and participate in the consensus mechanism.

In the introduction of the liquid white paper, the authors mention the three options available to support a peg. One is similar to Drivechain (discussed earlier), in which many are afraid of a possible angle of attack of the sidechain by well-funded miners. The second is the use of ZK-STARK that would definitely increase the decentralization aspect. But both options require significant changes to the existing bitcoin protocol, requiring soft forks, and so have yet to occur. For ZK-STARK, however, the chances are good it might be adopted and integrated. The last one, the one chosen by the Liquid Network developers due to its rapid implementation speed, is the creation of a federation, effectively using PoA. It is definitely a compromise which many do not like, but because they are using a peg of bitcoin, they are not getting the same rage from "bitcoin maximalists" as XRP and others do.

You might wonder what the Liquid Network's purpose is other than perhaps having the ability to support a higher number of transactions. Indeed, it can support more transactions - only one-minute elapses between each block, with final settlement within two minutes. There are other functionalities of interest as well, including supporting other assets by creating tokens such as those in Ethereum.

One of the significant advantages of using the Liquid network is the confidentiality it provides in transactions, well at least when it regards to the general public as they are not private but rather known by the functionaries, and by extension possibly the government. See the questions asked to the Blockstream team later in this chapter. The amount and asset type involved in a transaction are hidden by default, and only the involved parties and the foundation know about them. A full confidentiality would be very desirable, of course. This feature is particularly noteworthy in light of the increasing importance of privacy, as demonstrated by the arrest of a Tornado Cash smart contract developer. Tornado Cash operates on Ethereum and was utilized to enhance privacy by allowing the mixing of ETH.[92] Because these smart contracts allowed for a decentralized way of anonymizing your crypto transactions by mixing them with others, the authorities were not pleased. Tornado Cash was officially sanctioned by the U.S. Treasury Department admonishing anyone who would use it would be in violation of U.S. laws. But the arrest of a 29-year-old developer in Amsterdam for helping to create the open-source code, not for using it personally, is a step too far. We wonder if this might be the reason why Satoshi Nakamoto was afraid it could happen to him and, therefore, decided to remain anonymous. Technology has always been used by crooks,

---

[92] https://www.coindesk.com/layer2/2022/08/12/an-alleged-tornado-cash-developer-was-arrested-are-you-next/

and so are guns. This endless argument that the misuse of something by criminals justifies authorities banning its use by everyone else, except the government, is a long-standing issue, dating back to the era of prohibition, if not earlier.

But considering the Liquid Network is not permissionless, you wonder if eventually the authorities will knock on the door of all registered members of this federation to either remove the transaction privacy, or apply pressure behind the scenes to help identify the users involved. Regardless of its drawbacks, this bitcoin sidechain opens the door for more experiments. I hope, however, that in the near future, a decentralized peg and sidechain will become operational through the introduction of new opcodes in a potential soft fork. If LBTC was a coin and a blockchain in itself, with 3,567 BTC currently pegged and with BTC priced at about $21,000 (as of this writing in January 2023), it would be an equivalent market cap of $74.8 million and would be ranked at #280 in market cap on coinmarketcap.com. Measured this way, it indicates the importance of the network is not significant yet, although the number of pegged BTC rose more in 2020.

I have asked the Blockstream team, the team responsible behind the creation of the Liquid Network, a set of questions. They gave me permission to publish their answers.

Q.1) How would you compare the Liquid Network set of features and type of users to that of Ethereum? I've heard many exchanges use LN in certain conditions, if so, what are these cases?

> **Liquid is built to prioritize security, reliability and a sound foundation. It uses confidential transactions by default and uses bitcoin as its native token rather than an equity-like native share token. That means there is no privileged class of early adopters seeking to extract value for holders of the native token. Liquid also inherits from bitcoin's battle-tested consensus logic, meaning Liquid security benefits directly from the scrutiny on bitcoin itself. Liquid supports greater user pri-**

vacy through confidential transactions and encourages safer and more predictable smart contract development than other networks.

Q.2) I see that since 2020, the number of L-BTC has increased, meaning more bitcoin have been pegged to the network.How do you see adoption going forward?

> **Liquid adoption will continue to grow steadily both in terms of the size of the L-BTC economy and the breadth and diversity of assets that participate in it.**

Q.3) In a move to make it permissionless, have you considered moving your consensus to Proof of Stake, where the LBTC are staked? Of course, the only gain for stakers comes from the transaction fees since no new LBTC could be created if the peg to BTC is to remain.

> **Security on Liquid is provided by the federation model and does not require staking to provide consensus and finality. We view the federation model as having better trade-offs than Proof of Stake and hence have no plans to transition the network to Proof of Stake. There are lending products on Liquid for users seeking to earn L-BTC denominated yield.**

Q.4) If a future bitcoin soft fork introduces an opcode allowing for easy pegging of BTC to another sidechain like yours, would you switch from your current custodian holding of BTC to using this new pegging ability?

> **We will continue to evaluate any new emerging technology to see whether the trade-offs it enables would be valuable for Liquid.**

Q.5) Have you received any kind of pressure from any government in regards to the confidential transactions?[93]

---

[93] https://docs.blockstream.com/liquid/technical_overview.html#confidential-transactions

We'd prefer not to comment on communication with governments. Confidential transactions are a benefit for users to
minimize front-running and public disclosure of an entity's
financial positions. They've been designed with auditability
in mind.

Q.6) The liquid federation has currently more than 60 members. These
members decide who can join. Do they have equal votes and do they have
to vote unanimously to accept a new member?

Any company may apply to become a Federation member, a
decision discussed and voted on by the Membership Board.
Adding a new member requires a minimum of 3-of-5 to vote
in favor of adding the new member to the Federation. When it
comes to the criteria for approving a new company to become
a member, there are guidelines that the Membership Board
checks.

For new membership, the applicant is assessed by the following guidelines:

1. A clear objective to join the Liquid Network with
   a demonstrable use case and plan to be an active
   participant

2. Applicant agrees to the principles set forth in the Liquid
   Federation Member Charter

3. Technically capable of supporting the Liquid Network

4. Does not diminish the reputation of the Liquid Network

5. Operating a legal entity in a jurisdiction other than a Restricted Jurisdiction

6. Provides a copy of company registration or business license

The easiest way to apply to become a Federation member is to send an email to business@liquid.net and introduce your company and explain what you are working on.

As a member, enterprises gain the ability to peg-out of L-BTC back to BTC through the inclusion of a Peg-Out Authorization Key (PAK), run for election to become a member of one or more of the Liquid Federation boards, and gain access to internal resources, communications, and participate in discussions on future network upgrades.

Q.7) You have a requirement of a quorum of 67% of the functionaries, same quorum as Ethereum and other PoS blockchains. How many functionaries in total are there in the network currently?

There are 15 functionaries operating the Liquid network.

8

CLOSING REMARKS

Over the course of this book, I'm hoping you have come to understand the importance of decentralization and that the network effect is above everything else to keep as it is and therefore help to maintain bitcoin's value. A coin with bells and whistles and high transaction speed that works great but lacks decentralization should be considered a high-risk investment. Centralization opens the door for cabals to gradually and covertly take control of a system by altering its blockchain, enabling them to impede transactions, manipulate the supply, or engage in illicit activities on coins they do not even possess by altering the blockchain ledger.

> A cryptocurrency's ability to be resilient against manipulation is as strong as its consensus mechanism and its network effect.

Does that sound like a bitcoin maximalist talking? Perhaps, although I don't identify myself as such. I have traded altcoins before and invested in some. I do recognize their experimental value, but from the perspective of a currency that could potentially become the most-used one worldwide, I cannot imagine many of them stepping into this role except for bitcoin. I anticipate that bitcoin will evolve into a dominant global currency, while a few other coins will persist for their unique utilities, a credit to their pre-existing infrastructure and investment that confines these altcoin survivors to niche markets. We probably won't ever see a frenzy of new coins launching every week again like we did in 2017, but new coins might still be released, just at a much slower pace. At least it seems copycats like dogecoin, litecoin and others are quite rare nowadays and likely to remain so, or hopefully disappear in the future. The only value the majority of these types of blockchains brought to the table was for speculation and trading – and to some minor degree before the advent of the lightning network – reducing the transaction load on bitcoin's blockchain.

The entrance of NFTs on the crypto scene has shifted the focus of those folks looking to make a quick buck by becoming early investors and perhaps running pump-and-dump schemes. Granted, not all NFTs have been this way, and I certainly cannot talk much about this considering I know very little about the field of digital art collectors, as I personally have no affinity for digital art or collectibles. Nevertheless, the cryptocurrency space has opened up new developments and opportunities beyond the walls of regulation, allowing a free market to evolve. As we have seen for many past decades, people make bad investments no matter how many thousands of regulations the government puts into place. In nearly all cases, these regulations have favored certain players in a specific industry or investment sector, more so than protecting the public.

With the emergence of this new financial landscape, where the SEC declined to take action at the time of Ethereum's ICO – whether intentional or not is speculative – allowed this wild west frenzy that attracted not only people with good intentions with sometimes wrong beliefs, but also scammers and deceitful people. Some simply dreamt of being the next Satoshi with a better coin. Most bitcoiners are in favor of a free market and accept – although reluctantly knowing bad projects lead to the financial demise of so many – this competition. I'm surprised to see others hoping for the SEC action against the altcoins, knowing very well the SEC couldn't go after bitcoin, given its dominance and the fact there is nobody to sue. Even if Satoshi Nakamoto were still around, could the SEC really sue him simply for distributing software source code for free and shortly later for donating 1 bitcoin to Hal Finney?

A similar regulatory battle took place in 1976 when the Arms Export Control Act (AECA)[94] made it illegal to import and export defense articles and services, which included cryptographic programs, without a presidentially issued license. For the government, making cryptography part of arms export control was just a continuation of their effort during World War II when they actively worked on deciphering the Axis powers' encoded messages. With today's computing power, any resourceful organization could create new encryption technology that would be nearly unbreakable. The Allies were successful because of the weak computing power available to the Axis at the time. The movie *The Imitation Game*[95] depicts the work of a group of UK cryptanalysts to decipher German strategic messages encoded with the help of the Enigma machine. Although a sophisticated encoding machine for the time, looking like an odd sort of typewriter, the UK team demonstrated that cracking the Enigma code was possible with the use of their own electro-mechanical device called the Bombe.[96] Similar to cracking a short password for our modern computers; considering the Nazi government was sending a weather report every morning that started with the same text, it was just a matter of brute force to crack the password. As for the AECA of 1976, the regulatory battle on cryptographic programs ended in the 1990s after a criminal case against Phil Zimmerman, including a three-year investigation, was dropped with-

---

[94]https://en.wikipedia.org/wiki/Export_of_cryptography_from_the_United_States
[95]https://en.wikipedia.org/wiki/The_Imitation_Game
[96]https://en.wikipedia.org/wiki/Bombe#:: text=The%20bombe%20(UK%3A%20%2Fb, messages%20during%20World%20War%20II.

out filing charges. We can draw parallels between the SEC and the AECA; both entities are attempting to adapt outdated regulatory frameworks to a changing environment, while also seeking to demonstrate their importance and justify their continued existence.

So far, we have covered how the network effect is so important and how very few altcoins will maintain their value... Perhaps some will do so against the dollar but certainly not many against bitcoin. With few exceptions, like ether – although its value against BTC has never surpassed its 2017 high – altcoins, thus far all end up losing valuation against BTC, if not vanishing entirely.

I am still astonished by the number of XRP enthusiasts who wish for the demise of the Federal Reserve and invest in gold, and yet, still have the expectation that XRP will improve the current fiat system by replacing the outdated SWIFT system. Their idea is if you can't fight the banking cartel, one might as well make money investing in a coin that might benefit the cartel, even if this "bank coin" is trying to steal the limelight from bitcoin. XRP attracts a unique set of people who elevate the original issues with bitcoin - like high energy consumption and slow transactions - and overlook its potential. Bitcoin has the potential to play a role similar to gold in the 1800s under the gold standard. But, unlike gold, bitcoin doesn't need a derivative to represent it in everyday transactions, such as banknotes or electronic forms.

When I talk to people who have only heard of but never invested in bitcoin (or any other cryptocurrency), they are naturally unaware of this ongoing debate about "Bitcoin vs Altcoins." Granted, many current investors prioritize speculating in any coin that they believe has the potential to rapidly increase in value, without considering its long-term potential. To these investors, purchasing bitcoin and other cryptocurrencies is akin to investing in commodities; it is a means to enter and eventually exit with the objective of amassing more fiat currencies, such as US dollars. (Yet as the meme goes, "You invest in bitcoin to have more dollars; I invest in bitcoin to have less dollars. We are not the same.")

Since the Nixon shock in August 1972, we have been living in a fiat paper world, and the banking cartel has successfully convinced the majority of the population that the current dollar system is superior, especially homeowners who purchased their homes with a mortgage. Most homeowners believe that their mortgage decreased in value over this last decade, because their pay has increased. In other words, rather than holding the perspective that their mortgage has *decreased* in value, home owners perceive that their house has increased in value. Whether that is really true depends on how much their house is worth when priced in dozens of eggs, or ounces of gold, or barrels of oil, for example. The devaluation of the dollar provides an artificial gain to property owners, as their mortgage is devaluing in real (absolute) value. But on the other hand, this valuation adjustment comes at the expense of the inflation tax that is affecting everybody but more acutely by renters rather than homeowners. It is one of the first arguments I bring to proponents of the fiat system, that if they are truly compassionate for the poor and lower middle class, they would agree with this perspective. But typically, they reply with the claim that it is worth it to improve the economy by helping business expansion with fiat creation.

Human perspective is always a key factor in debate. What do people want to see the most? Why do they have this bias? Do they have a personal vested interest or old wound that prevents them from seeing the other side? Can anyone be truly unbiased? I tried as much as possible while writing this book to simulate a dual personality, if I may put it that way. I challenged myself to examine things from many angles to gather the complete picture. If you only see a Rubik's cube from one side, you might only see a blue square while somebody else might only see a green square.

But in the end, what really matters to a project longevity is its network effect, and many altcoins are likely to slip away with no one to maintain or keep interest in them. However, some of the projects created have value in themselves. They push the envelope towards new fields of study that bring tremendous value and influence to bitcoin developers showing them ways to improve bitcoin, now and in the future. I see a great value in the decentralized exchanges that were initiated with Ethereum's smart contract. Nothing is perfect at first, and they should all be viewed as experiments. Embrace the new concepts inspired by the research; it's likely some ideas will eventually work their way into bitcoin via a second layer.

It is fascinating to see how many of the gold bugs – or rather, many of the folks invested in gold and silver that are mocking bitcoin who are often followers of the Austrian School of Economy – are not able to come to term with one of its fundamental pillars of the Austrian School, that being, it is the market that decides what is money. They are stuck with Carl Menger's first theory of money that it starts from something that has utility. However, as we have discussed, Ludwig von Mises showed how its value is based on its usefulness as a commodity in exchange. That's why so many strange things have been used as money by different cultures in the past, including things that have never had any form of utility like giant rocks[97] (rai stones) in Micronesia.

The mistake that is often made is to imagine that improvements and new discoveries are over and it's pretty much static from now on. But we are just at the beginning of amazing new cryptographic discoveries. Critics of bitcoin and even cryptocurrencies in general are going to be greatly surprised over and over again by the redefinition and new ways of understanding money in the coming years.

> Imagine horse breeders in 1910 looking at the Ford Model T and saying it won't displace horses since it is too slow, difficult to start, not enough gas stations, not practical in snow without realizing major additional improvements in the cars themselves and the infrastructure supporting it will be coming within a few decades.

But what is important to realize is how few cryptocurrencies running their own blockchain will eventually exist. Think of it this way: How many telephone network systems do you think would still be in existence today if a bunch of competing telephone networks had been created in the

---

[97]https://en.wikipedia.org/wiki/Rai_stones

1920s and 1930s? Or how many internet protocols would we still have if hundreds had been at its inception? And even with IPv6's inclusion of backward compatibility to support various protocols such as TCP and UDP, IPv4 remains an important protocol in use today. These examples of network effects offer a strong indicator that bitcoin's dominance is here to stay, regardless of how much "better," how many more transactions, or how much more convenient that flashy, new blockchain purports to be. Remember the point about what the gold bugs are missing, when they say gold has "intrinsic value" because it is used in jewelry and computers? Value comes from the market. Sure, if an element is used in jewelry, that use imbues some value, but the fact that the market has chosen this element rather than another is actually the key. Oil has utility, but the market is unlikely to ever choose it as money. I can't imagine someone carrying crude oil in their pocket.

It's not Mother Nature that sets the value, Mother Nature only sets the properties, while the market sets the price. Similarly, the market will choose something that has the most convenient properties to serve as money.

Gold was chosen as money for thousands of years not because of its utility in jewelry or other products but because of its rarity and convenience once melted in coins. The same principle applies to bitcoin. Although it has no utility outside of its use as money, it is its convenience in transacting in the electronic world that has led to its ever increasing adoption.

Bitcoin's dominant market cap and very conservative approach are two key factors that make it strong. The best minds in cryptography are actively working on improving the network and the user experience, and more individuals and companies are piling on every year. Had bitcoin and its blockchain had never been invented, it's likely that fewer young mathematical minds would have explored the bitcoin-type concepts and cryptography.

The important lesson is how few cryptocurrency projects remain relevant even a few years after they launched. As time passes, the cryptocurrency graveyard fills with heartbroken investors. Do yourself a favor and visit https://coinmarketcap.com/historical/ and select any random year after 2012, and see if you even recognize projects in the top 20. Are they still in the top 100, or perhaps far away on the fourth page, or perhaps not even listed anymore?

Since its inception, the Ethereum blockchain has demonstrated some resilience, and anyone claiming it will still claim a top five spot in the next 10 years might be making a good guess, considering the Ethereum network's importance. It might be, but Ether's development path is more complex and its changes are not as conservative as bitcoin's development. Ask yourself this question: If you had to invest nearly all your wealth into a single cryptocurrency that will be locked up for the next 20 years, which one would you choose and why? The why is very important. Let's tackle the why first, then work backwards. To me, the cryptocurrency that is most likely to be still valid in 20 years possess the following qualifications:

- A money with little chance of interference of its protocol, including its inflation rate, and zero censorship of transactions;

- In the top in terms of recognition (market cap);

- A sound, proven consensus algorithm; and

- A very conservative approach by its software developers to avoid catastrophic meltdown

We have detailed these elements in earlier chapters, so you already have a good idea of my personal choice on this important question, bitcoin obviously. It doesn't mean the protocol will never change drastically, but any important alteration would likely be for extremely critical reasons — say for example the discovery of a potential weakness in SHA256! Proof of Work has demonstrated its resilience despite its simplicity and massive energy requirement, or rather because of it.

We also covered the importance of decentralization in avoiding censorship of transactions, manipulation of the supply, and other related dangers. We have shown what it would take for bitcoin to be subject to this, but we also demonstrated how much easier it would be for a group of cabals to use any number of proof-of-authority coins to censor rogue transactions and actors. Although XRP holders are excited about how its technology could support the current banking system, they should be vigilant about guarding its vulnerability to censorship. XRP will likely secure a favorable outcome from the SEC lawsuit, so, in terms of a trade, there is some potential gain to capture once it is adjudicated or settled. But for the long term, I would be wary. Considering proof-of-debt is a horrible system that favors a few, I would classify any "coins" intended to support the fiat system as an absolute "shitcoin," just like Federal Reserve notes are. There is no denying that if an altcoin were controlled by a single organization with the ability to manipulate its supply, apply censorship, and change the rules on the fly, it would be considered a "shitcoin." As stated earlier, more often than not people love this system for how their house "increases" in value, or rather how their mortgage slowly reduces because of the dollar devaluation. If decision makers were truly honest about their compassion towards the poor and lower middle class, they would despise this system and accelerate any effort to get rid of it. This doesn't mean I'm against anyone investing in real estate … this is the system we live in, and people need a place to live. In fact, I'm also a real estate investor myself, and although I understand very well the advantage this unfair system brings me in artificial gains, I know it would be much better for all of us to be out of it.

You might find bitcoin "maximalists" harsh and uncompromising, but some began their journey to maximalism by trading altcoins, then got burned/scammed/rug-pulled before switching their focus to bitcoin only. Others who now proudly call themselves "toxic bitcoin maxis" came to change their perspectives largely on philosophical grounds, adhering to mantras like "Came for the gains, stayed for the revolution" and "Fix the money, fix the world." With wisdom rooted in a bitcoin-only philosophy and experience or familiarity with various blockchains, bitcoin maximalists shun the shiny claims of altcoins and support the dismantling of the central banking cartels.

That being said, the central banking cartel will not go down without a fight. To maintain control, they will likely seek to track every bitcoin transaction. They will also attempt to create their own central bank digital currencies, with draconian regulations that will impede the development and blockchain activity on exchanges. Although they cannot control bitcoin's supply, they do recognize their ability to interfere with it by tracking bitcoin transactions, enacting heavy regulations, and amplifying know-your-customer rules at any point of entry and exit from bitcoin to fiat rails (e.g., exchanges). They will probably continue to crack down on bitcoin mixers and other such tools, while at the same time try to erect restrictions on bitcoin miners. But higher inflation and its associated pain might awaken even more people to bitcoin. Countries like El Salvador and the Central African Republic are establishing a financial safe haven from price inflation by making bitcoin legal tender. For many, it might not have sounded like a good idea at the time, but when much higher inflation kicks in worldwide, (and it might be worse by the time you read this) they will get a sample of how Weimar Germany felt during its period of hyperinflation from 1921-1923.

Essentially, from the view of bitcoin maximalists, PoW is the best, most secure decentralized consensus algorithm available. Because any other blockchain using PoW with a lesser amount of hash power is at the mercy of a 51% attack from bitcoin miners that could redirect their hardware and resources toward that blockchain, they will always be less secure. Proof of Stake is more complex, and as such, it requires more time to establish itself as a solid alternative consensus algorithm. So far it has demonstrated some form of resilience, as many have been operating for a few years without successful hacks or interference. But its complexity makes it harder to evaluate its long-term resiliency and formulate game theories involving it. A thought worth pondering: Does the government tacitly support PoS or is it employing a stealth strategy of letting PoS coins run, hoping they will entice investors to migrate away from bitcoin's PoW before they implement coordinated restrictions?

Obviously, what the cryptocurrency landscape will look like in 50 years is anyone's guess. But even with bitcoin developers' conservative approach, I am sure bitcoin's changes will surprise us all ... its layer 2 will definitely be unrecognizable from the limited one we have today. What the future reserves for us depends heavily on the degrees to which politicians meddle with the free market and impose government regulation, but I'm confident bitcoin will remain in place. As for PoS and PoW, or any others, it is difficult to foresee all the possible attack vectors, including increased government regulations, cryptocurrencies could face in the coming years.

With the complex amalgam of game theory mixed with government power, I just hope we get to decentralize the government one day in opposition to a world where the United Nations makes and enforces laws for the entire planet. Know that in such a dystopian society, powerful people will interfere in any way they can with any cryptocurrency competing against their own system. I just wish the masses could recognize that powerful central entities are always hijacked by cabals to control the rest of the population, typically in a subversive manner, ensuring that the masses are distracted by the crisis du jour, while their freedom covertly erodes. The proof-of-debt system incentivizes strong, centralized control. Think about it, the more central and powerful a government is, the more of a target it

becomes to corrupt individuals, politicians, bankers, and corporate entities. Adolph Hitler himself worked to centralize and direct power toward
Berlin. As more precise news and information disseminates through various internet channels, people are increasingly inclined to prefer a decentralized government over centralized rule - a trend I am personally pleased
to see. We've established, bitcoin's development is conservative and for
a good reason. For many, bitcoin is a long-term store of value, like gold,
but with additional properties and abilities intrinsic to its electronic nature.
The short-sighted trader looks only to transaction throughput, smart contracts, and other bells and whistles that are of no interest to core developers
of bitcoin, at least not on bitcoin's blockchain. Returning to a sound money
system should be our main priority, and bitcoin is positioned to become the
global standard currency. Those who are fans of XRP or ether, for example, are hoping for the so-called bitcoin "flippening," meaning that XRP or
ether overtakes bitcoin's market capitalization. Sadly, they do not realize
the drawbacks this would cause. If bitcoin can be dethroned, any coin can
be dethroned. With this instability at the top, long-term store of value can
never be associated with any cryptocurrencies. I personally do not believe
this situation will manifest, but if it does, it will be a very short-lived occurrence. At the time of this writing, the bitcoin blockchain is just less than
one-half a terabyte, meaning that a bitcoin node can be run with an ordinary computer on less than a single terabyte of disk space. And remember
that small bitcoin node operators are participating in the overall process
by not forwarding invalid blocks and transactions. As for XRP, I certainly
hope holders of this currency grasp how much power Ripple has over the
currency, despite how many times the word "decentralized" shows up on
the xrpl.org website. We do not want to enable the central banking cartel
to maintain their horrible system, we want to get rid of it.

If you are still not convinced, I recommend you read these books and
in this order:

- *The Creature from Jekyll Island,* by G. Edward Griffin

- *The Case for Gold, by Ron Paul*

- *Confessions of an Economic Hit Man,* by John Perkins

- *The Bitcoin Standard,* by Saifedean Ammous

Of course, I should add *The Book of Satoshi* to this list if you are interested in learning more about Satoshi's written conversations on the Bitcoin Talk forum, opinions, and views during his short two year "public life."

Frequently Asked Questions

How long did it take you to write this book?

I started around March 2022, so a little over a year before everything was done. This is a dynamic field and I could have kept writing for years to come, but at the same time, we are witnessing cracks in the banking system so it comes at a particularly interesting time.

What made you think about creating this book?

I realized many who were interested in bitcoin, and cryptocurrency in general, were confused and had no idea why there was a debate around what they considered simply an investment. Through this work, I offer them context on this unexplored debate, including an analysis of the information and sometimes misinformation spread by gold bugs and supporters of altcoins.

What was your background?

I started investing in real estate in 2003 and was focused on cash flow as the core concept of my portfolio. Then around 2008, I started learning about gold and silver, and to reorient my perspective, I had to delve deep to wrap my head around the economics of these metals. Initially, I saw them as pointless investments that do not provide dividends or rental income. After a few books, I was introduced to the Austrian School of Economics, and I loved it. Suddenly, the subject of economics was no longer the boring topic presented by mainstream media news and documentaries and was now intriguing and dynamic. Being a software engineer, I was readily able to grasp the concept of bitcoin when I ran across it in 2012. I became fascinated by the idea and quickly saw it as the digital, functional equivalent of both gold and silver. Considering we live in an electronic world, I reasoned that the implications were massive, as it opened the door to a new world of possibilities. That's also when I decided to write The Book of Satoshi. The anonymity of bitcoin's creator and the fact that we likely will never hear from him again was captivating. His mysterious existence made his sole source of communication, his writings, utterly enthralling.

Have you personally invested in altcoins?

At first, I was very much annoyed by altcoins. Later, I decided to at least trade some of them. I traded silver futures in the past and was burned by the manipulations by the big banks; I now stay away from such trades. But what was impressive to me is how much easier it was to trade these altcoins. considering the other traders were often not experts themselves. Sad to know many are getting slaughtered with their bad trades, but that's the nature of the market and why many cannot resist the lure from the fear of missing out (FOMO). Additionally, many of these coins' price movements were manipulated by other players, but that was often more recognizable than in the futures market.

I also invested in some altcoins as a long term trade with the goal to return to bitcoin, partially or fully. By investing rather than trading, it forced me to learn more about them. In particular, I invested in the Tezos ICO since I found the concept very interesting and intriguing, and I wanted to understand, in detail, how Proof of Stake works. I even got involved with a Tezos baking service (Hayek Lab) with a knowledgeable IT partner. In retrospect, had I put that cash into bitcoin instead, I would have had a much larger gain today, thus proving the point I often advanced in this book - over the long term, bitcoin will outperform altcoins. So my recommendation to my friends remains: Focus on bitcoin. But, if they cannot resist the lure of altcoins, they should only have minor investments in them, unless they intend to do short term trading with the goal of accumulating more bitcoin. Sure, one could invest in Ethereum as it sounds like it might be here for a while, but I'm more confident about where bitcoin will be in ten years than where Ethereum might be.

What surprised you most about altcoins and the evolution of the market?

I was surprised by how drastic things changed in 2017 with bitcoin's dominance taking a sudden dive as compared to Ethereum and other coins. But the most interesting part was the debate on the need for faster transactions with a higher number of transactions per second. This debate spurred the creation of Bitcoin Cash but also that is when SegWit and the Lighting Network appeared, demonstrating the ability for amazing innovation within bitcoin's ecosystem. When you think about it, the bitcoin community produced two major achievements in less than ten years. First the jump from not having any decentralized digital currency to having one with bitcoin's release. Then later having the ability to operate a layer 2 network, with instant transactions, on top of it. It is easy to imagine that within the next ten years fascinating, additional, and important improvements will once again appear and baffle bitcoin critics.

What part of the book was the most difficult to write?

The sections where I describe the lightning network and Proof of Stake. Both are complicated subjects, but it was an enjoyable challenge to ensure that they were described in a way to allow for as many as possible to understand their innerworkings.

Will we see new crypto currencies and blockchain popping up?

I firmly believe the 2016-2018 frenzy will remain unmatched. Regulators have been sharpening their knives, and they have scared many developers. Also, the landscape is so crowded, no one would try to create a "better Ethereum" and or "bitcoin-killer." The idea is cementing in the collective mindset that bitcoin is here to stay and will remain the dominant blockchain, regardless of how many bells and whistles other coins might have. The general public doesn't know why that is, but I hope those who read this book will have a solid understanding of why bitcoin has this position in the marketplace.

What will happen to altcoins in the future?

I think Ethereum is likely here to stay, at the very least for some time. A big difference in mindset between bitcoin and Ethereum developers is how the latter have shown they are not afraid to make major changes, in particular with the move to Proof of Stake. Bitcoin's decentralized nature makes it more difficult for important changes to be incorporated into the code. For a currency, an asset that you want to be strong and stable for the long term, this is good.

As for the others, I speculate there will be another few niche markets as well, but the great majority will slowly die off, regardless of how well-designed and -operated they might be. Displacing the network effect of the top dogs would require a drastic advantage embedded in the altcoin that I don't see evolving, particularly when you consider that everything in this field is open source.

Would you be offended by donations?

No.

BTC: bc1qq38959jg39qxttwvmgqagnw8jujtkq5nlmm50f

GLOSSARY

AML - Anti-Money Laundering, is a series of measures and procedures by financial institutions to prevent financial crimes described by the respective local authorities.

ASIC - An acronym for Application Specific Integrated Circuit. These are specialized hardware to run specific tasks. Some have been designed for the sole purpose of efficiently performing SHA256 for bitcoin mining.

Baker - In Tezos, the nodes that create blocks.

BIP - An acronym for Bitcoin Improvement Proposal. Any future improvement to the bitcoin software and protocol will have its details published and will be associated with a number. For example, BIP-141 was published to describe SegWit (Segregated Witness).

Coins - Generic term used to specify a digital currency embedded in a blockchain.

Consensus algorithm - A set of rules and procedures used in a distributed computing network to ensure that all nodes in the network agree on the current state of the network. A way for a network of computers to agree on a shared truth or ledger, even when some of the computers may be unreliable or malicious.

Cryptocurrency - A term used to describe a digital currency, typically that claims to be decentralized.

ECDSA - An acronym for Elliptic Curve Digital Signature Algorithm. This algorithm used a curve represented mathematically as the basis to generate a private key and its corresponding public key.

Epoch (or cycle) - In Proof of Stake, the rights to mine a certain number of blocks is allocated at the same time. This group of blocks will be declared as being part of the same epoch or cycle.

Hash - Hash algorithm produces a fixed output out of any size document provided as input. One can see it as a fingerprint of the document. Creating a document that will generate a given hash output is meant to be nearly impossible.

ICO - An acronym for Initial Coin Offering. Describes that a project is funded by the public rather than an investor group. The term is inspired from Initial Public Offering, the process when companies go public.

KYC - An acronym for Know Your Customer, a regulations requiring financial institution to collect identifying information about their customer

Market capitalization - Describes the total value of an asset, which is calculated by multiplying the total number of shares for a company, or coins in the case of a cryptocurrency, by its value per share or coin.

Mempool - The space in a node or miner's memory where unconfirmed transactions are stored before they are added to the blockchain. Not all miners have the same transactions in their respective mempool, as mempools are dynamic, and transactions are not received simultaneously. But for the most part, the contents of a mempool are similar.

Segwit - An abbreviation for Segregated Witness. It was a protocol upgrade that provides a protection against transaction malleability.

SHA256 - An abbreviation for a secure hash algorithm giving an output of 256 bits. See hash algorithm

Timelock - This type of operation provides a time restriction on when the content of transaction output can be executed.

Tokens - A term often used for cryptocurrency that are accounted as part of a smart contract on another blockchain. Ethereum is the dominant platform that has been used.

Transactions malleability - when SegWit is not used, the hash of representing a transaction will not cover all the data. This means the transaction could be changed in a way that invalidates the current hash, while the destination address will always remain the same. Resolving this, allowed the Lightning Network to be supported.

Acknowledgements

This book would not have been possible without the valuable input that came from many discussions I had with friends and family. I'd like to extend my gratitude and appreciation to them for sharing their thoughts.

- I am particularly grateful to my wife, Marie Gagnon, for her tremendous involvement and support along this project. I would like to extend a big thank you as well to my son, Samuel Champagne, and my daughter Vivianne Champagne (viviannechampagne.com) for their contribution in bringing this book to the world.

- Sincere thanks should also go to my friend David St-Onge, the author of "Bitcoin: Everything you need to know" as well as Olivier M. and S.A. Simmons for their beneficial comments and critiques during the early draft version of the book.

Thank you to Preston Pysh for agreeing to write the forward for this book.

In addition, a special thanks goes to Ricardo Galvão for creating the expressive cartoons that made this book more interesting and vivid. (https://www.instagram.com/ricardogalvaocartoon/)

I also want to extend my appreciation to Mary Graybeal who also contributed to the editing of the book and James Wheeler (www.ibrandpackaging.com) for his graphic design work.

Finally, I would like to acknowledge the excellent and valuable help I received from the team at Konsensus.Network for the editing and book formatting and I offer them my sincere thanks.

LIST OF FIGURES

LIST OF TABLES

INDEX

www.ingramcontent.com/pod-product-compliance
Lightning Source LLC
Chambersburg PA
CBHW040753220326
41597CB00029BA/4765